SECRET ACRES

Little Stranger © Edie Fake 2018.

First edition.

Printed in Hong Kong.

ISBN-13: 978-0-9991935-0-1
ISBN-10: 0-9991935-0-3

SA039

Library of Congress Control Number: 2017958125

Published by Secret Acres
200 Park Avenue South, 8th fl.
New York, NY 10003

LITTLE STRANGER

WITHDRAWN

For the Queerdos out there, David especially

Little Stranger

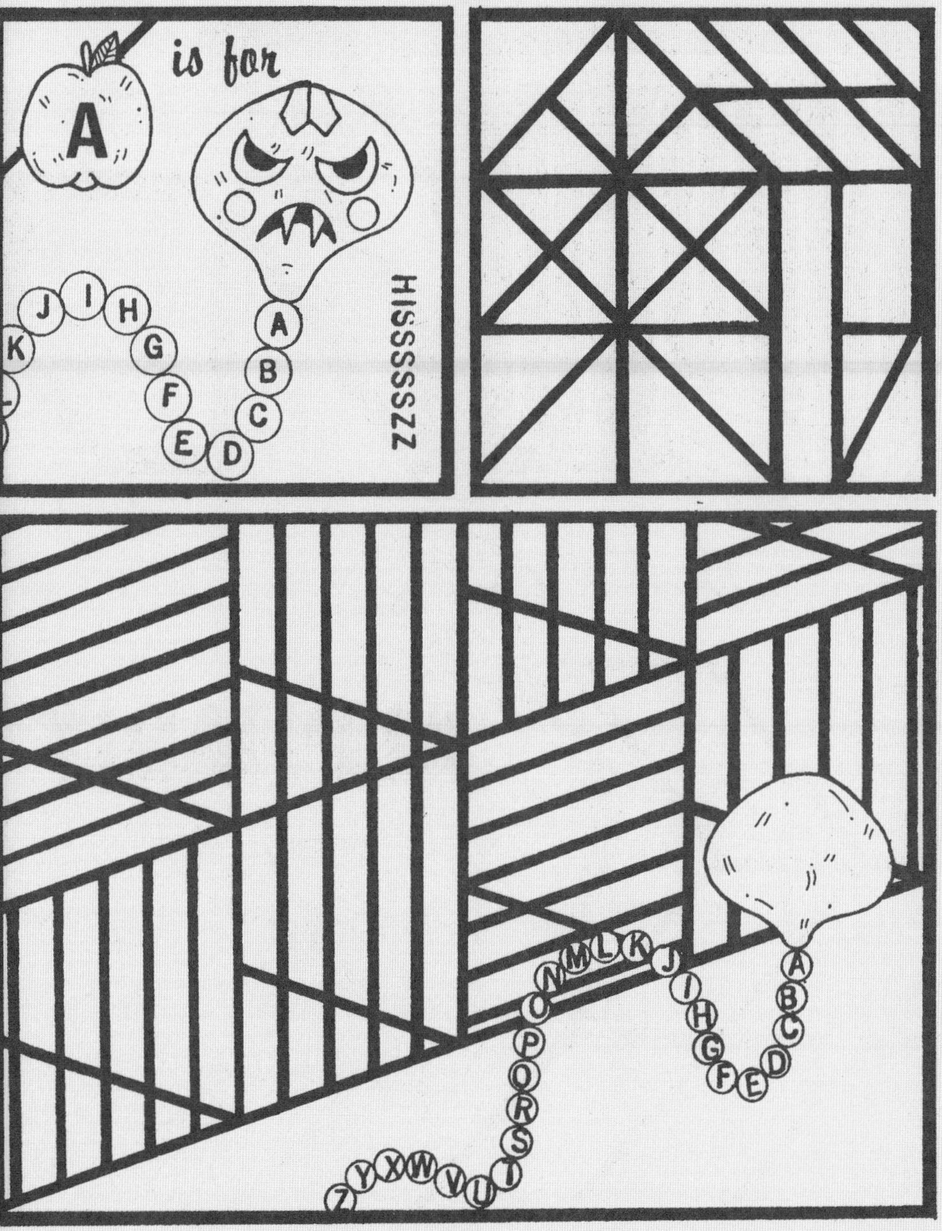
A is for
HISSSSSZZ

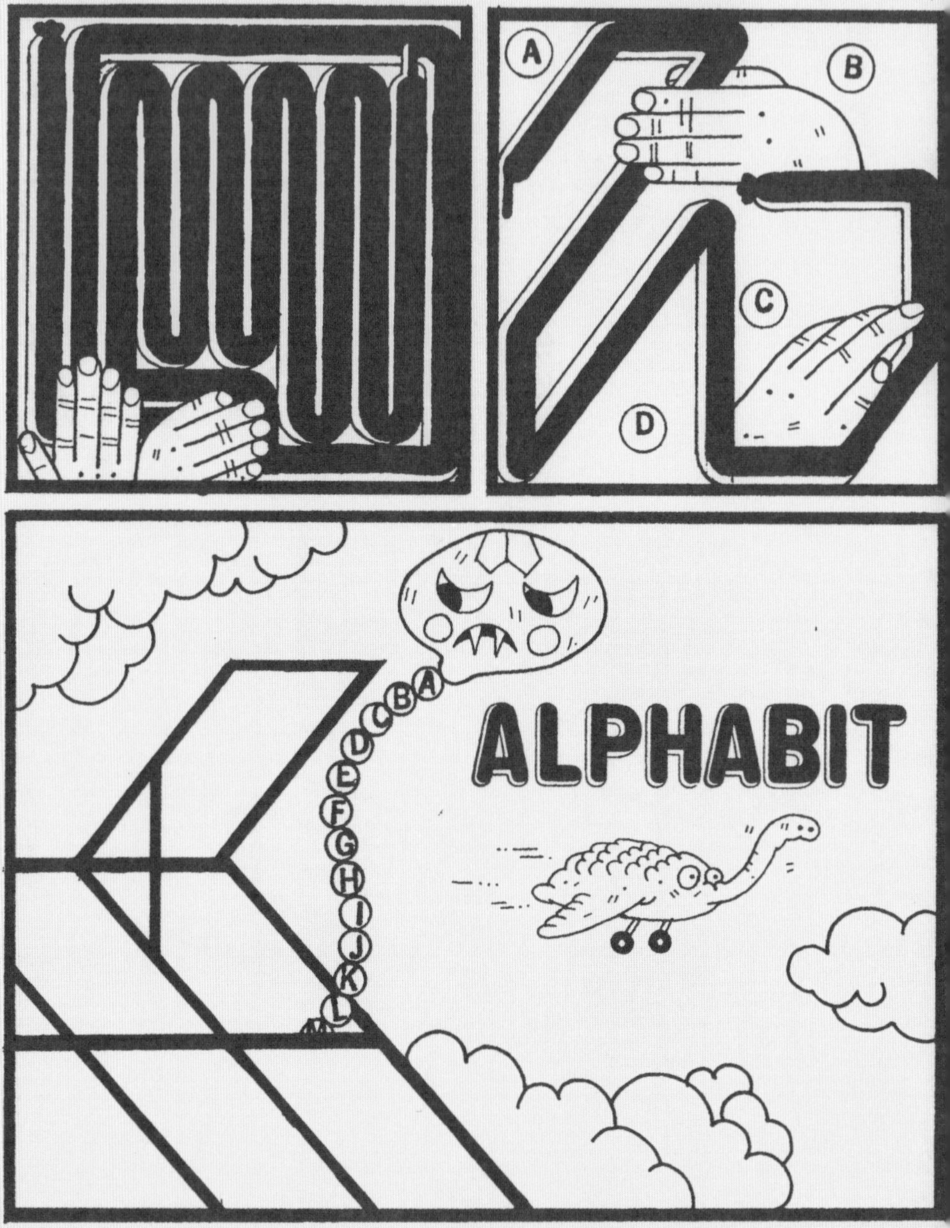
A
B
C
D
ABCDEFGHIJKL
ALPHABIT

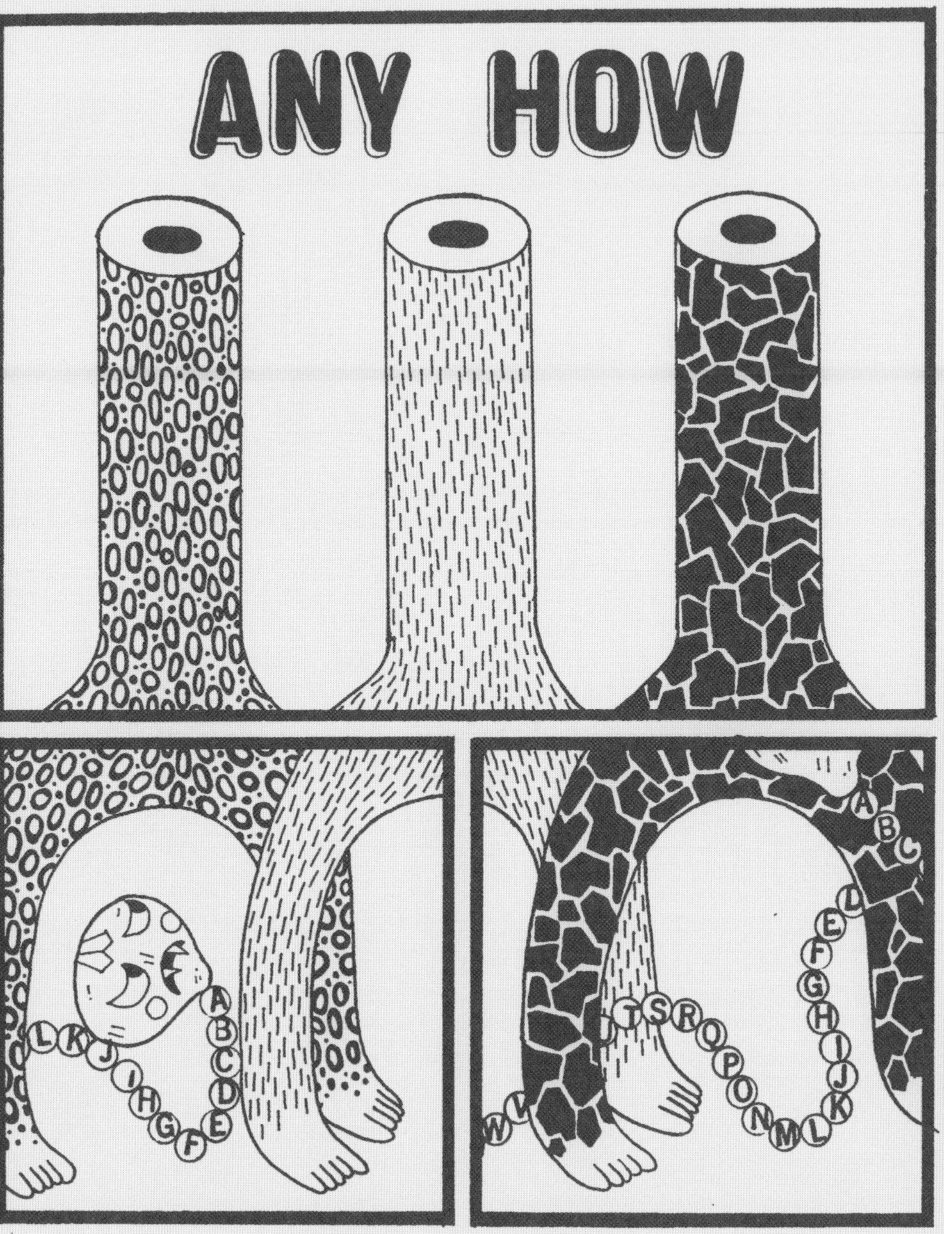
ANY HOW
A B C D E F G H I J K L

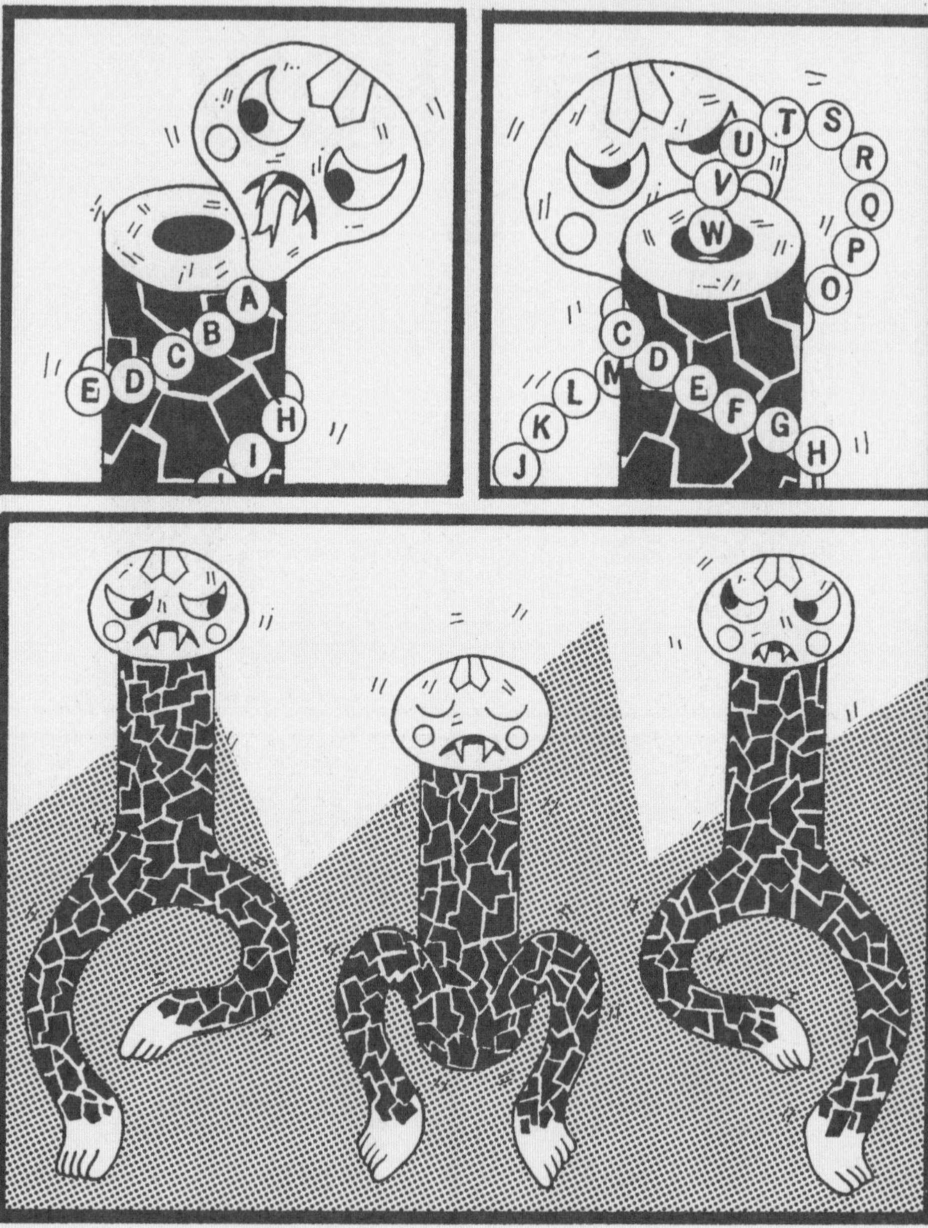
E D C B A
H I
J K L M C D E F G H
O P Q R S T U V W

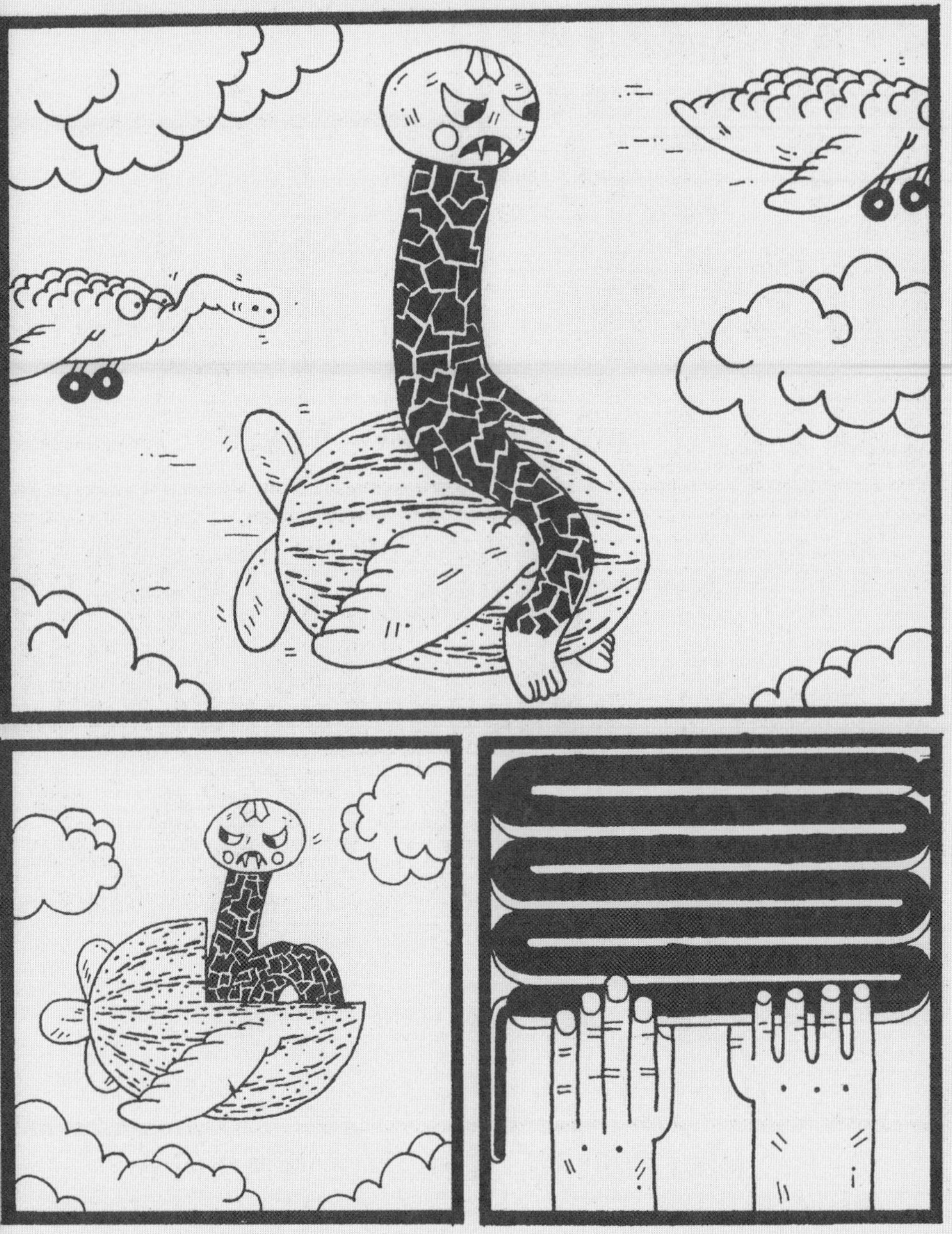

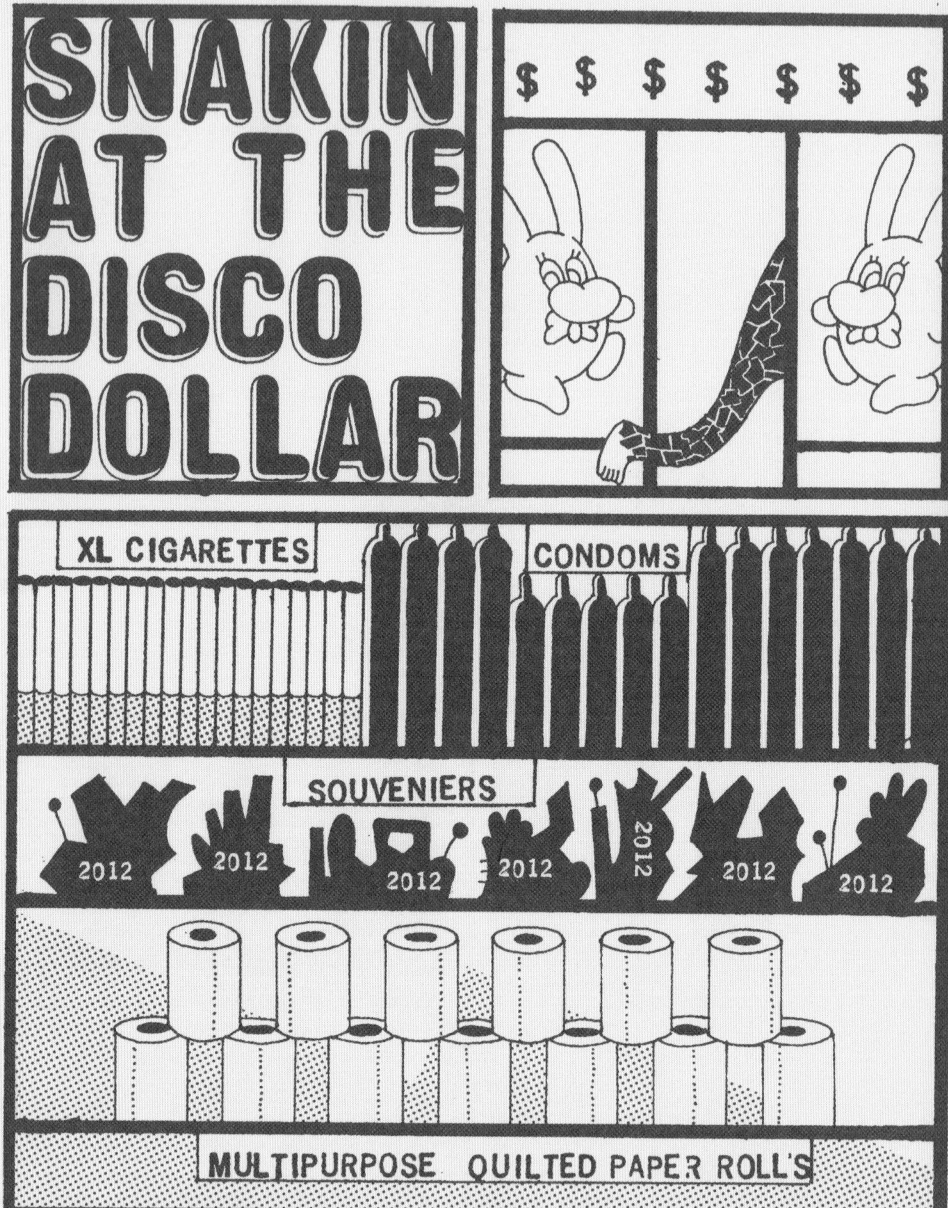
SNAKIN AT THE DISCO DOLLAR
$ $ $ $ $ $ $
XL CIGARETTES
CONDOMS
SOUVENIERS
2012
2012
2012
2012
2012
2012
2012
MULTIPURPOSE QUILTED PAPER ROLL'S

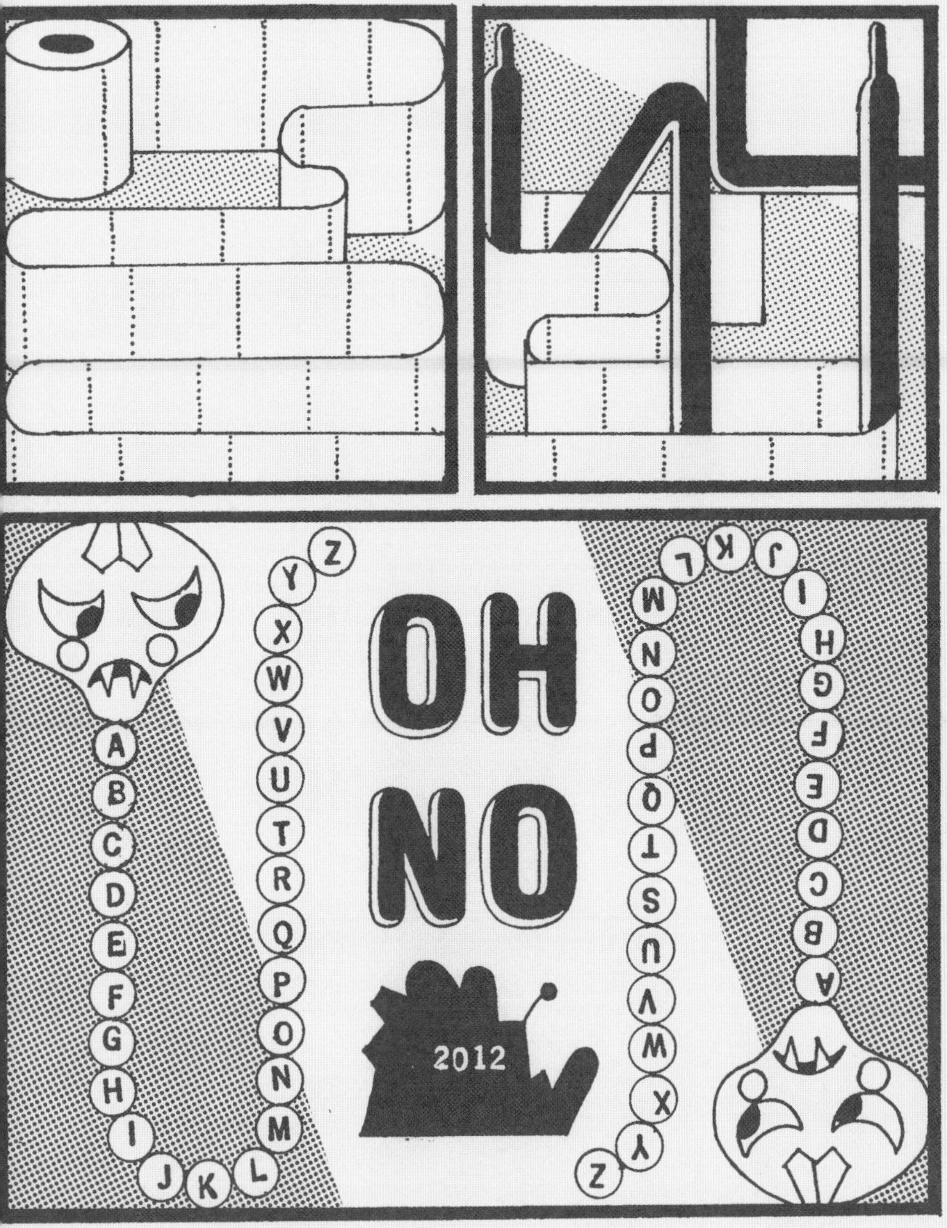
A B C D E F G H I J K L M N O P Q R S T U V W X Y Z
OH NO
2012
A B C D E F G H I J K L M N O P Q S T U V W X Y Z

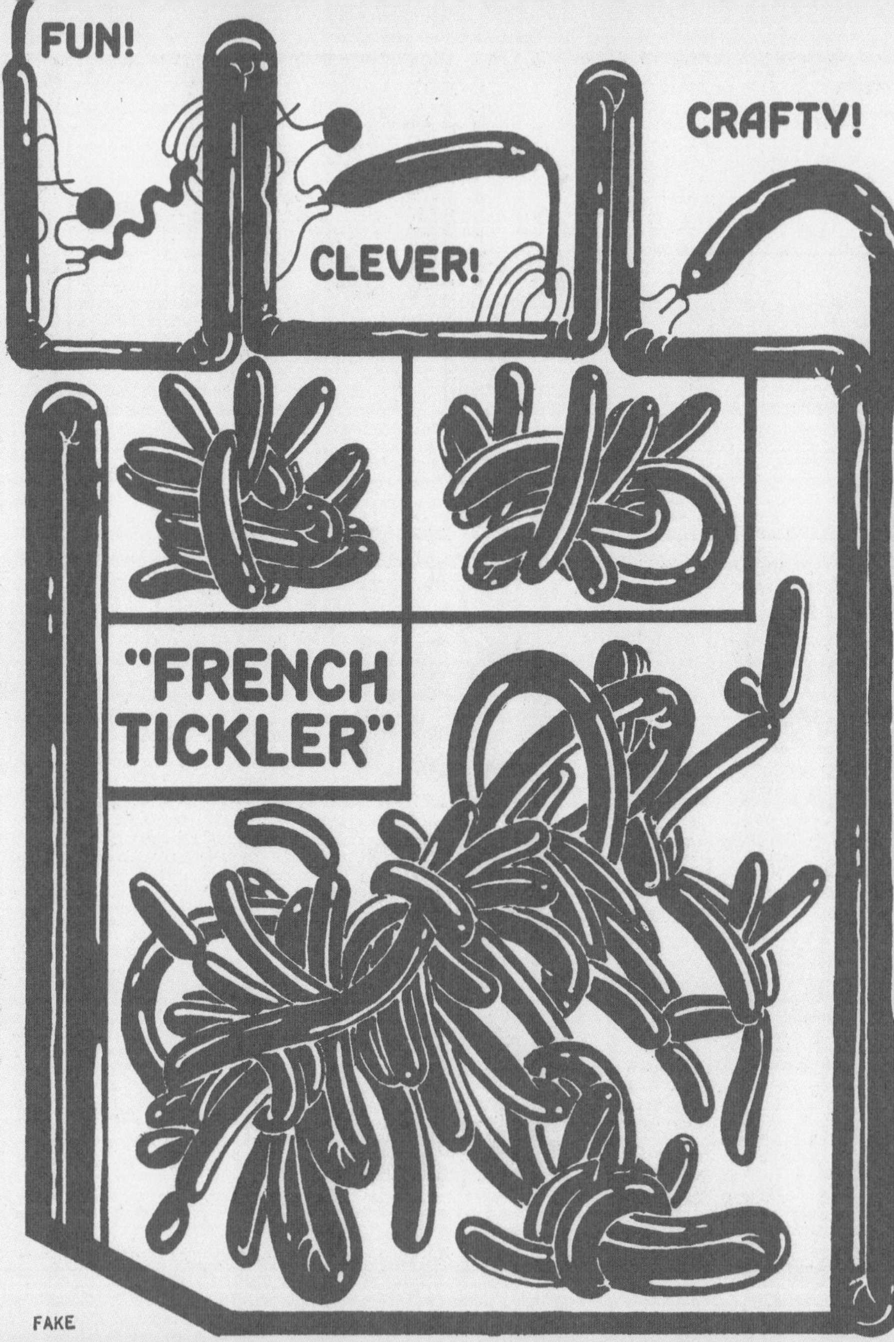
FUN!
CLEVER!
CRAFTY!
"FRENCH TICKLER"
FAKE

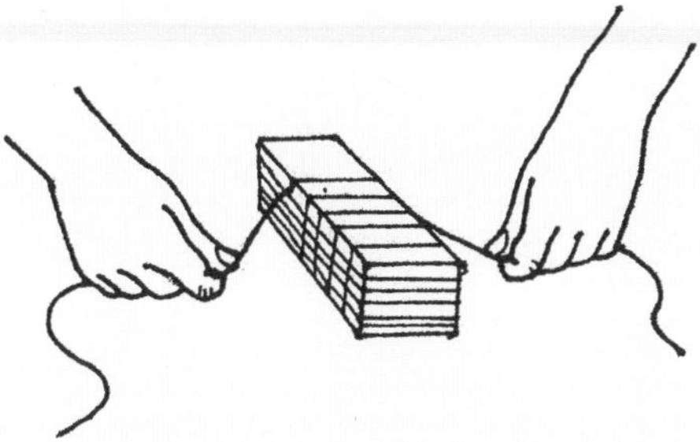

LET'S BUILD A HOUSE

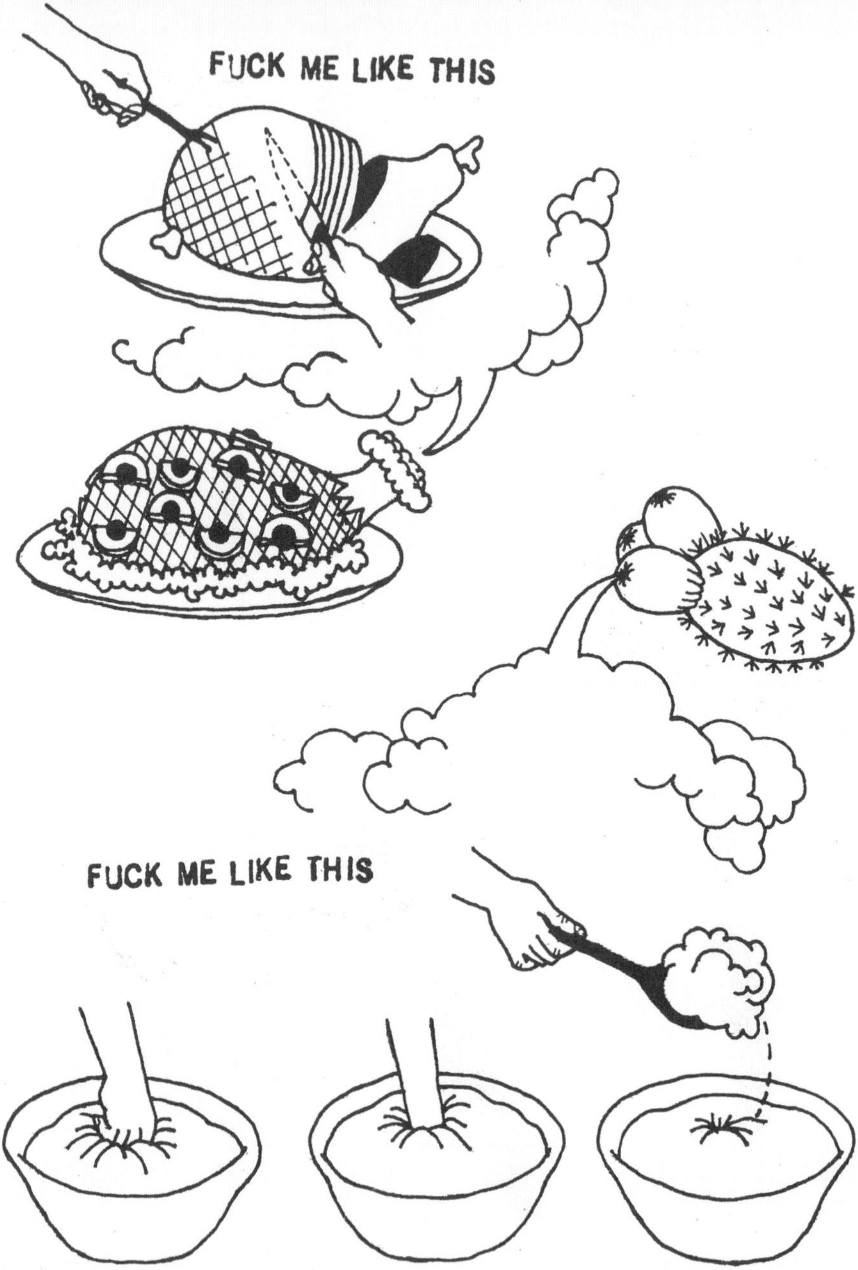
FUCK ME LIKE THIS
FUCK ME LIKE THIS

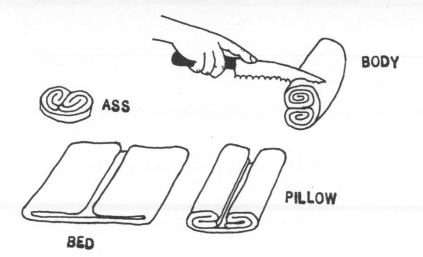

BODY

ASS

BED

PILLOW

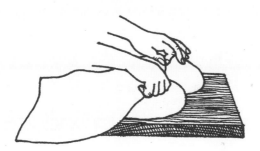

TENDERLY

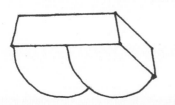
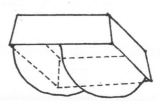

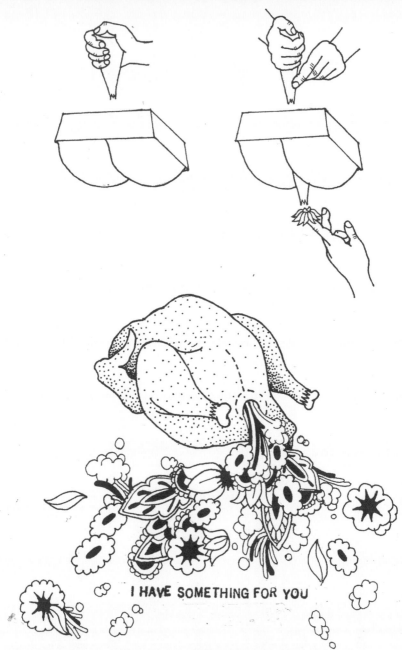

I HAVE SOMETHING FOR YOU

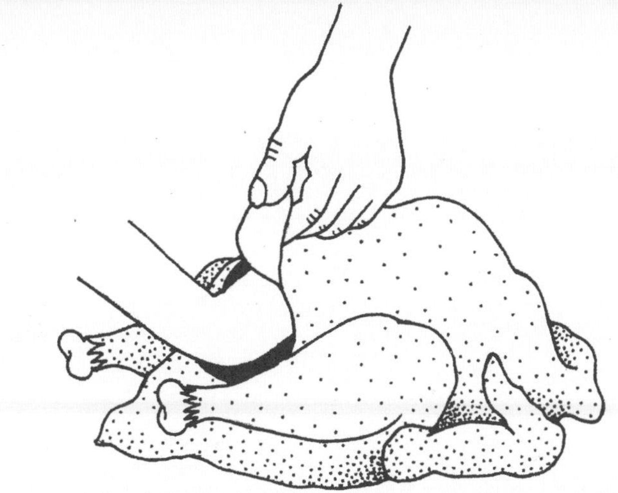

ABOUT MY BOYHOOD

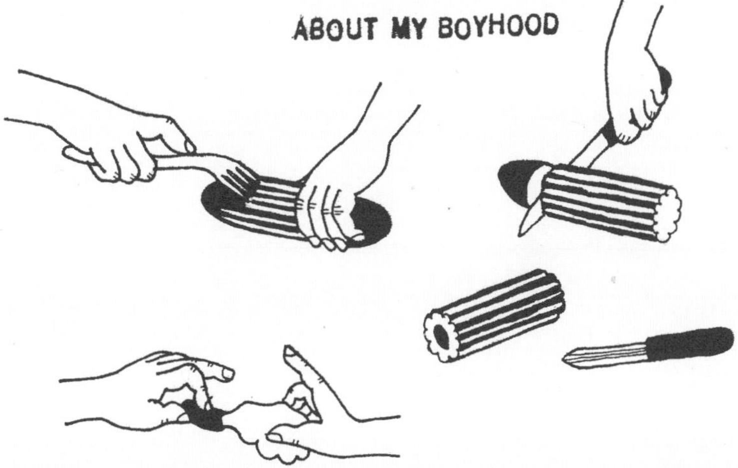

A PROSTHESIS

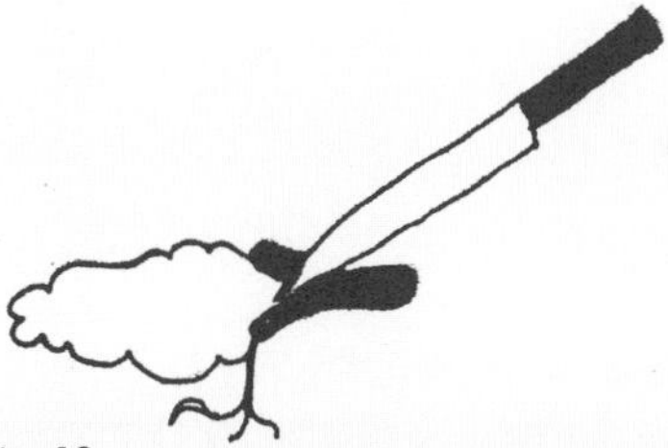

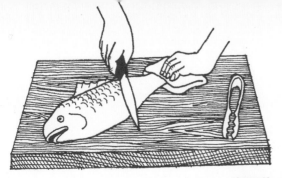

FIRST AN EXAM

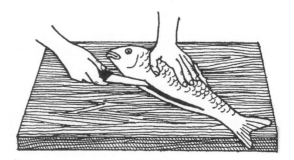

BLOOD CHECK

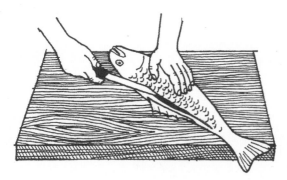

THIS IS NOT ATTRACTIVE!

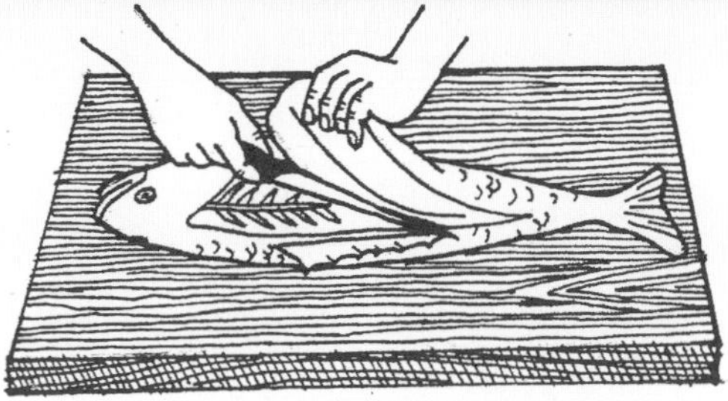

NOW SAY AH

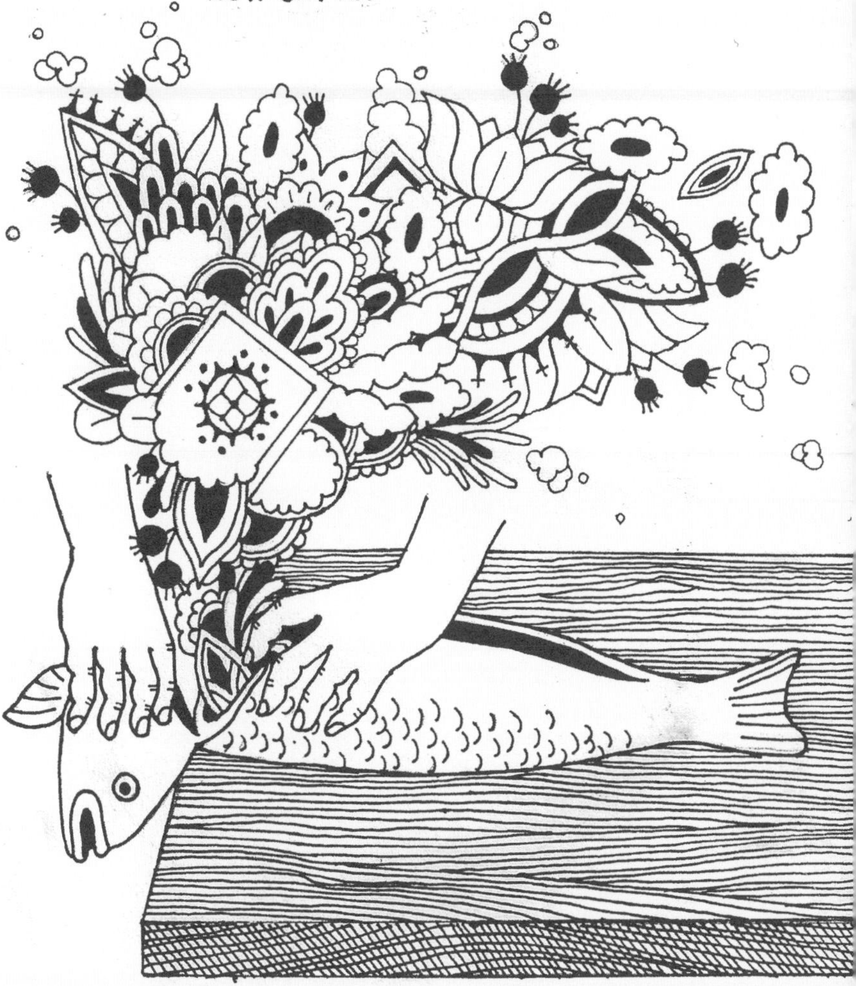

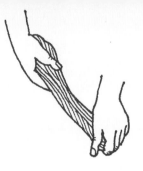

YOU WANT A...?

HERE, TAKE THIS

JUST TAKE A GOOD
LONG LOOK AT YOURSELF

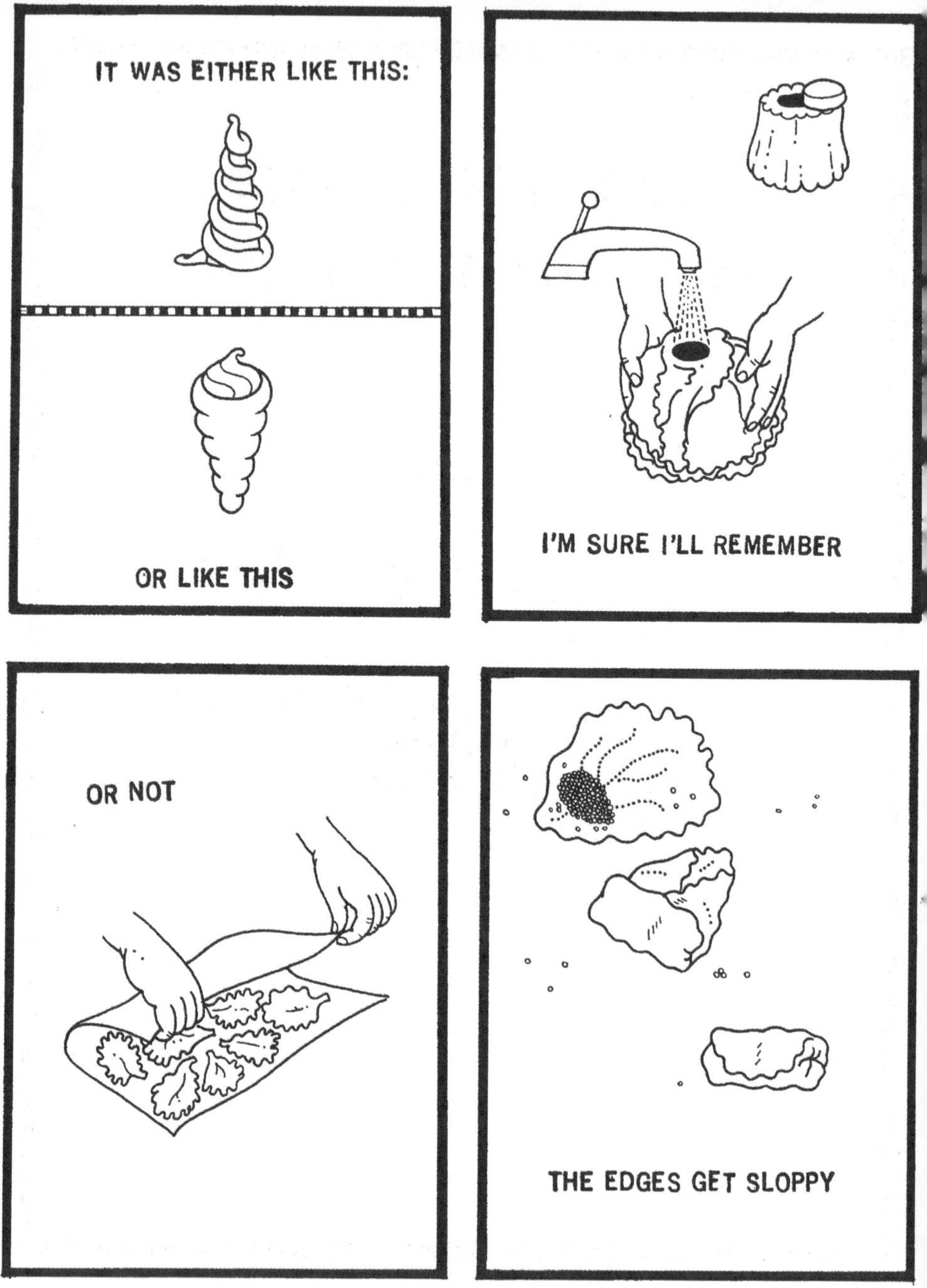
IT WAS EITHER LIKE THIS:
OR LIKE THIS
I'M SURE I'LL REMEMBER
OR NOT
THE EDGES GET SLOPPY

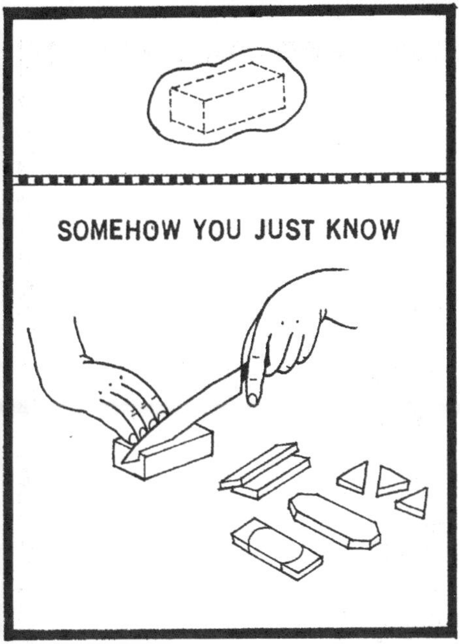
SOMEHOW YOU JUST KNOW

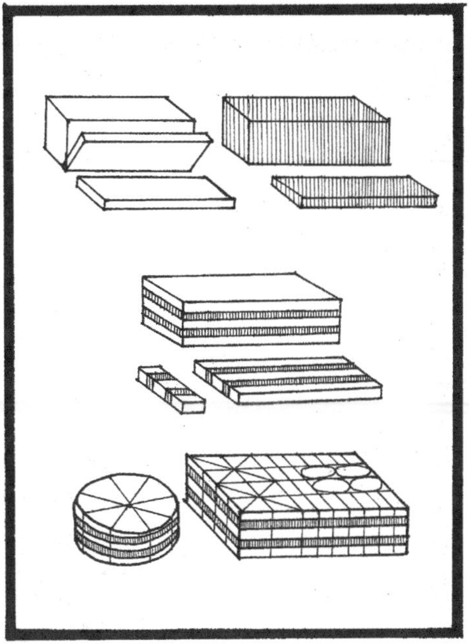

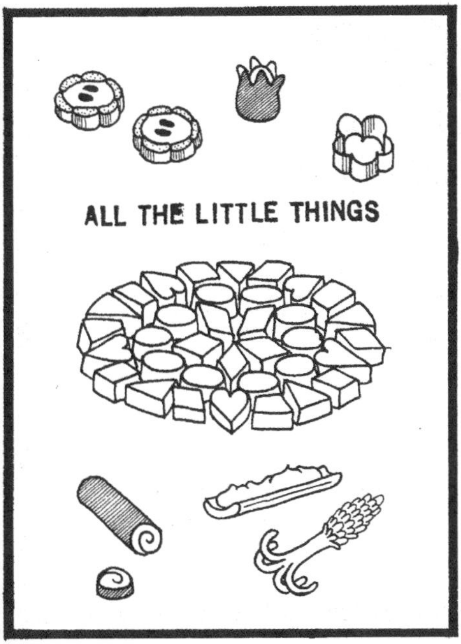
ALL THE LITTLE THINGS

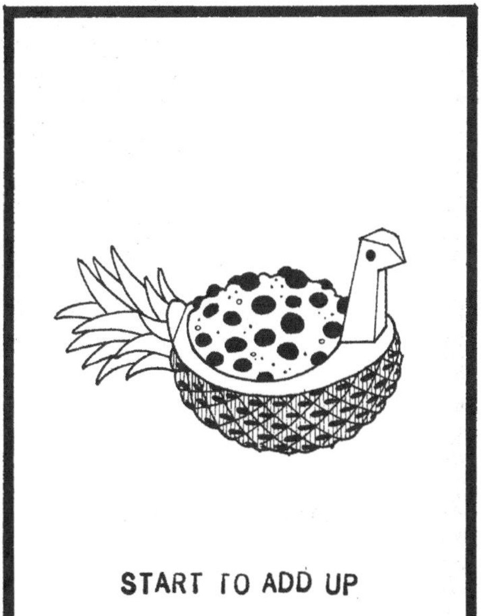
START TO ADD UP

WELL WHAT DO YOU THINK

I'M DOING HERE?

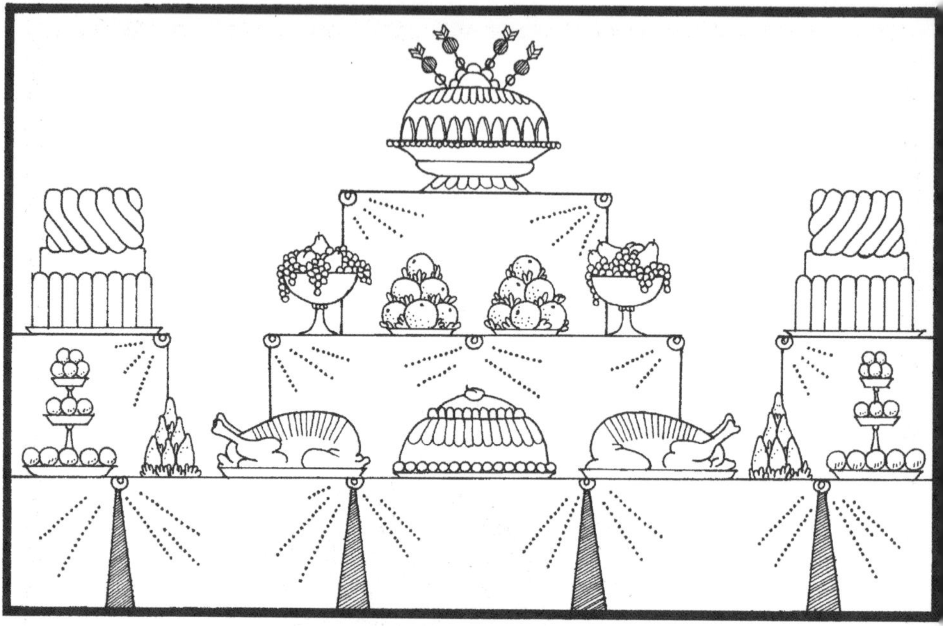

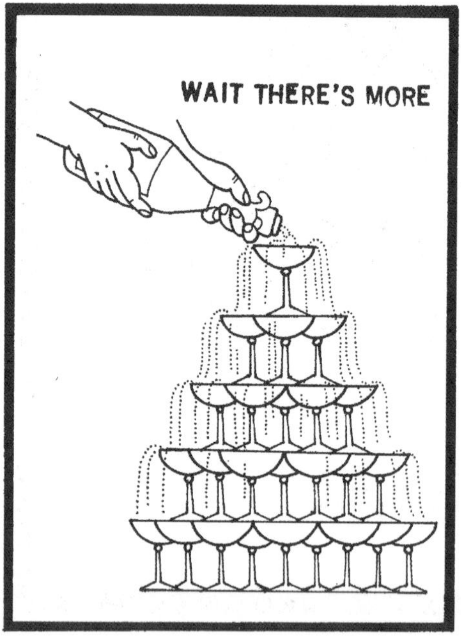
WAIT THERE'S MORE

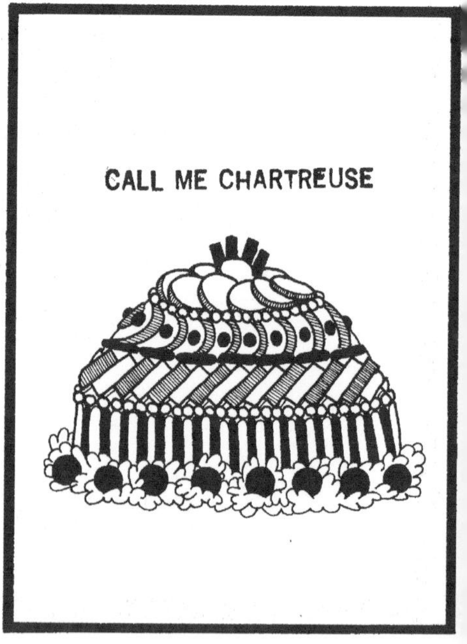
CALL ME CHARTREUSE

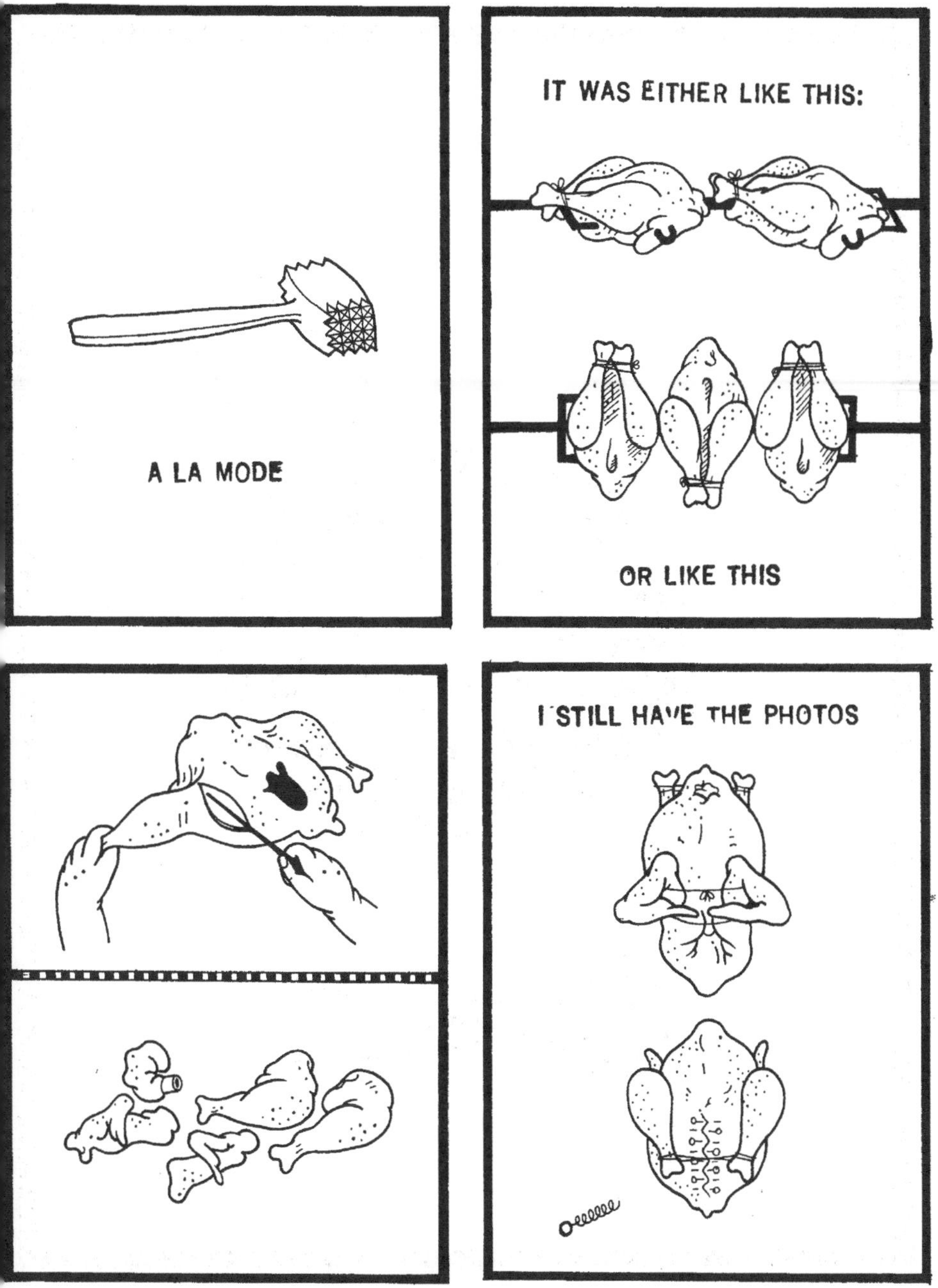
A LA MODE
IT WAS EITHER LIKE THIS:
OR LIKE THIS
I STILL HAVE THE PHOTOS

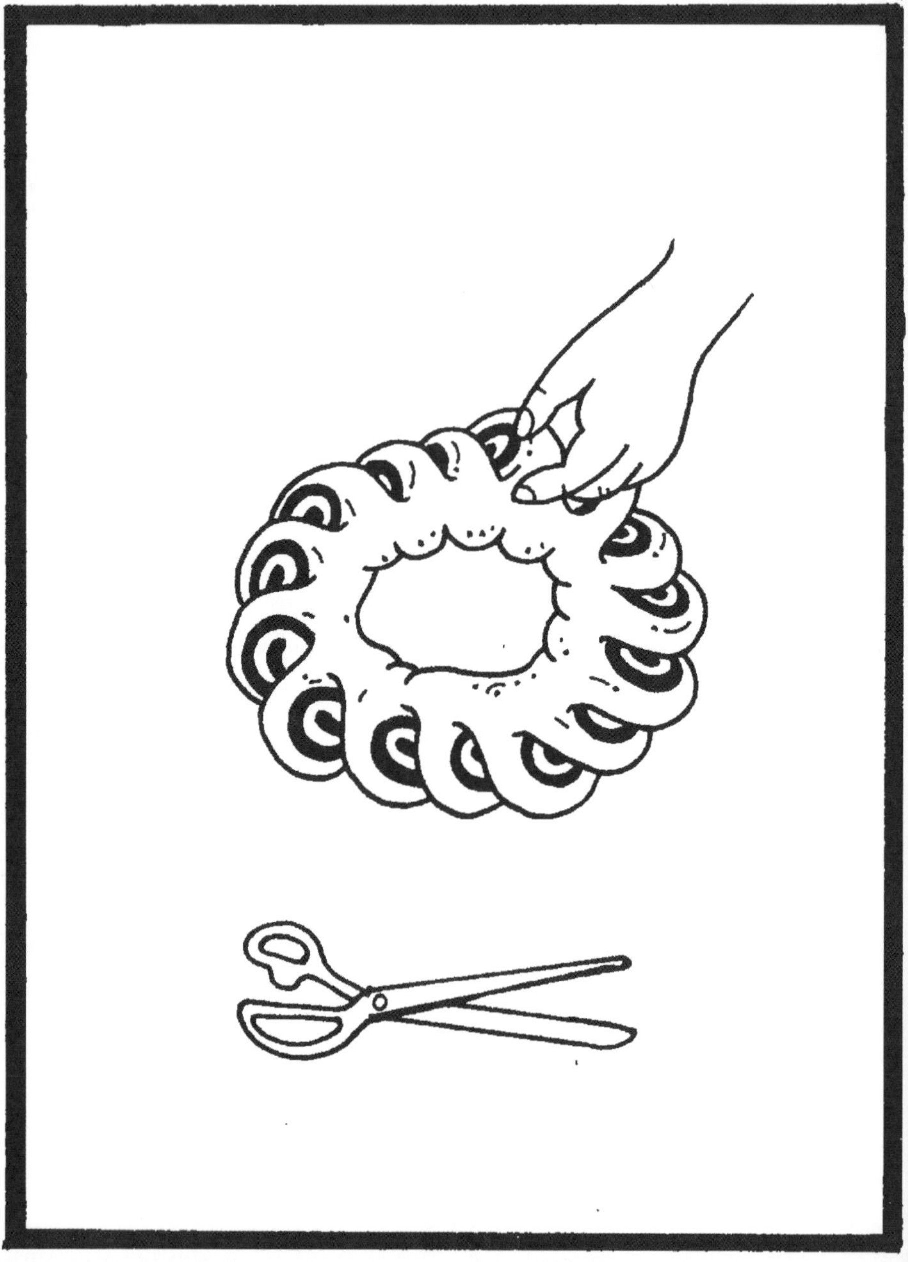

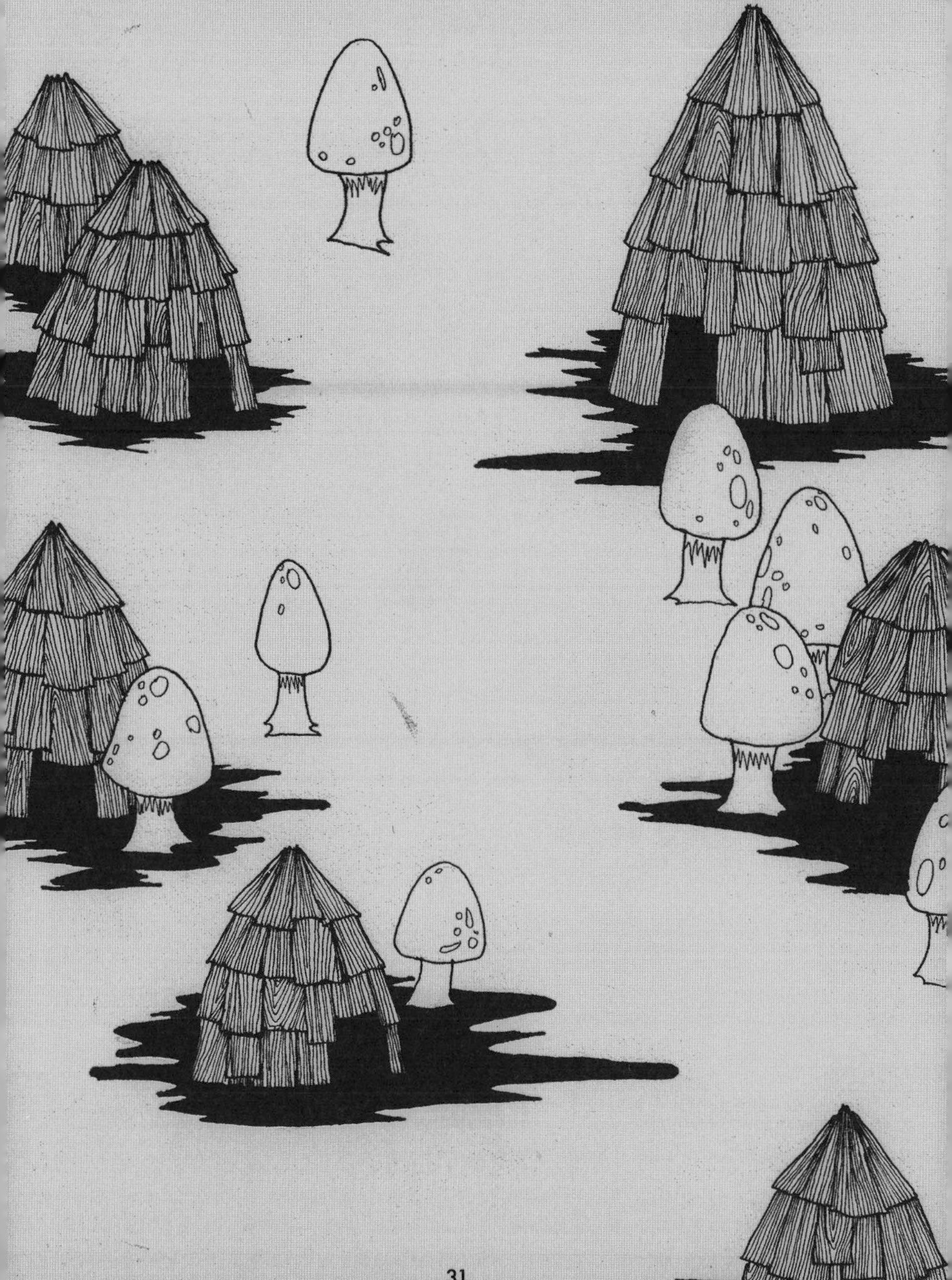

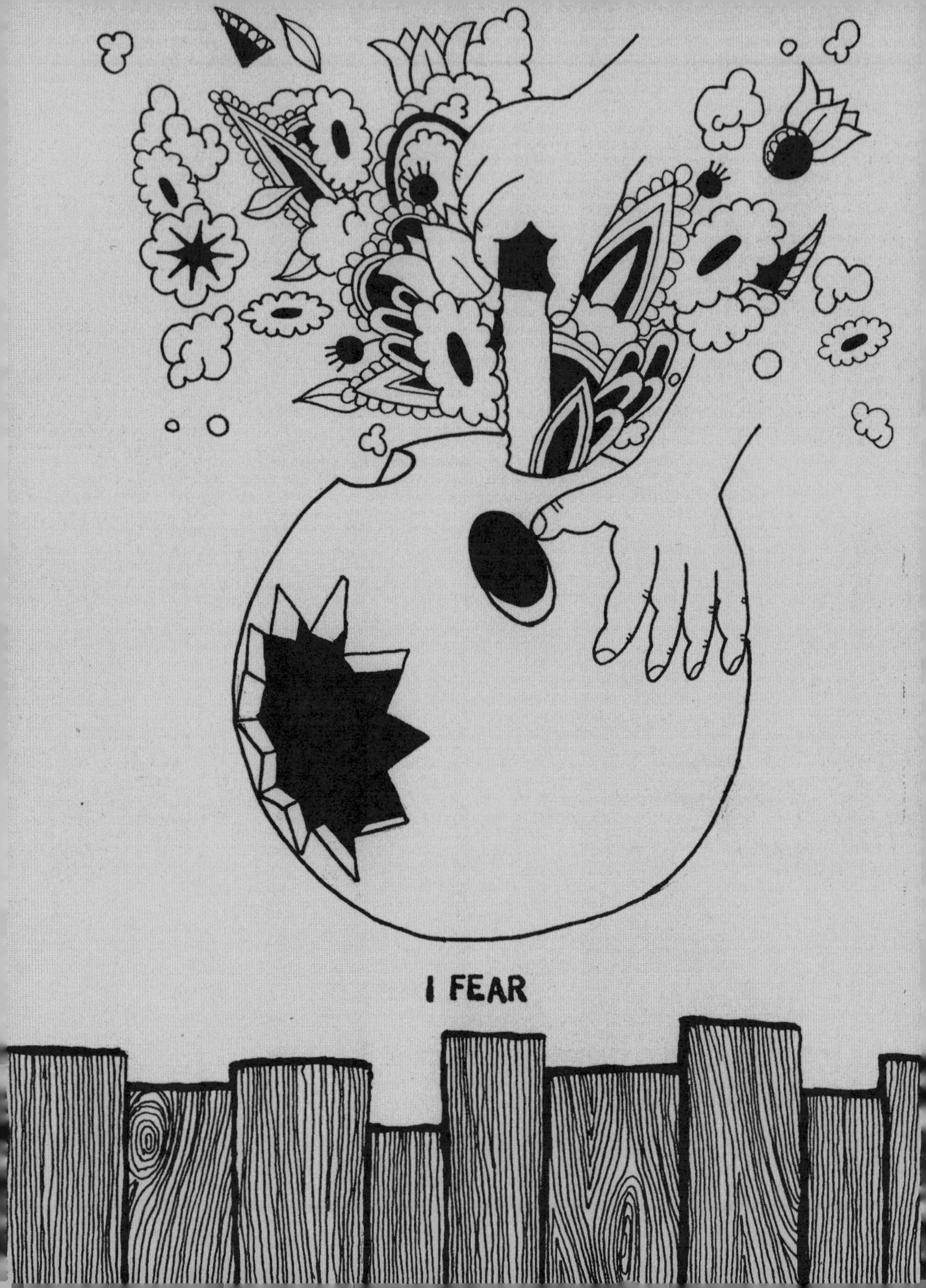
I FEAR

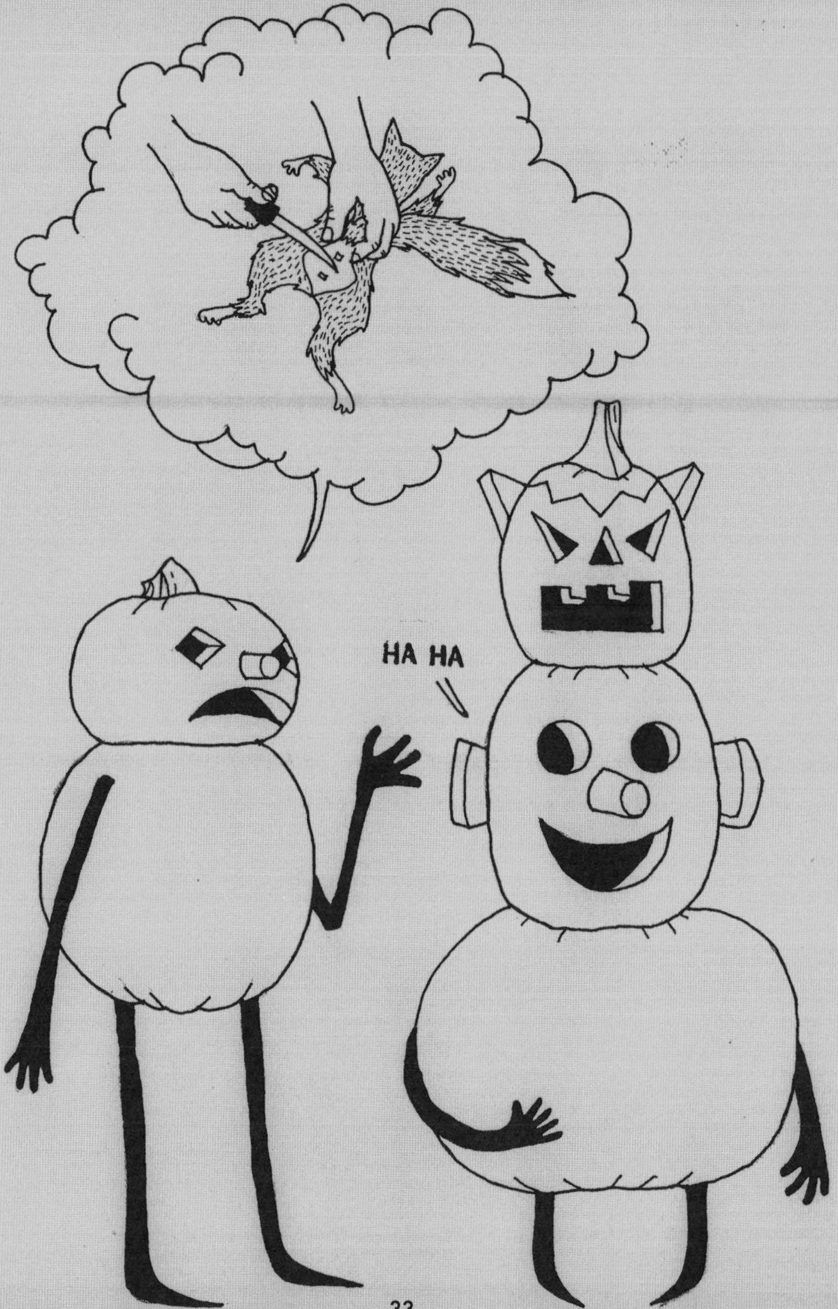
HA HA

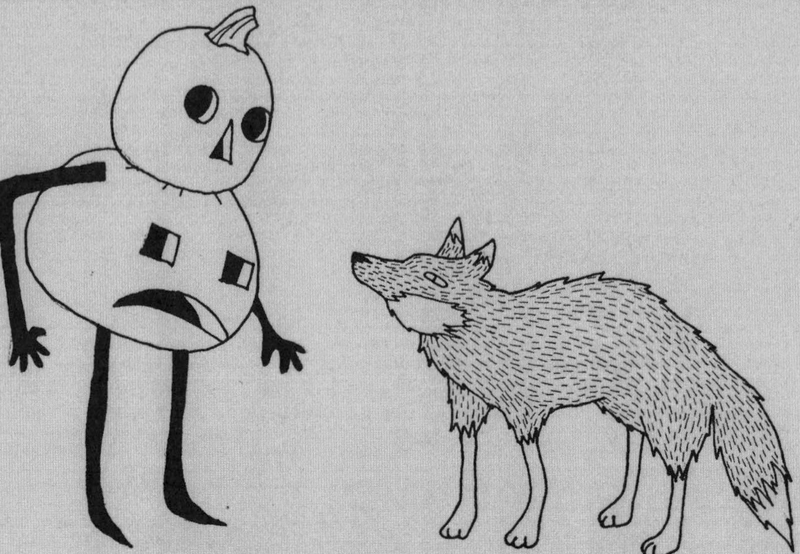

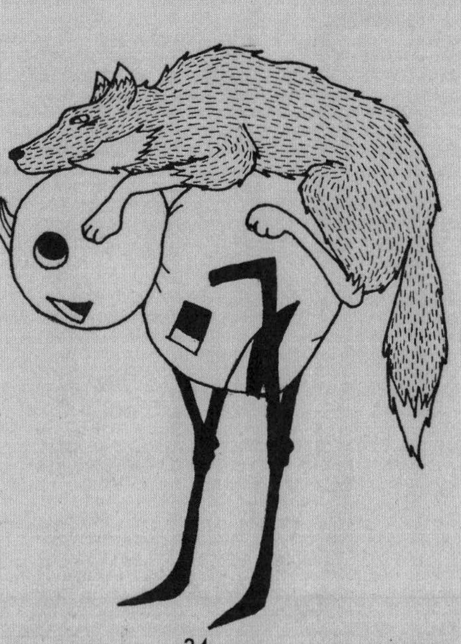

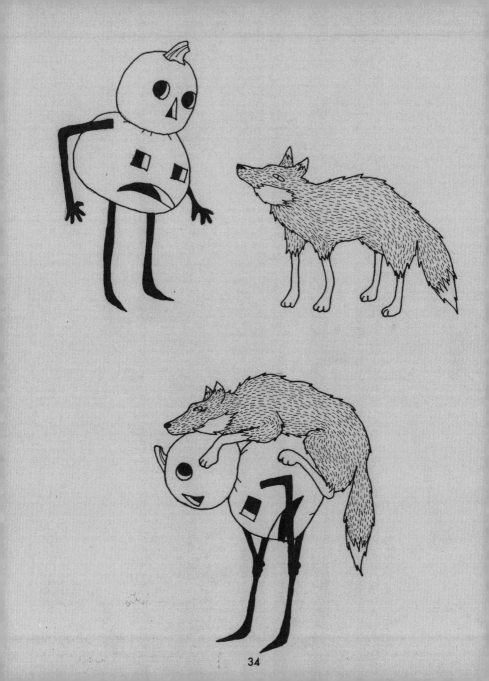

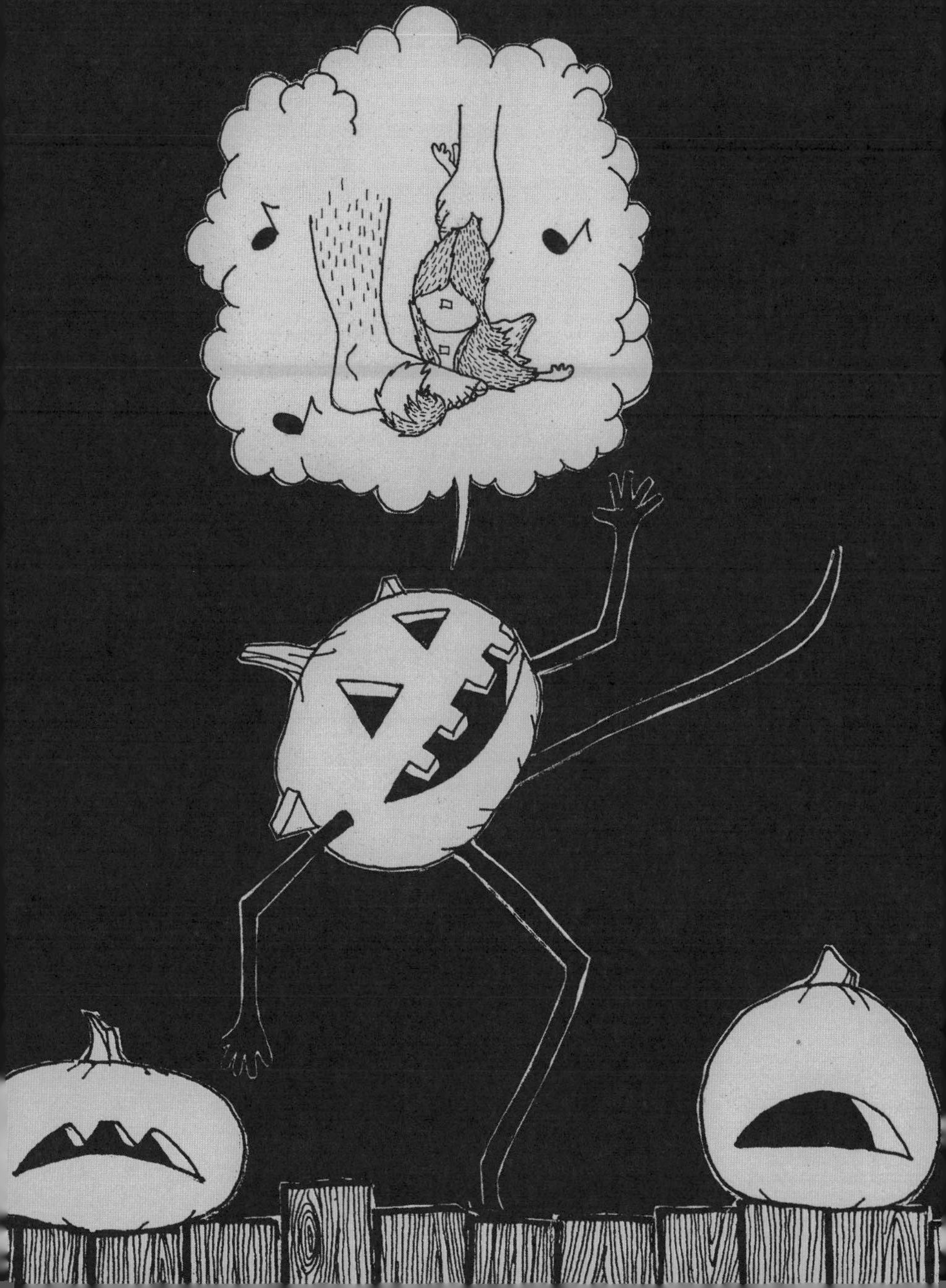

MULLIGATAWNY

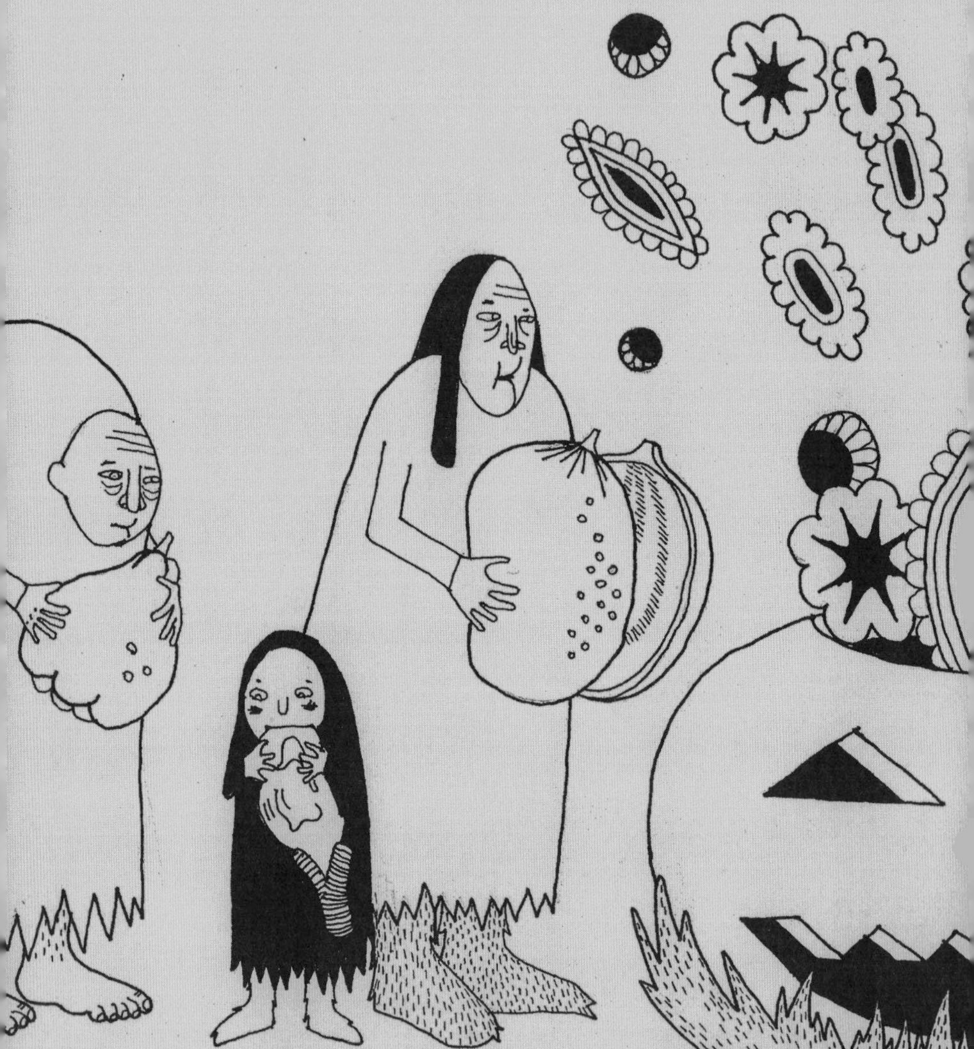

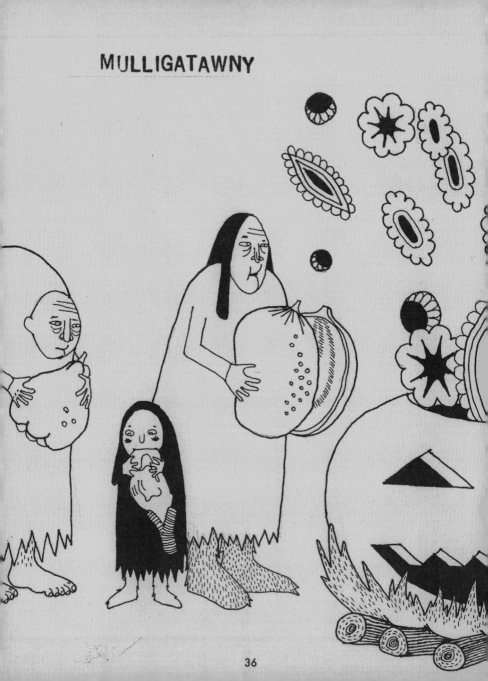

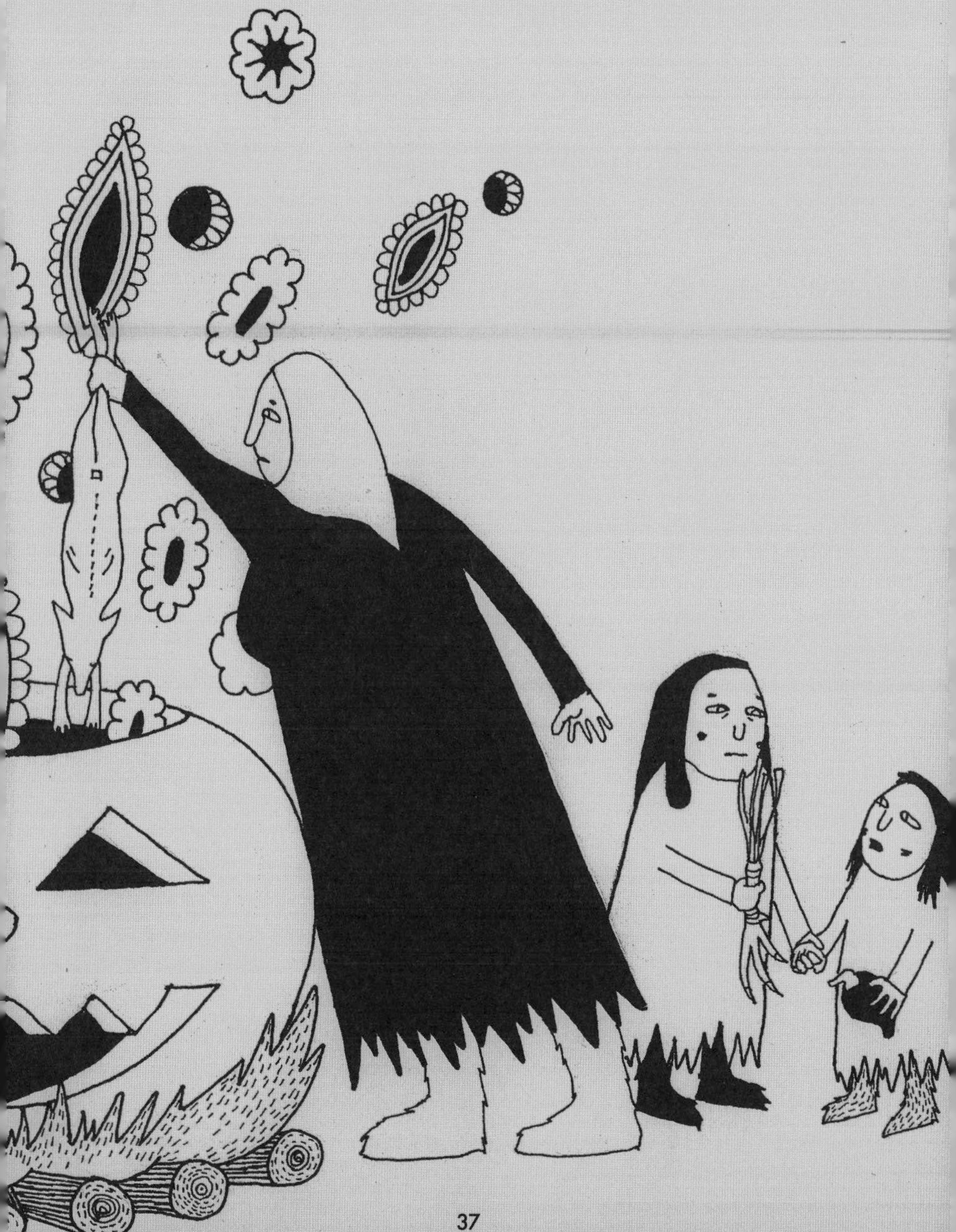

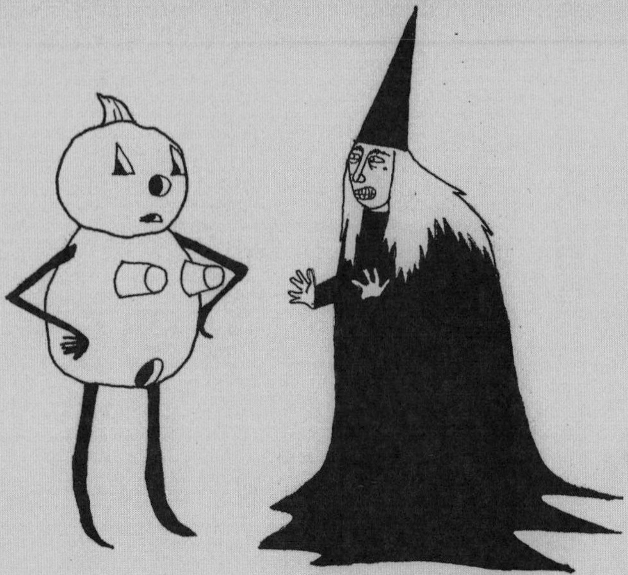

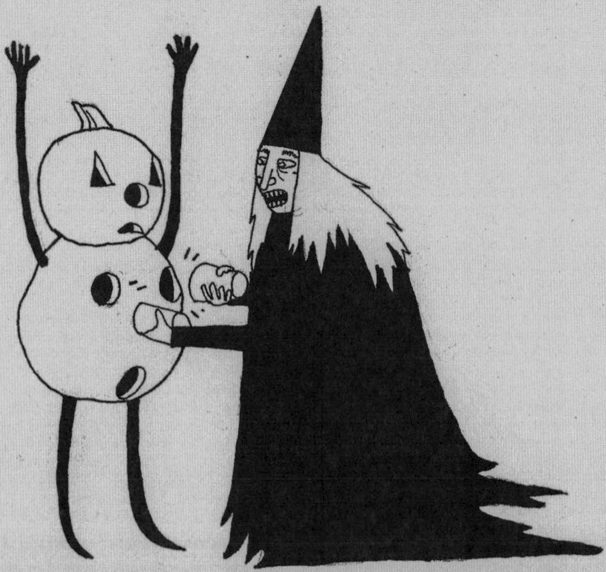

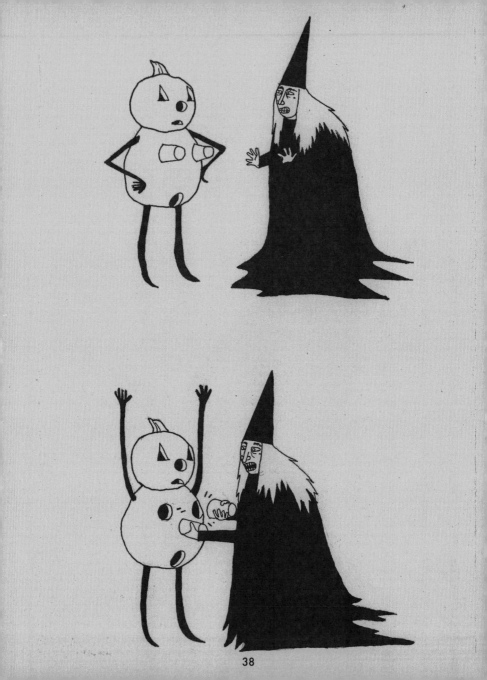

THE OL' SWITCHEROO

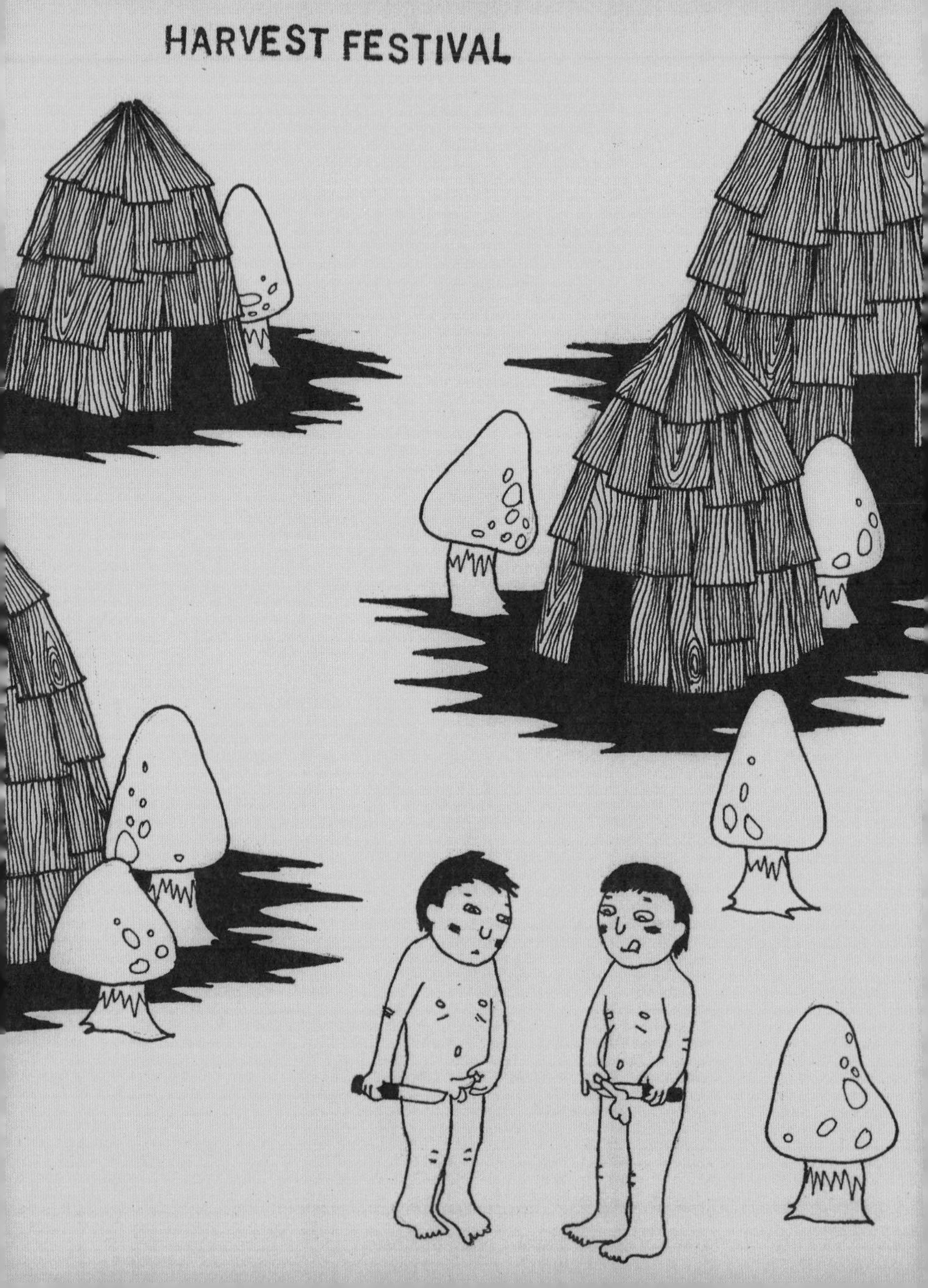
HARVEST FESTIVAL

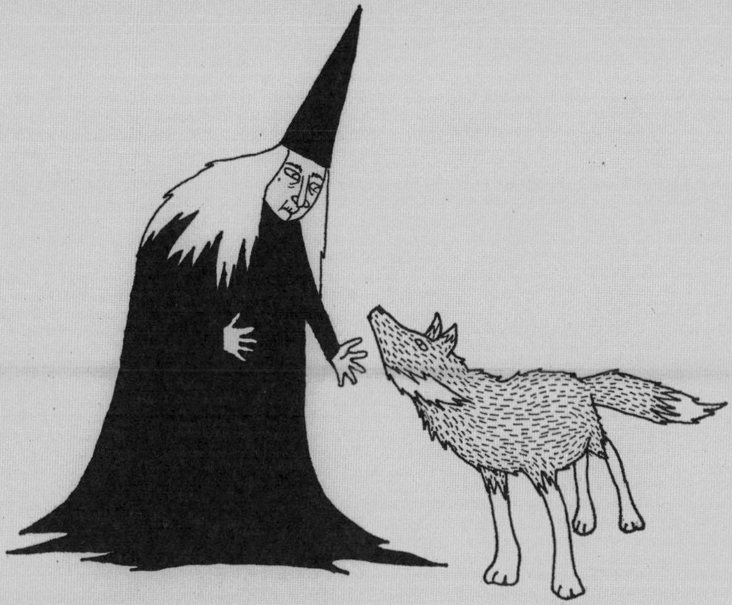

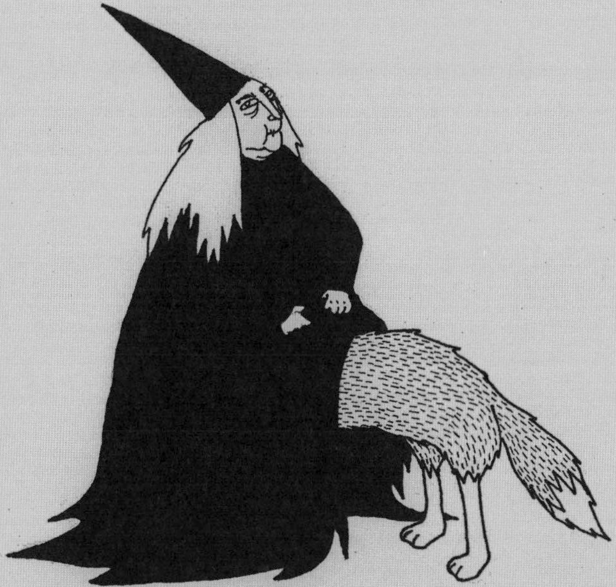

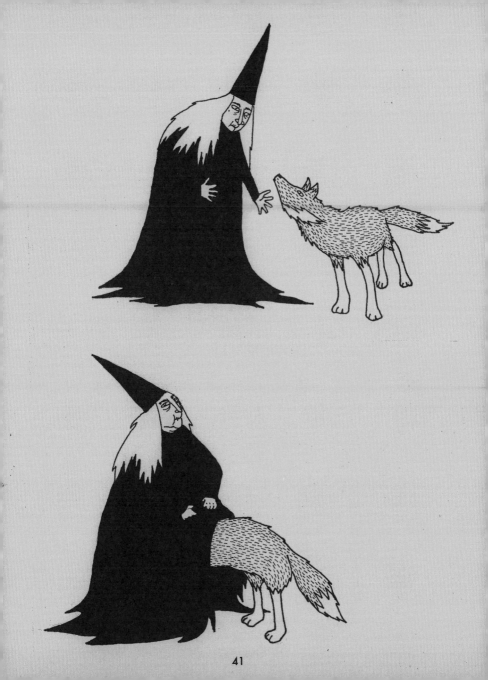

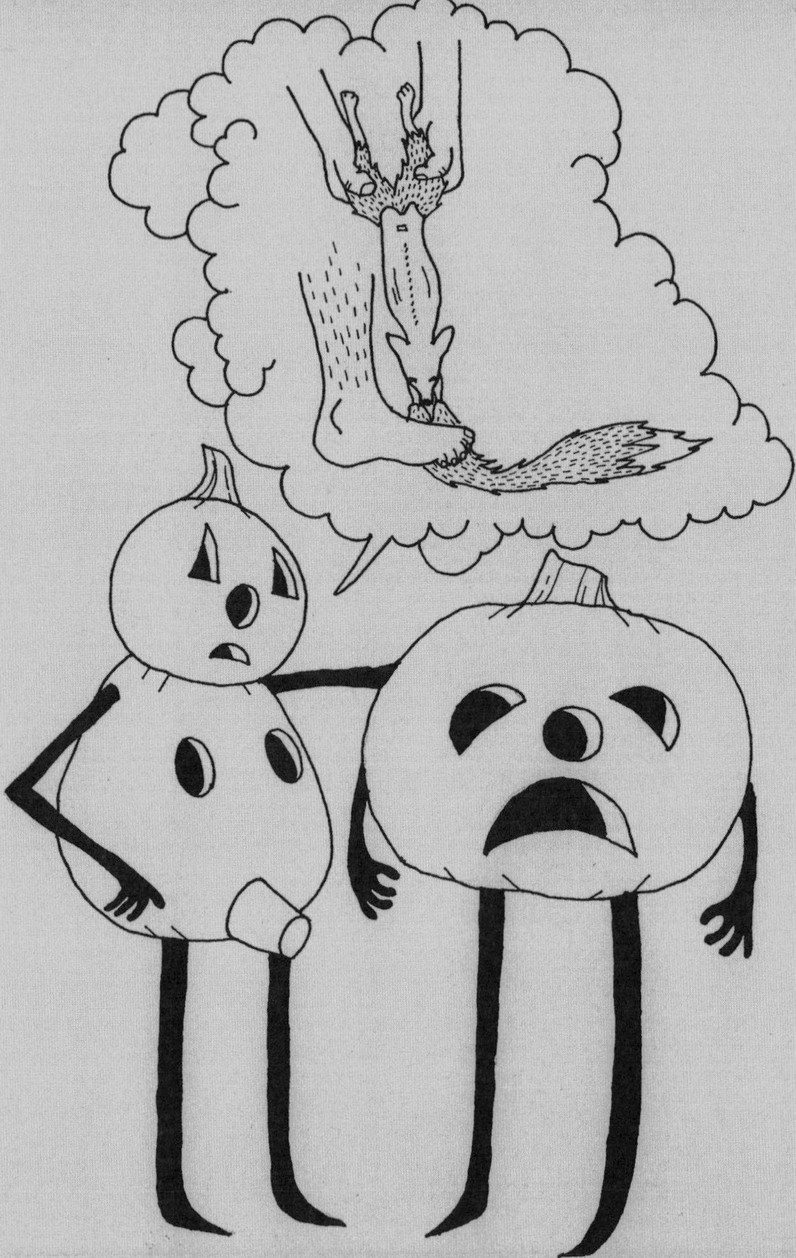

I FEAR NOT

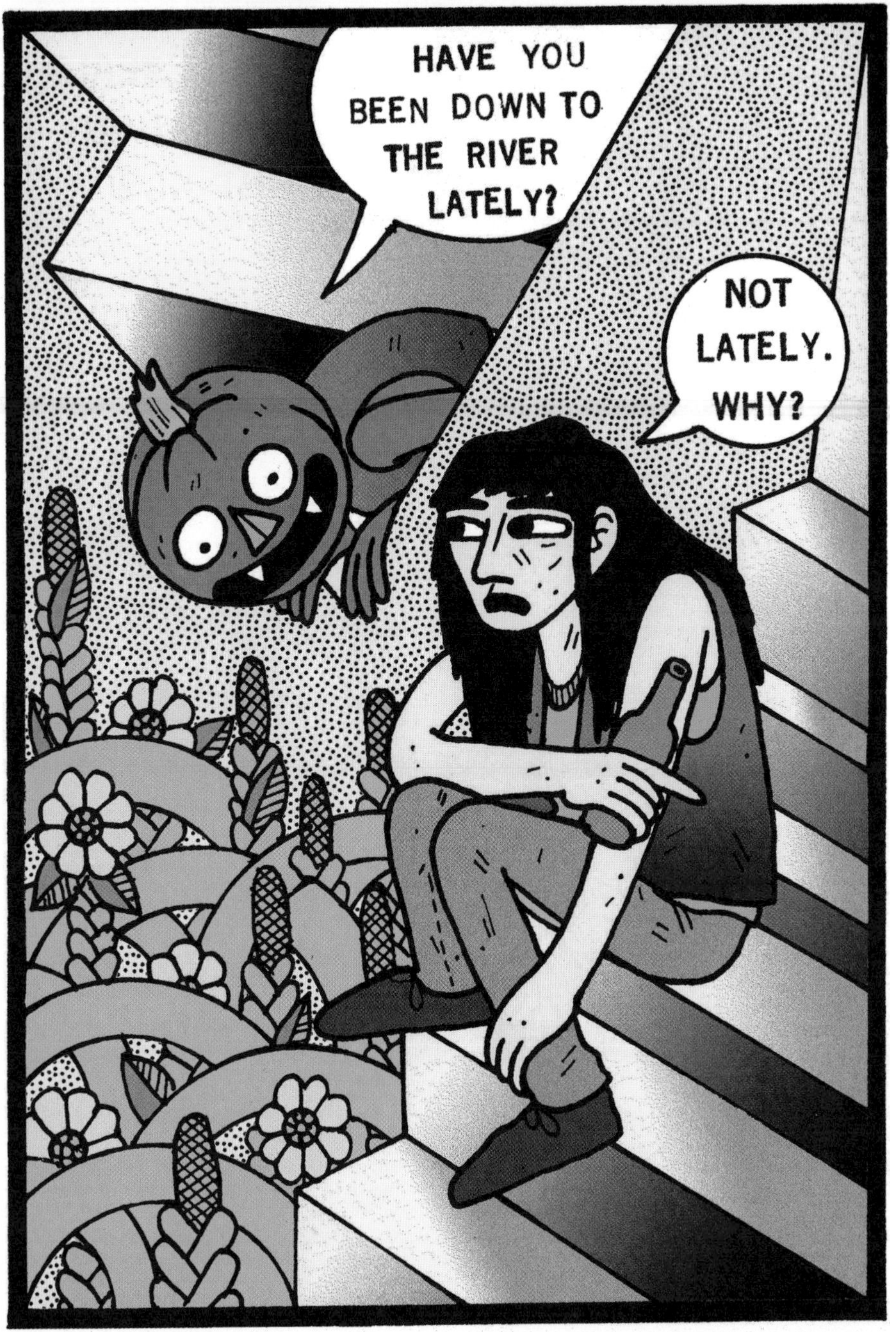
HAVE YOU BEEN DOWN TO THE RIVER LATELY?
NOT LATELY. WHY?

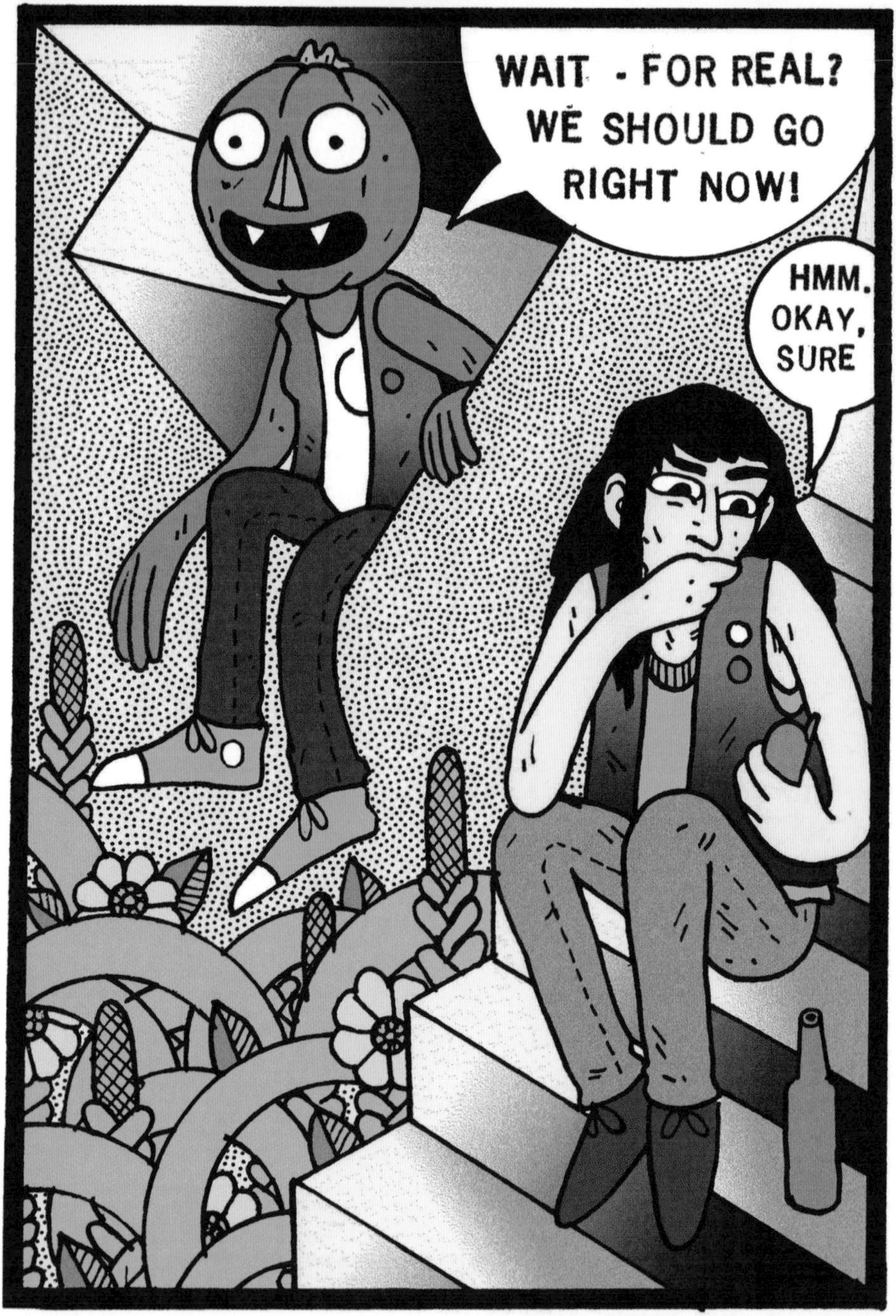
WAIT - FOR REAL? WE SHOULD GO RIGHT NOW!
HMM. OKAY, SURE

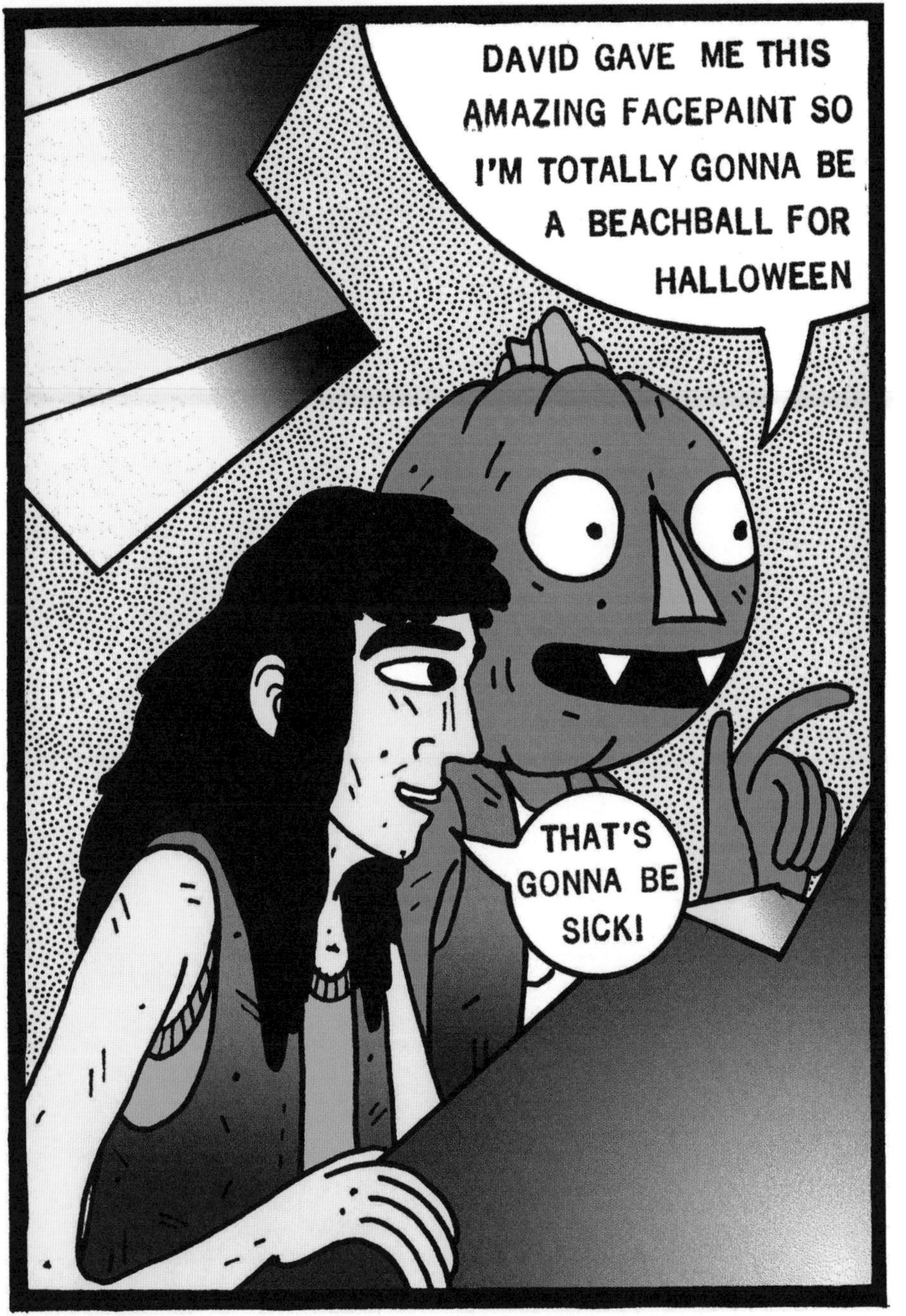
DAVID GAVE ME THIS AMAZING FACEPAINT SO I'M TOTALLY GONNA BE A BEACHBALL FOR HALLOWEEN
THAT'S GONNA BE SICK!

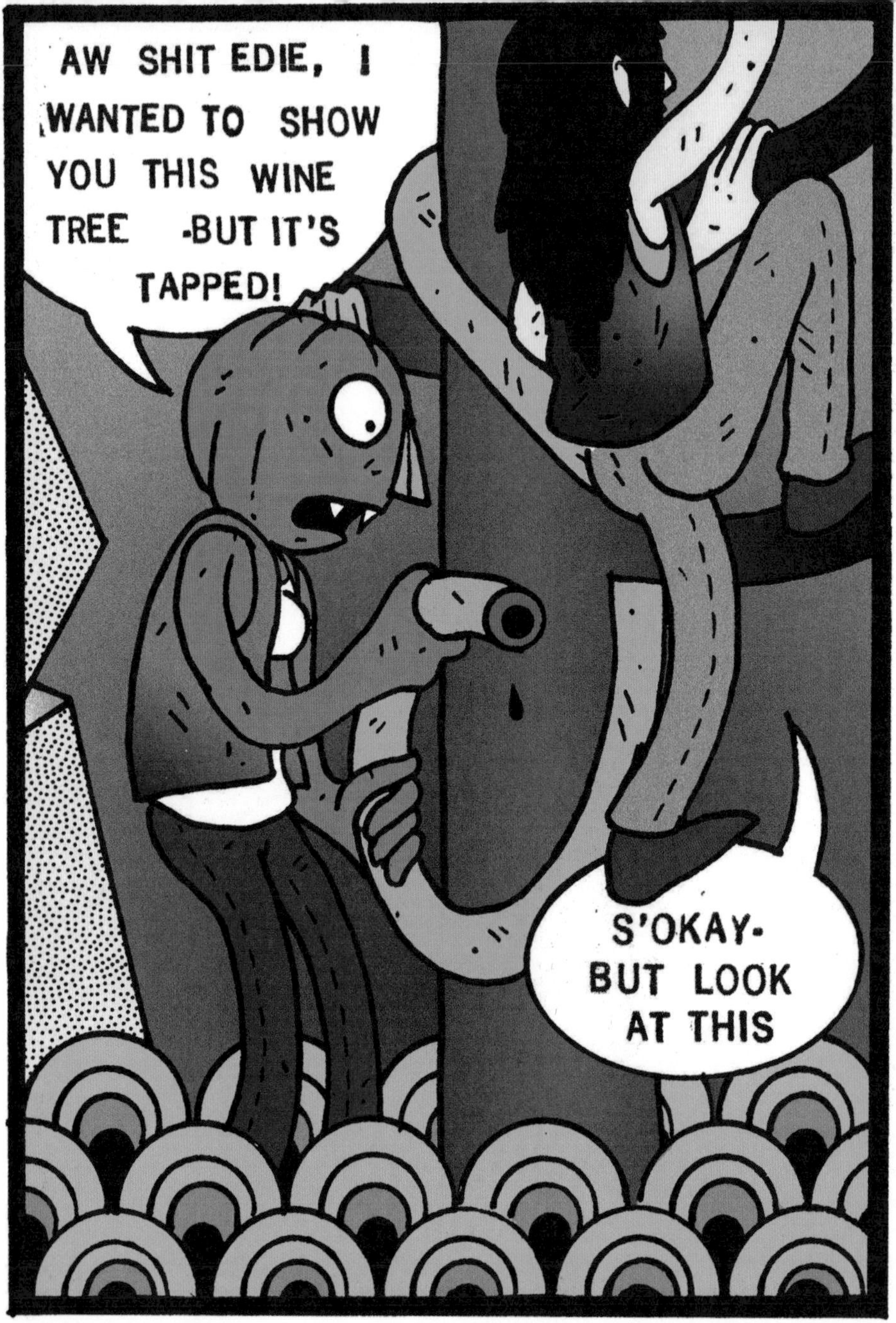
AW SHIT EDIE, I WANTED TO SHOW YOU THIS WINE TREE -BUT IT'S TAPPED!
S'OKAY- BUT LOOK AT THIS

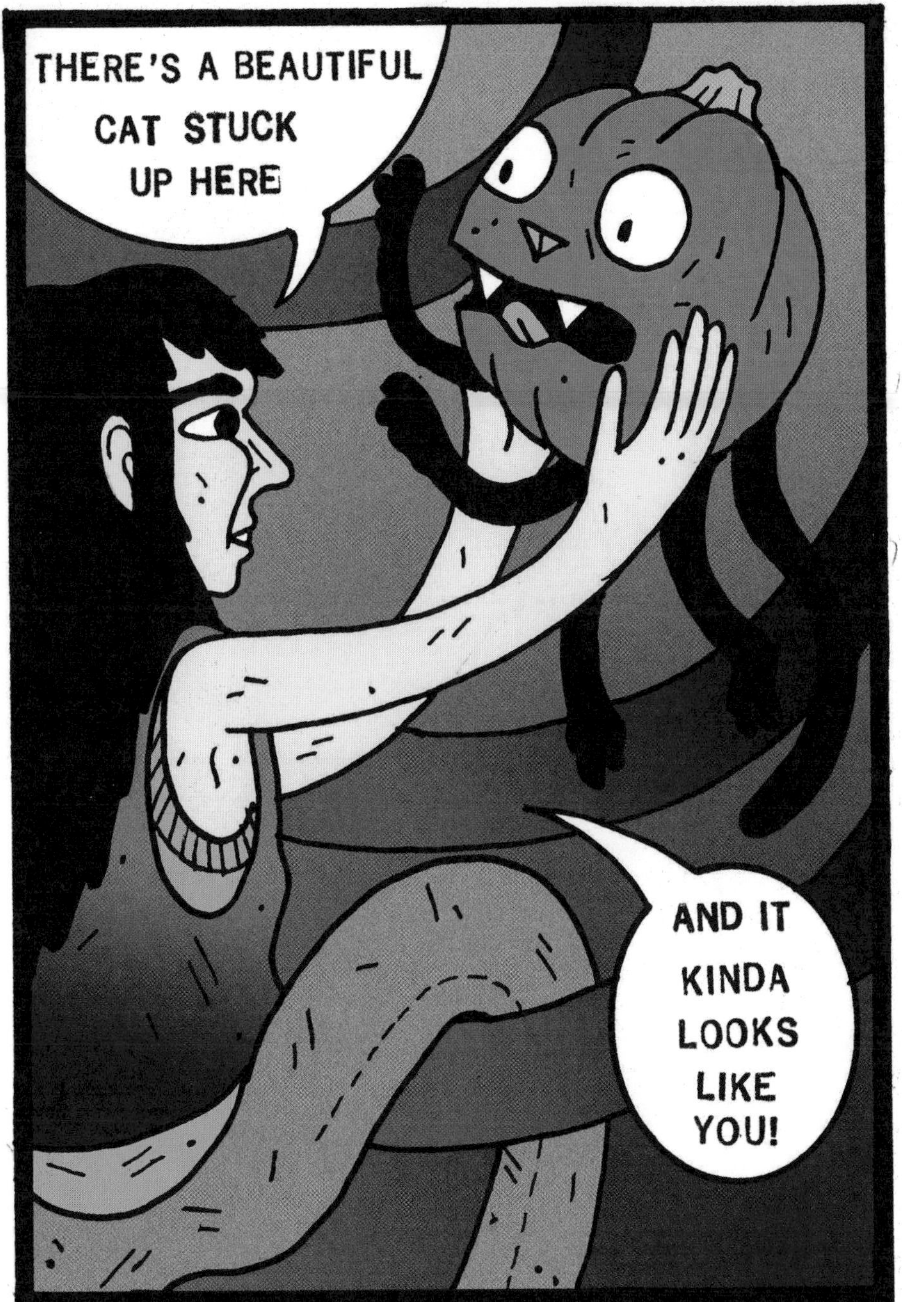
THERE'S A BEAUTIFUL CAT STUCK UP HERE
AND IT KINDA LOOKS LIKE YOU!

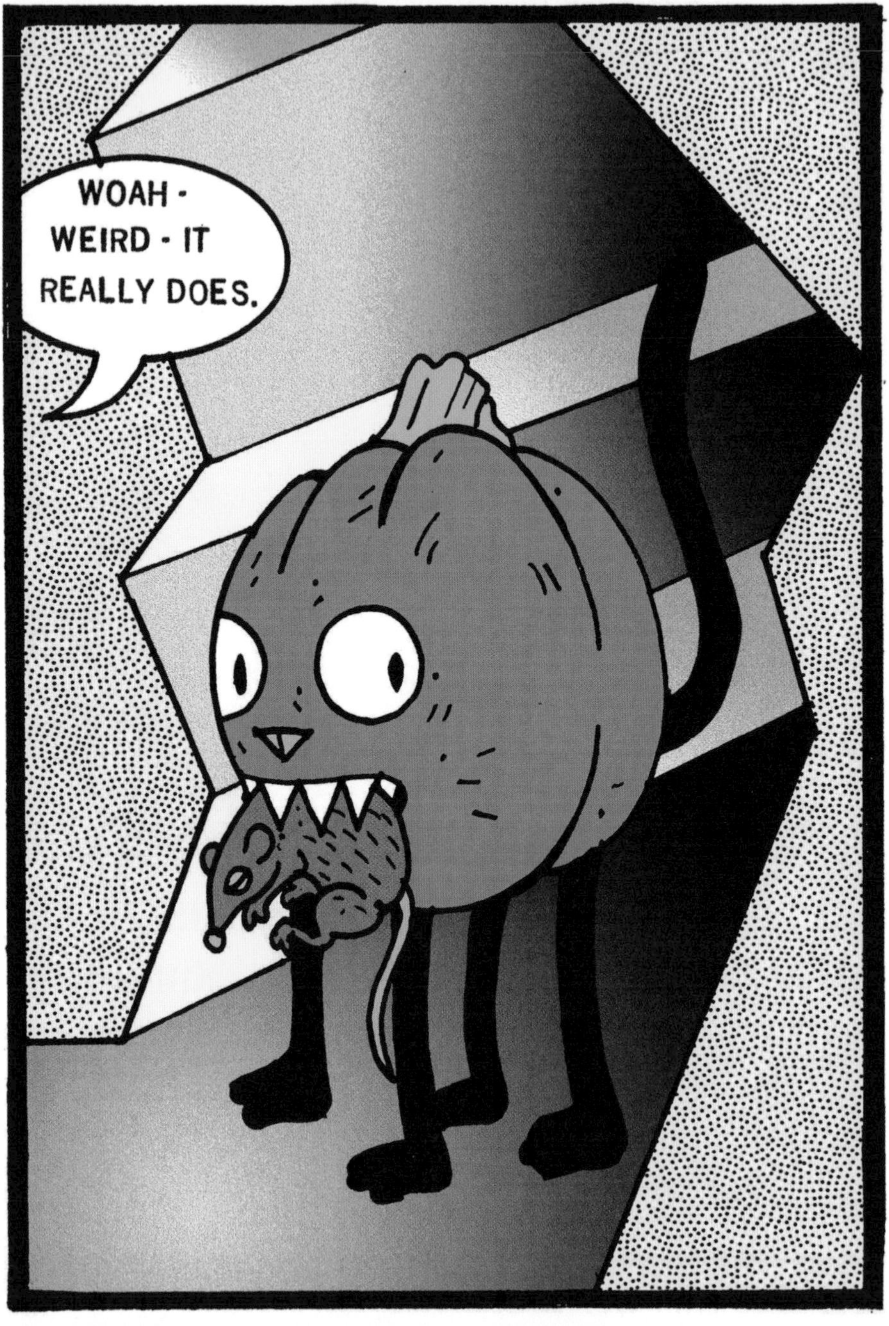
WOAH - WEIRD - IT REALLY DOES.

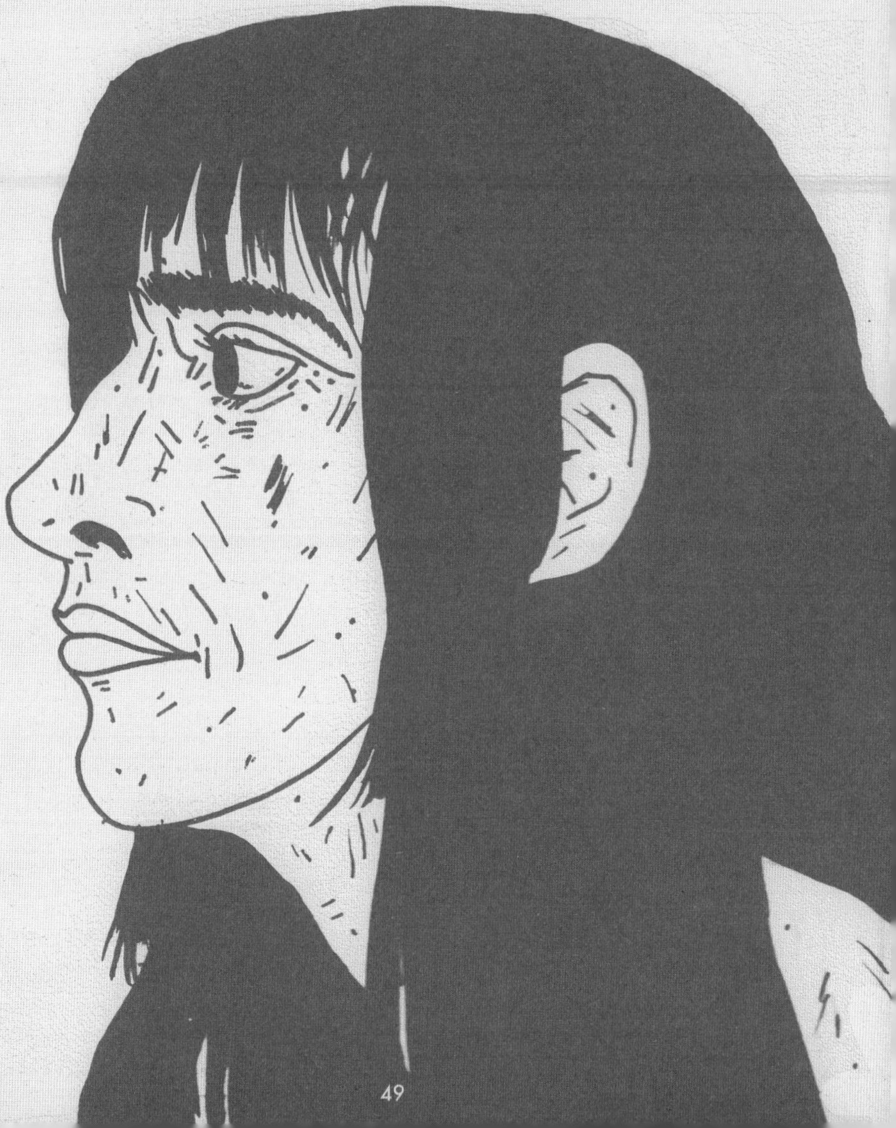

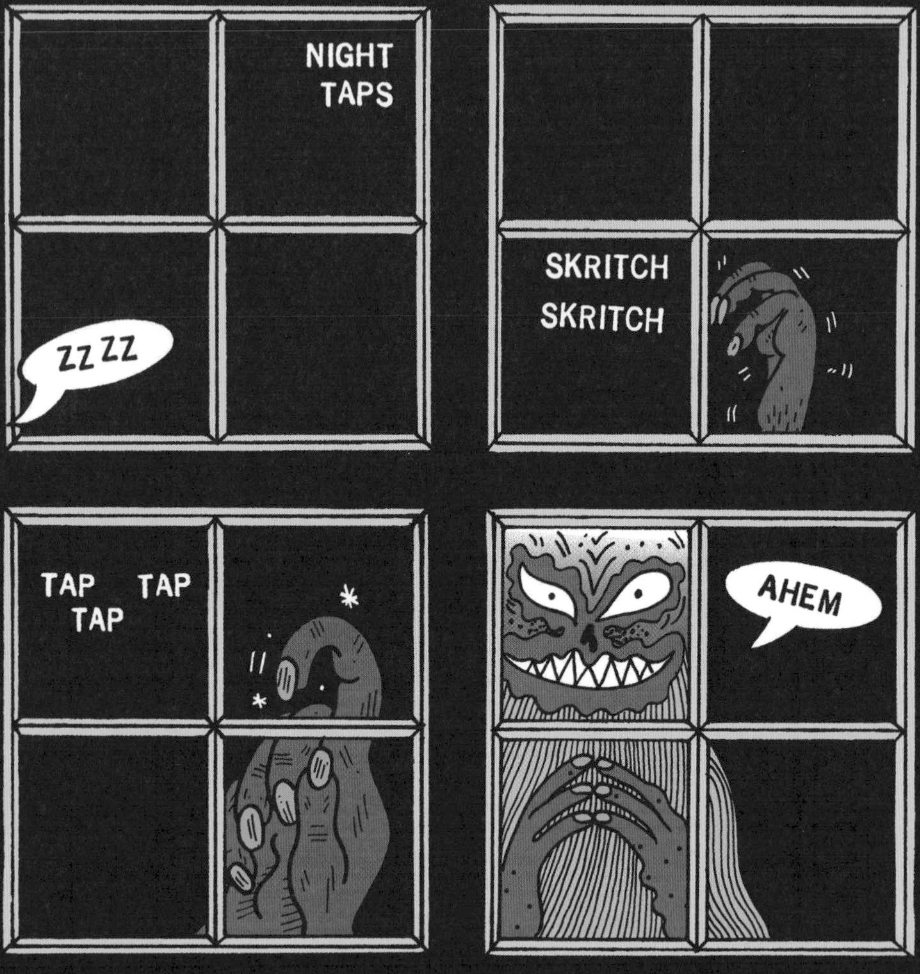
NIGHT
TAPS
ZZZZ
SKRITCH
SKRITCH
TAP TAP
TAP
AHEM

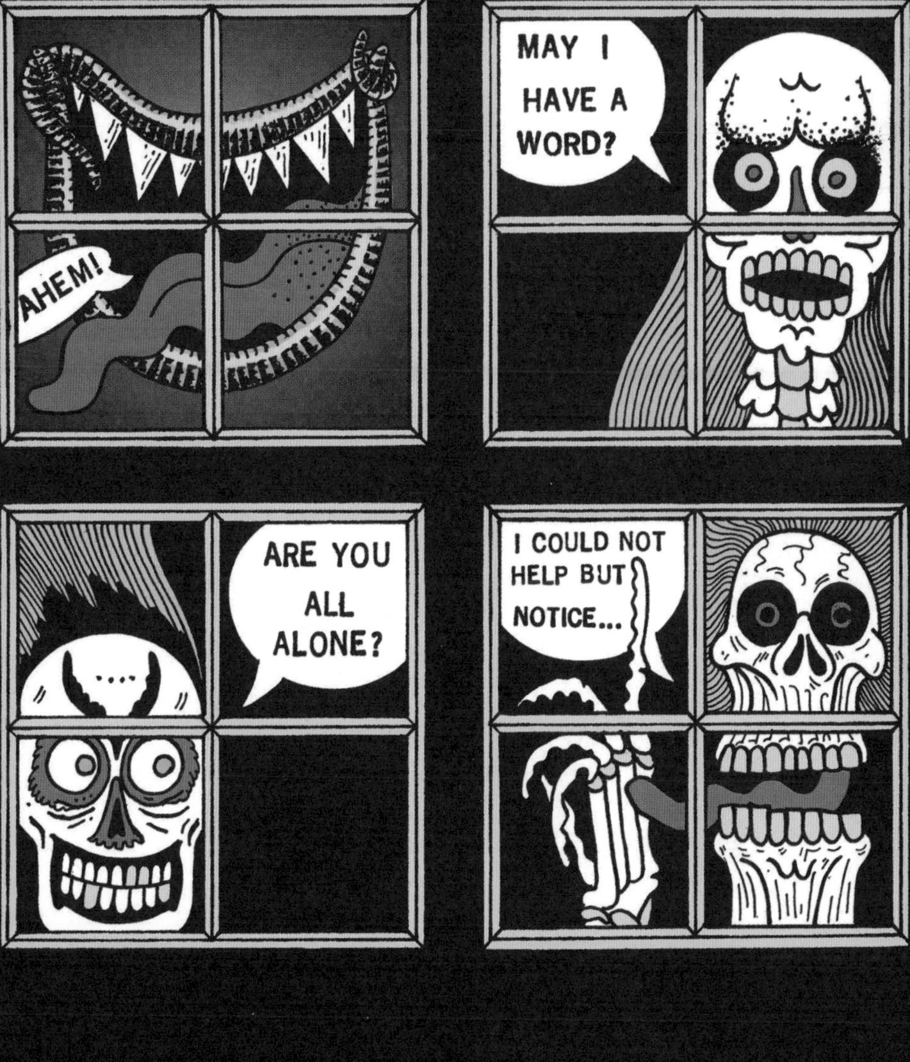
AHEM!
MAY I HAVE A WORD?
ARE YOU ALL ALONE?
I COULD NOT HELP BUT NOTICE...

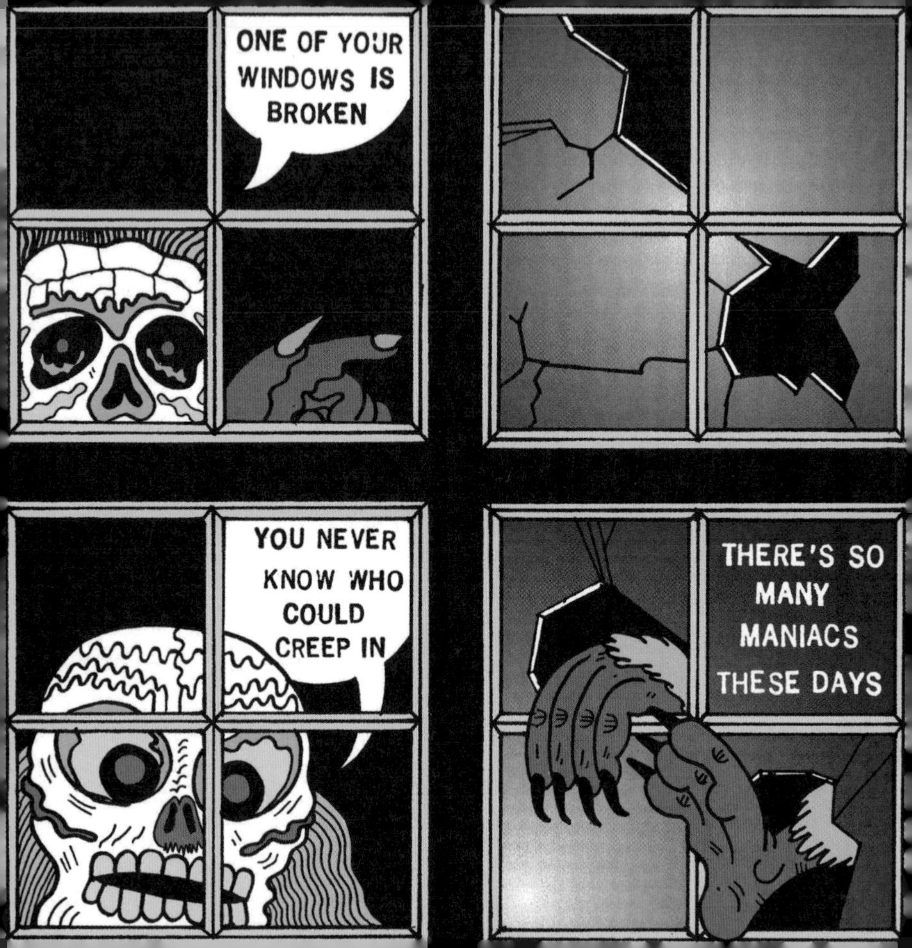
ONE OF YOUR WINDOWS IS BROKEN
YOU NEVER KNOW WHO COULD CREEP IN
THERE'S SO MANY MANIACS THESE DAYS

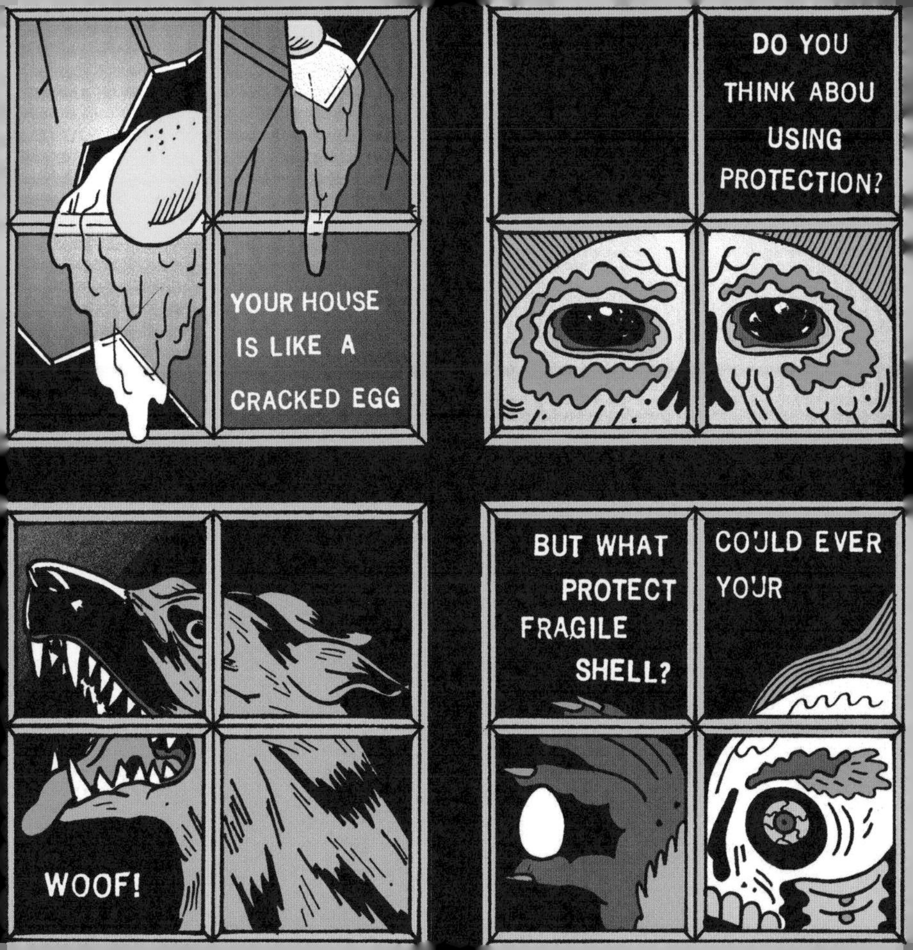

YOUR HOUSE IS LIKE A CRACKED EGG
DO YOU THINK ABOU USING PROTECTION?
WOOF!
BUT WHAT PROTECT
COULD EVER YOUR
FRAGILE SHELL?

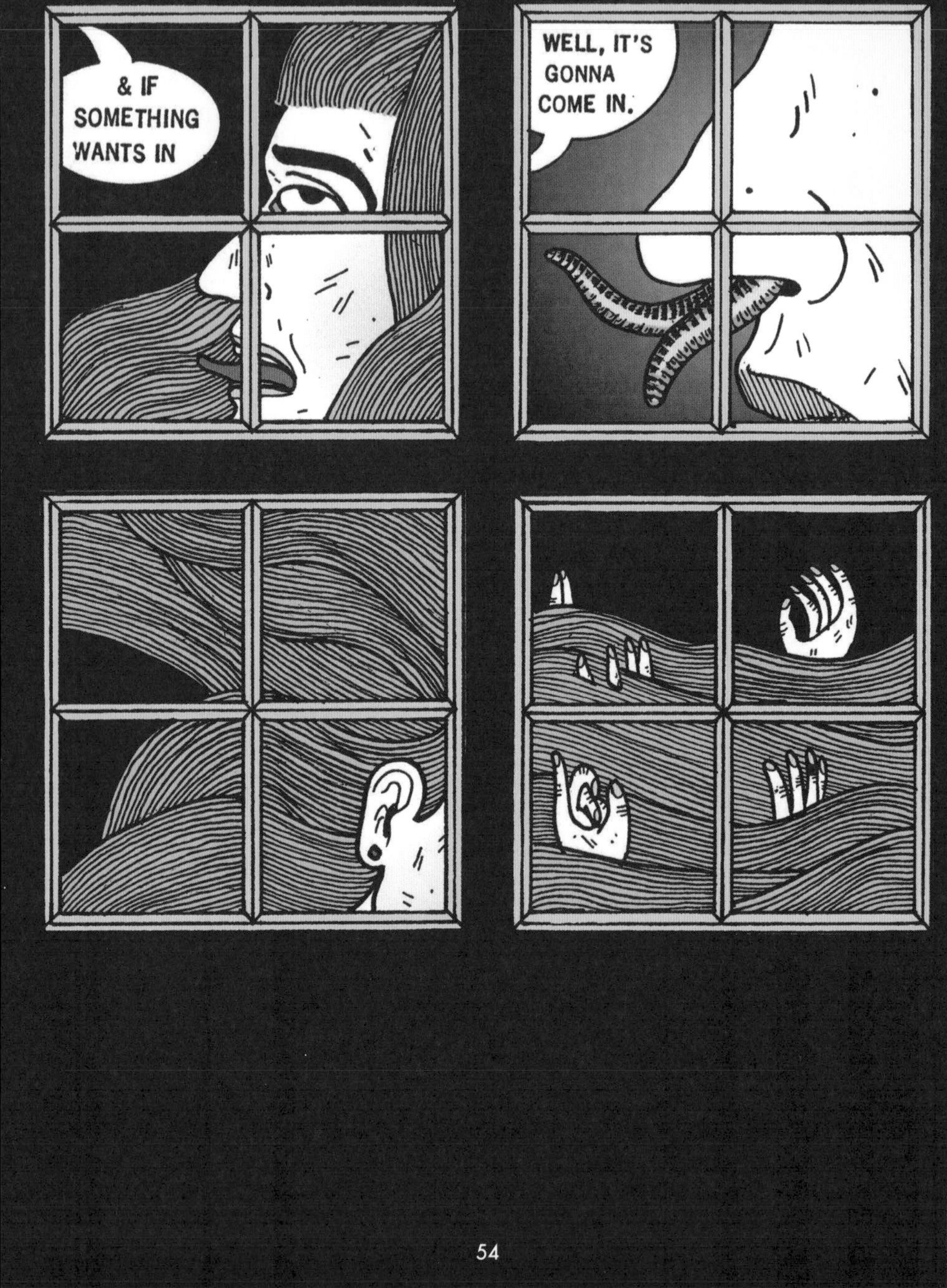
& IF SOMETHING WANTS IN
WELL, IT'S GONNA COME IN.

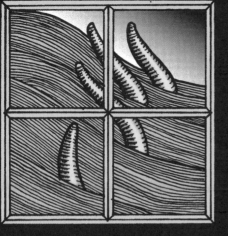
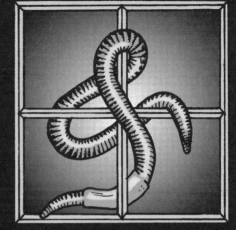
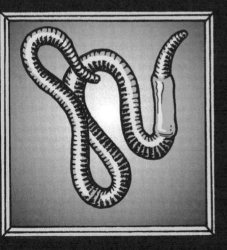

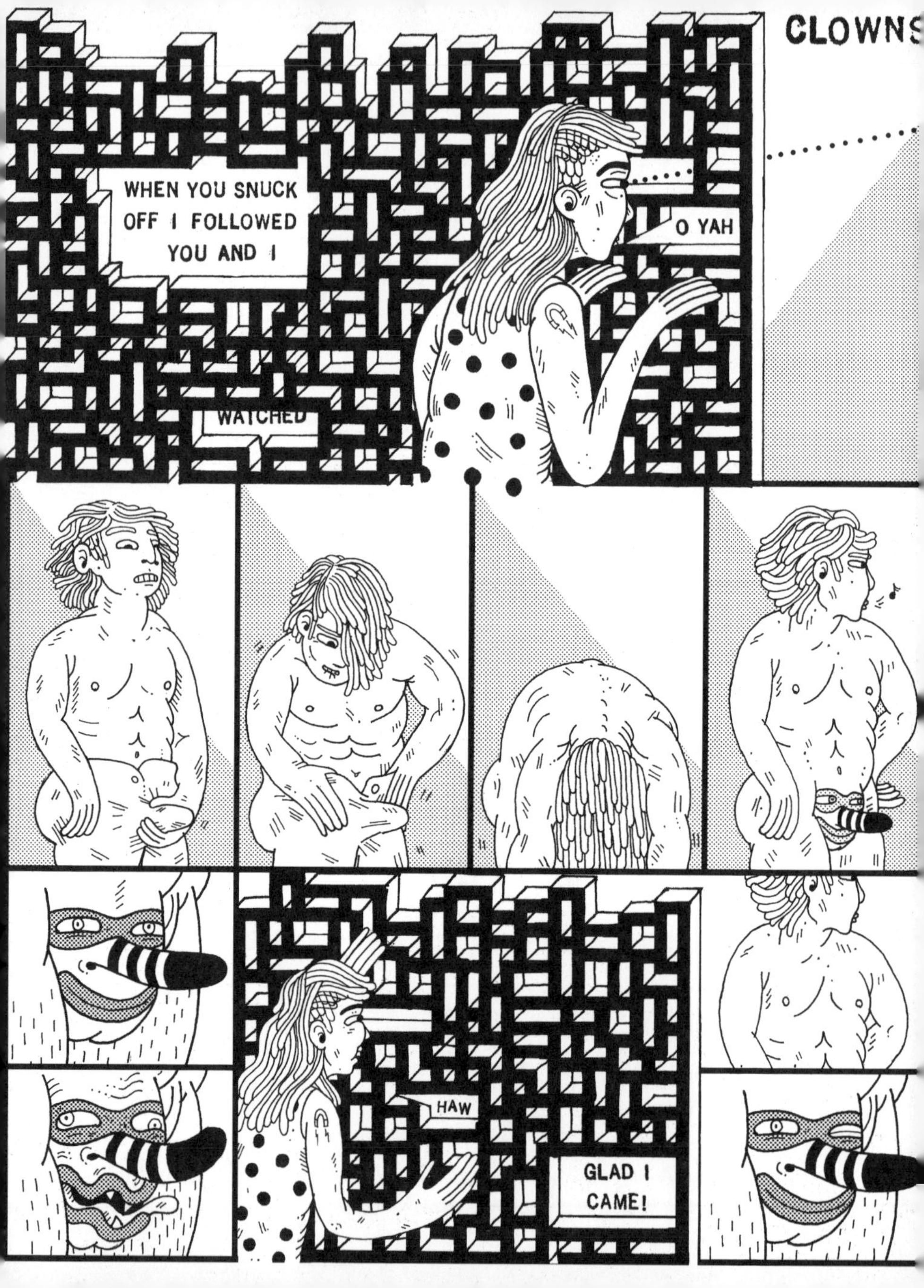
CLOWNS
WHEN YOU SNUCK OFF I FOLLOWED YOU AND I
WATCHED
O YAH
HAW
GLAD I CAME!

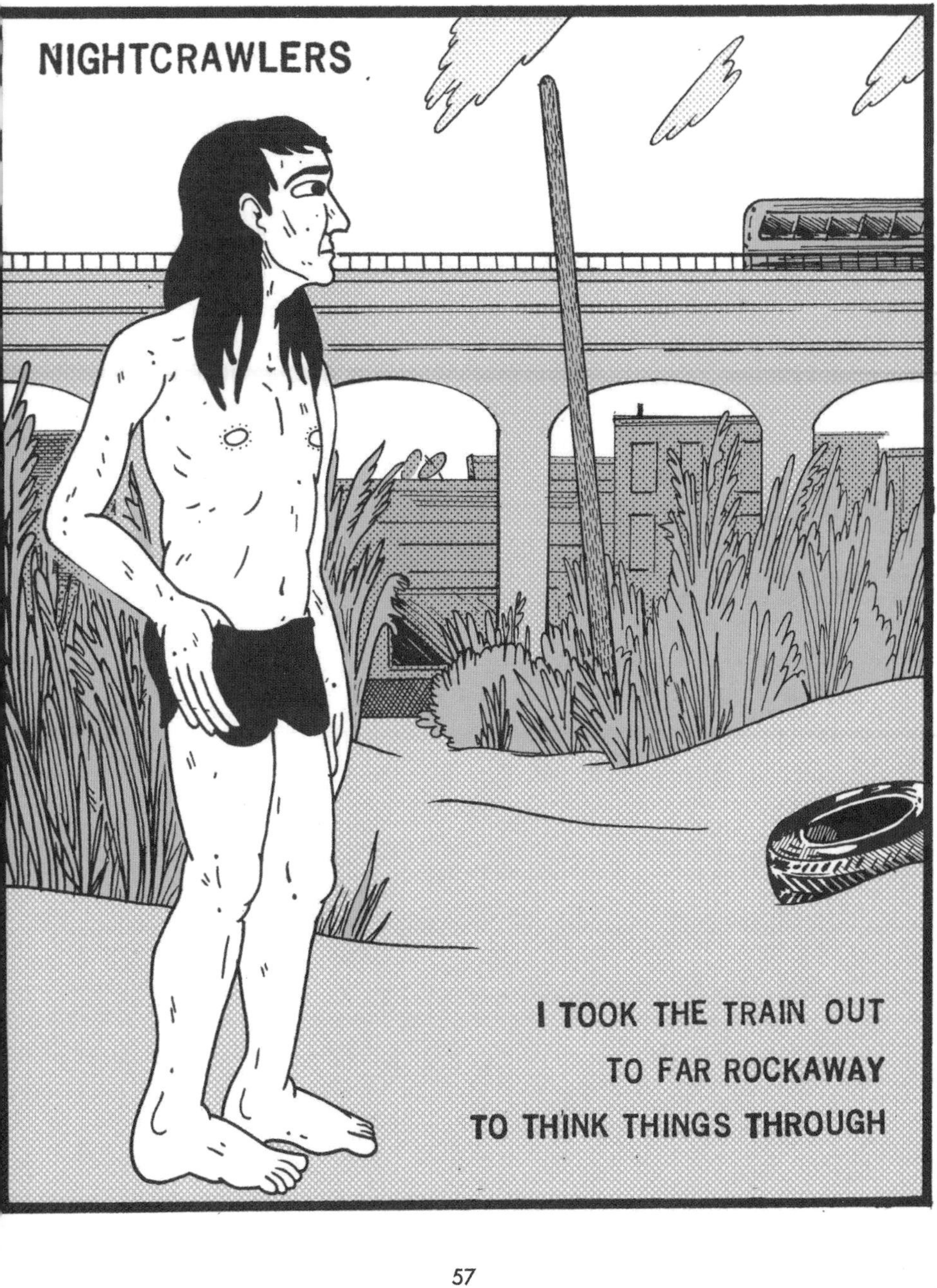
NIGHTCRAWLERS
I TOOK THE TRAIN OUT
TO FAR ROCKAWAY
TO THINK THINGS THROUGH

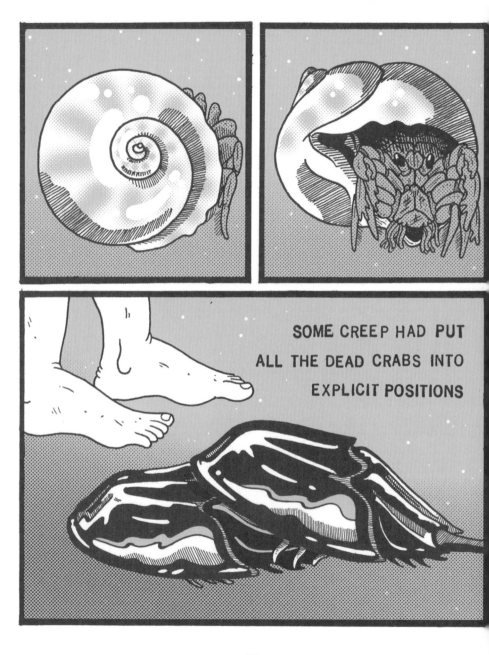

SOME CREEP HAD PUT ALL THE DEAD CRABS INTO EXPLICIT POSITIONS

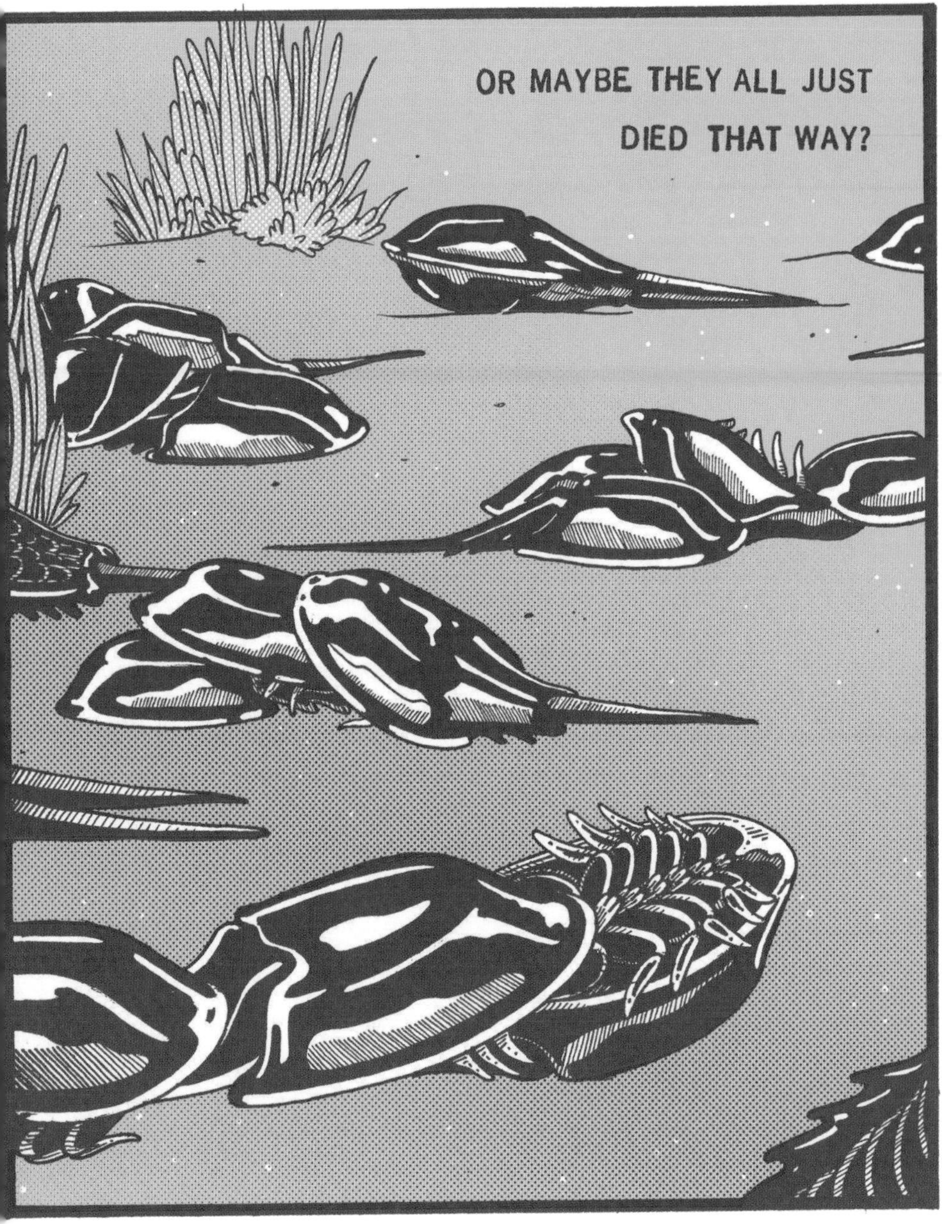
OR MAYBE THEY ALL JUST DIED THAT WAY?

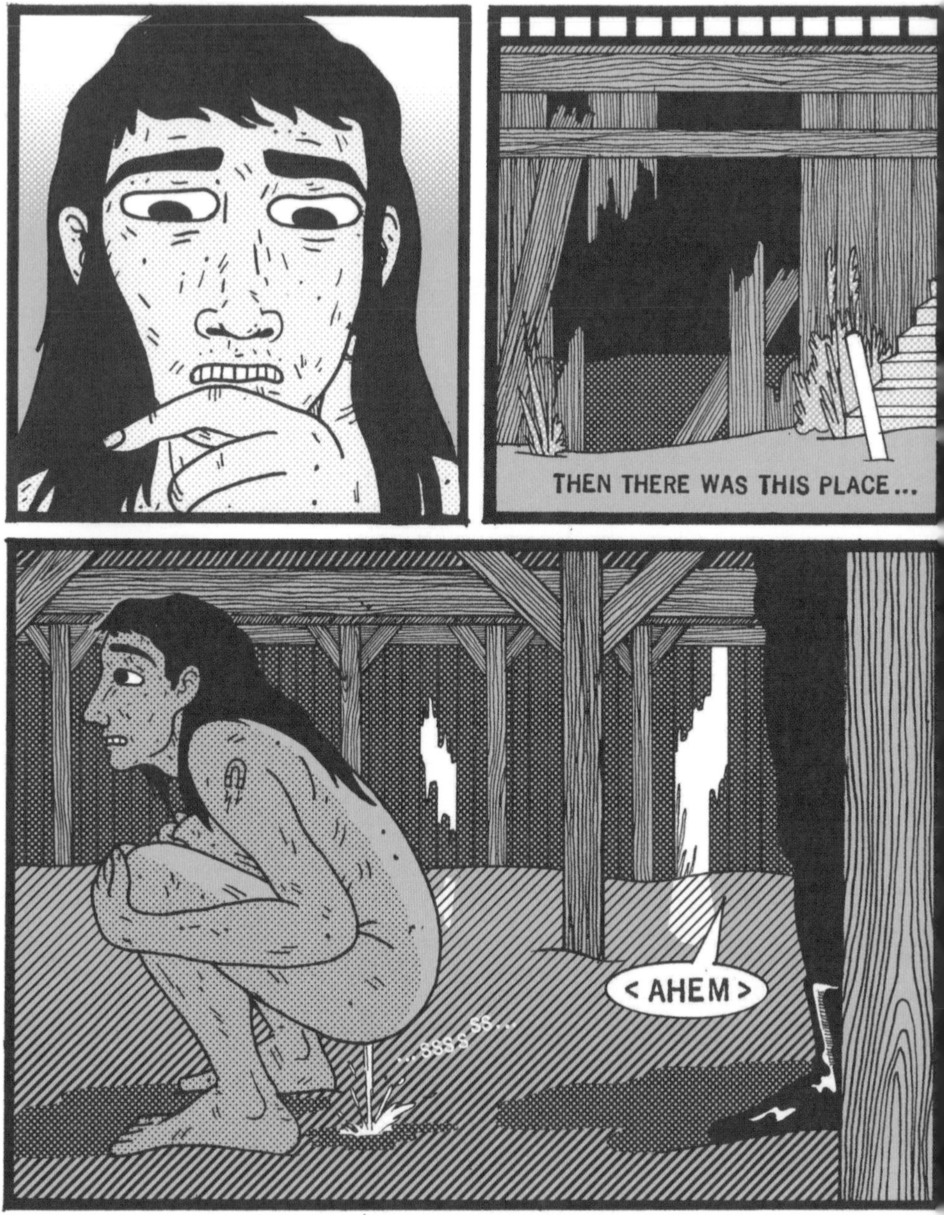
THEN THERE WAS THIS PLACE...
< AHEM >
...SSSS SS...

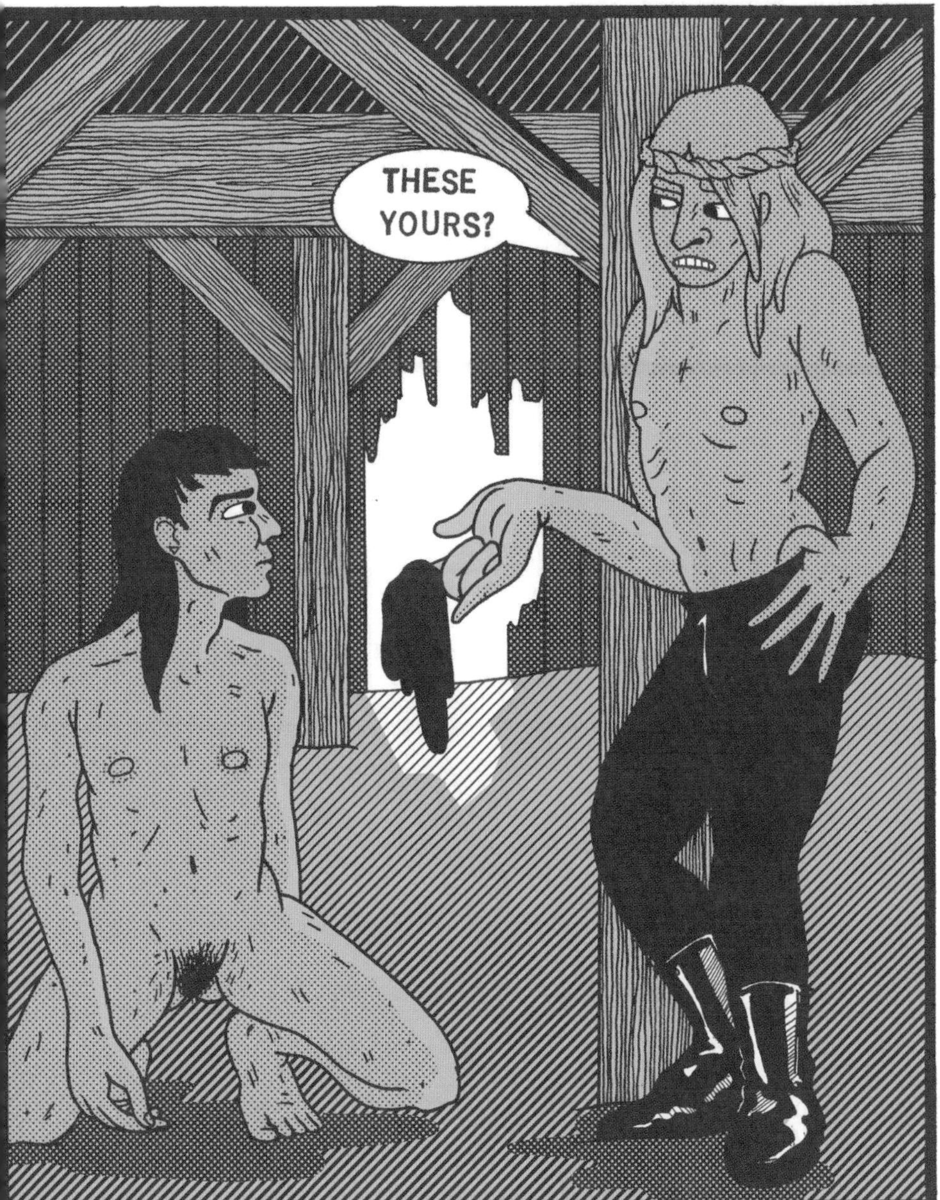
THESE YOURS?

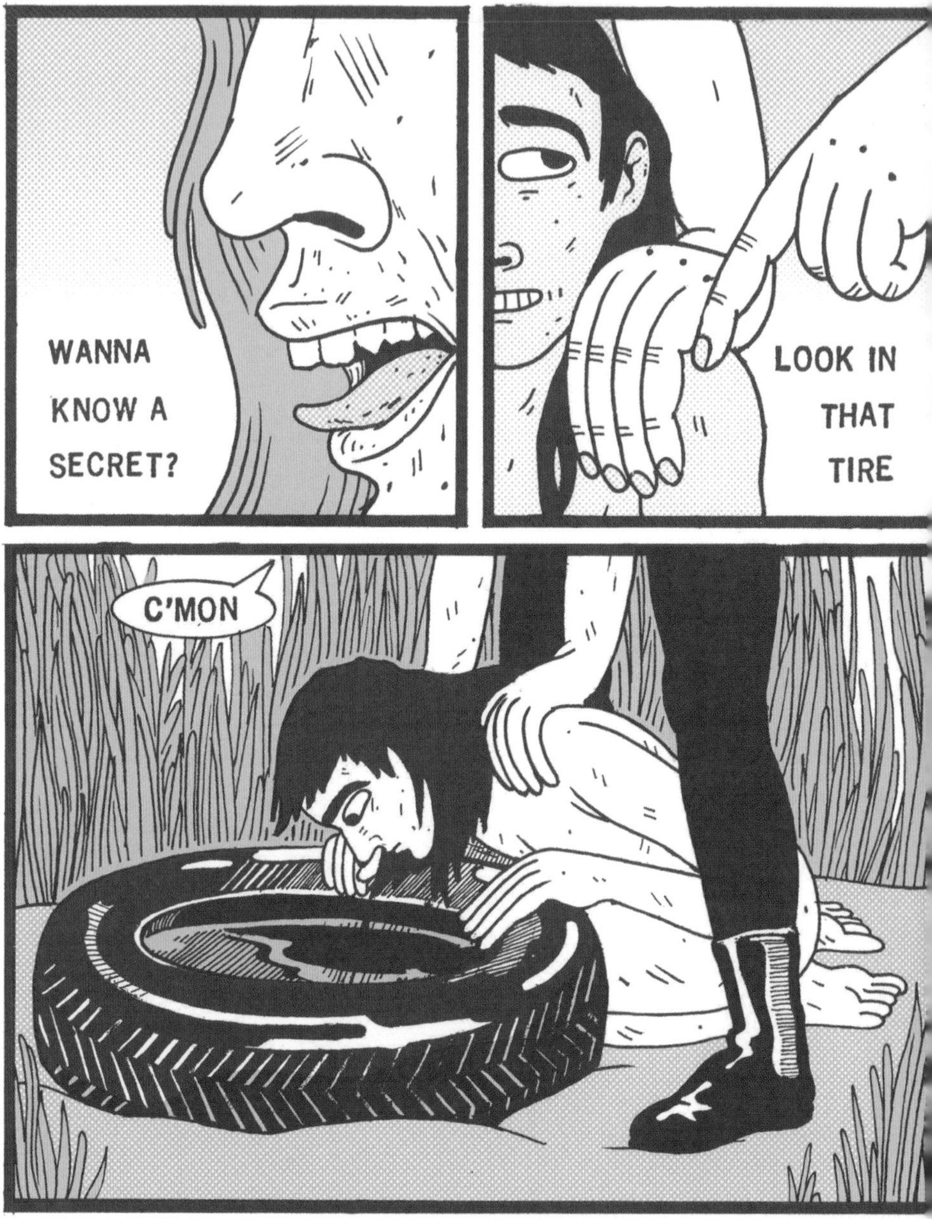

WANNA KNOW A SECRET?
LOOK IN THAT TIRE
C'MON

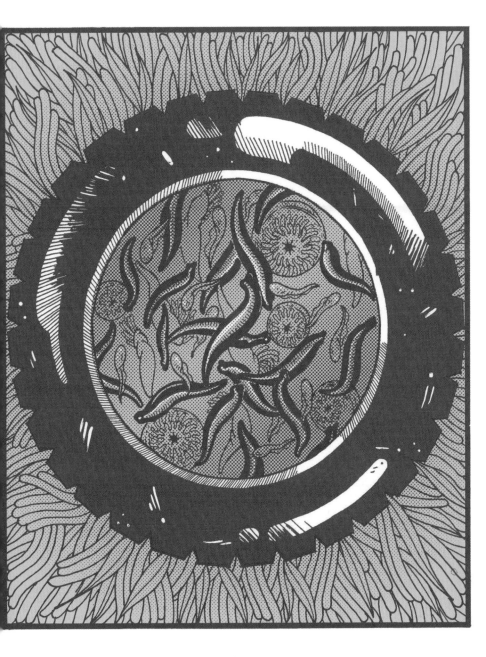

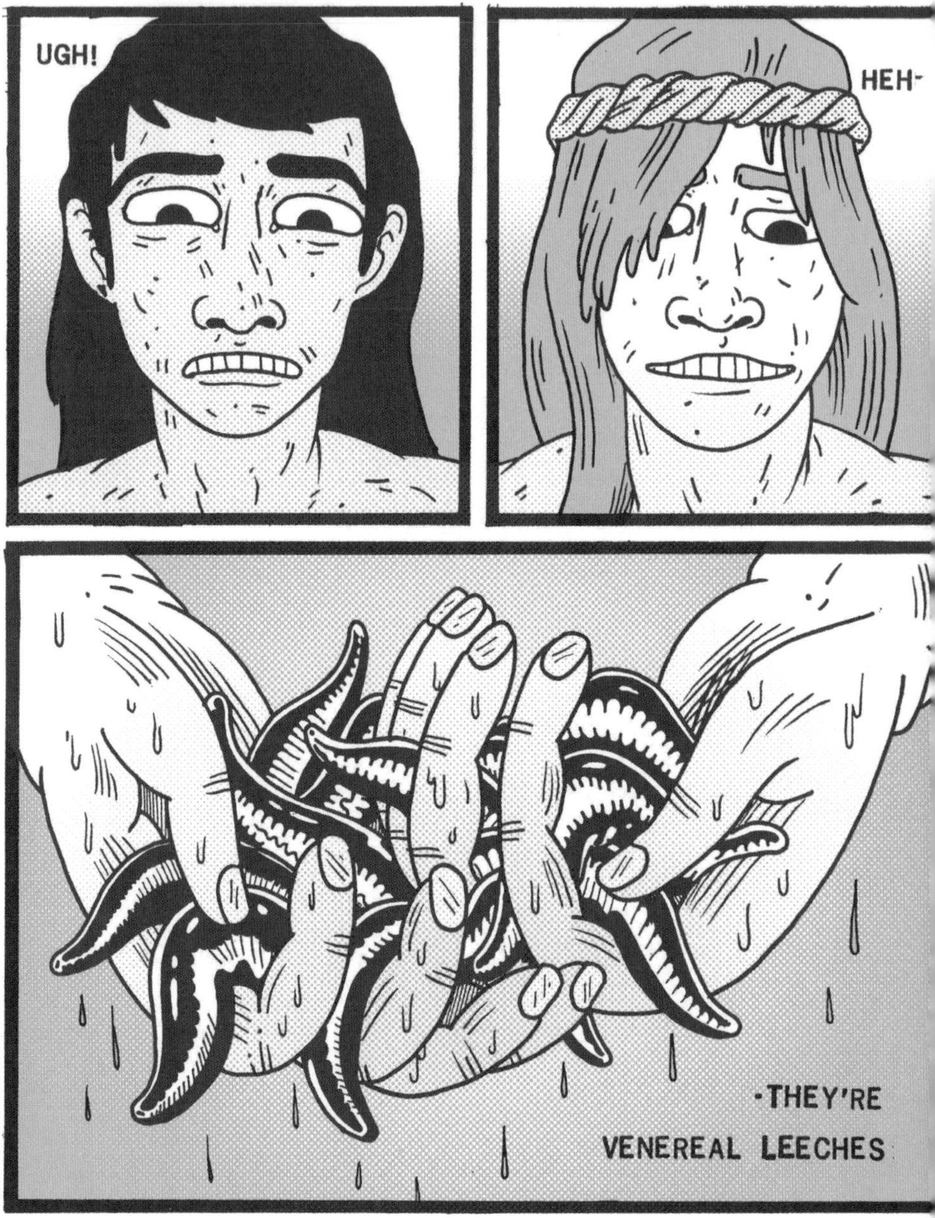
UGH!
HEH-
-THEY'RE
VENEREAL LEECHES

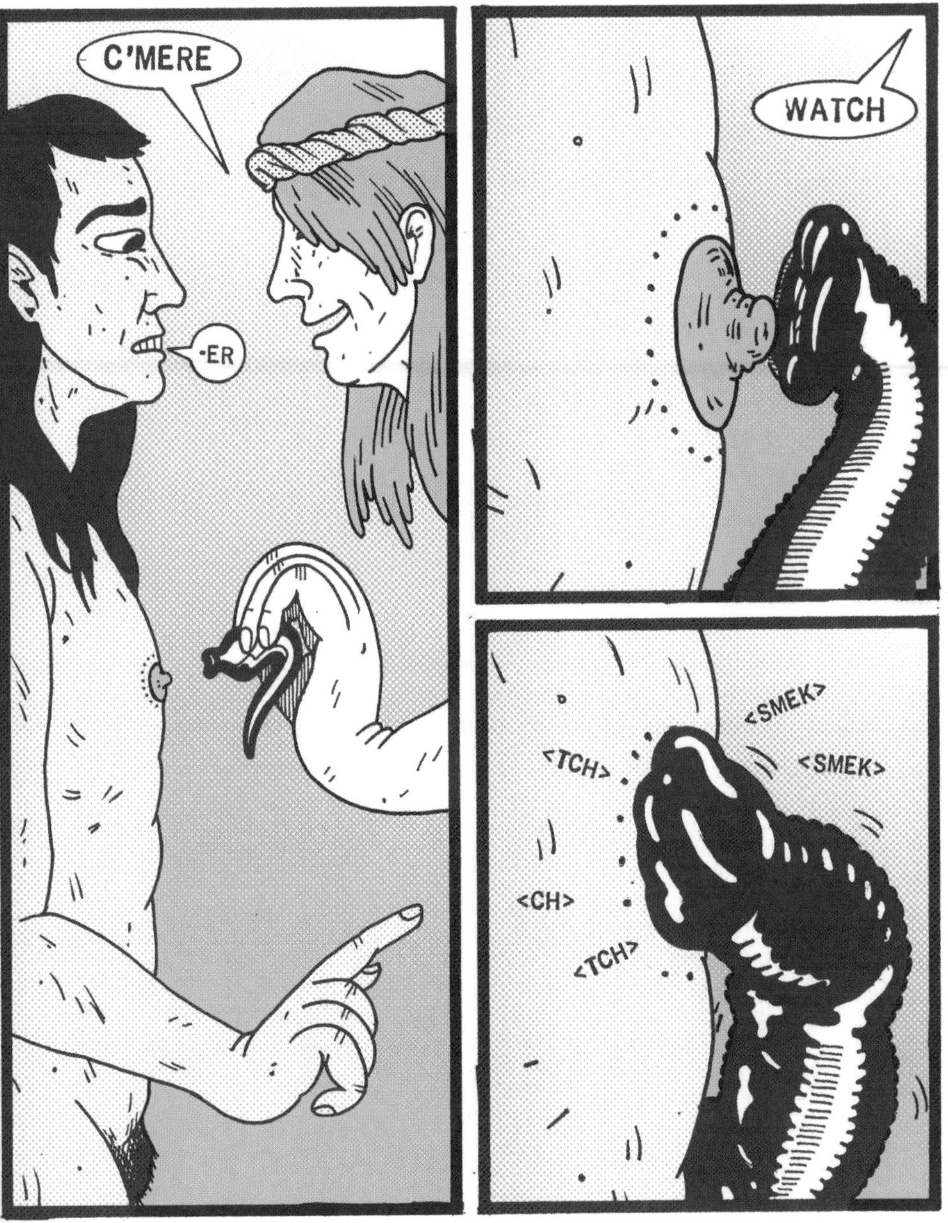
C'MERE
-ER
WATCH
<SMEK>
<TCH>
<SMEK>
<CH>
<TCH>

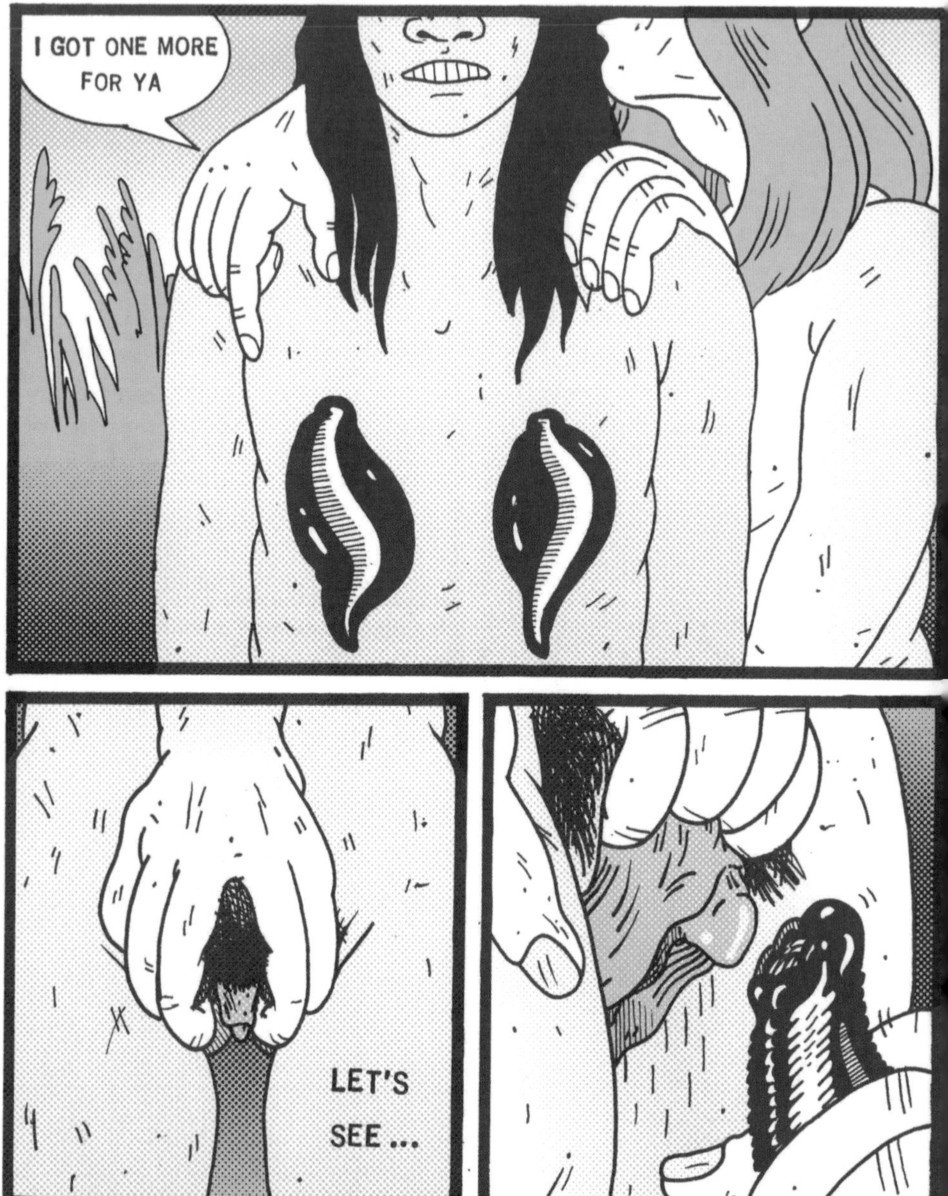
I GOT ONE MORE FOR YA
LET'S SEE...

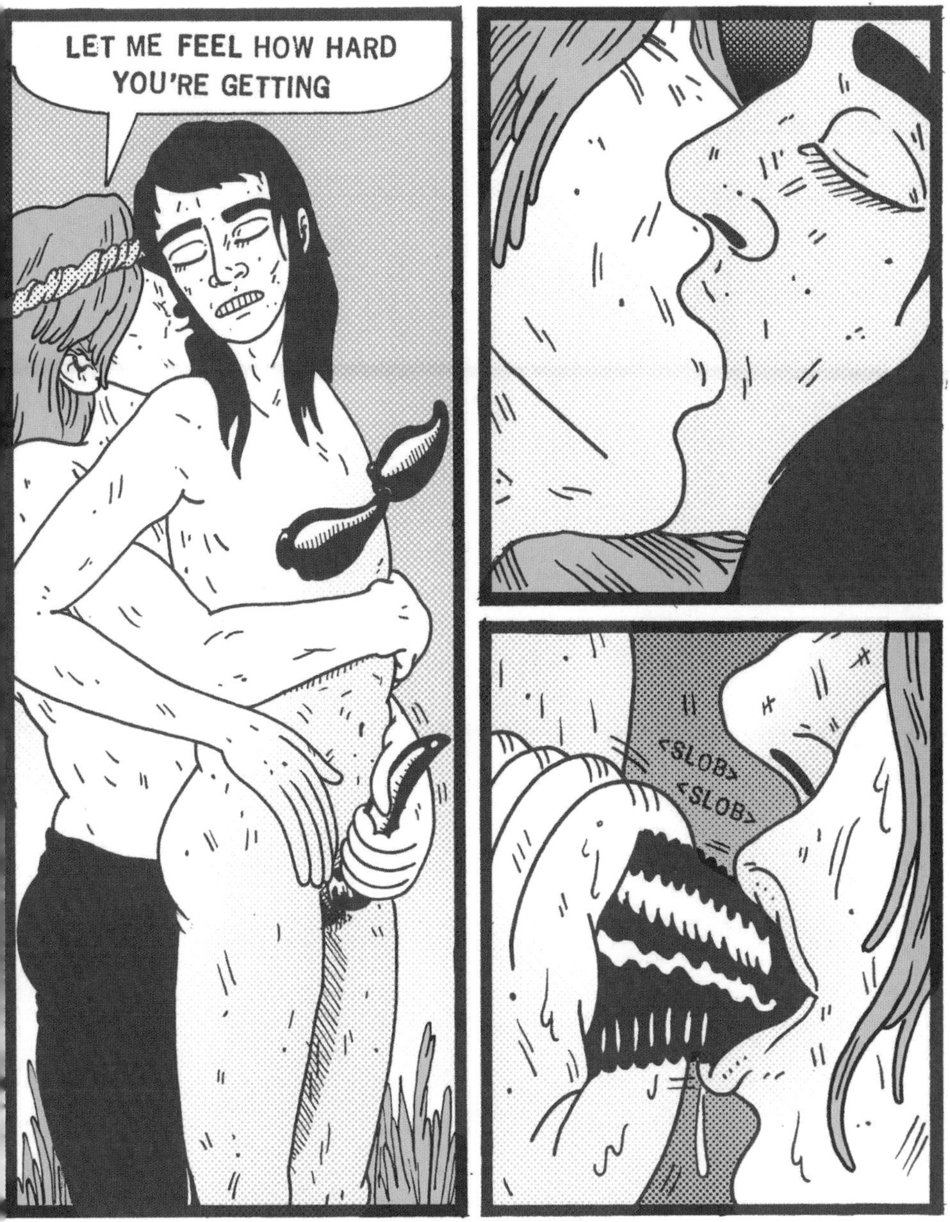
LET ME FEEL HOW HARD YOU'RE GETTING
<SLOB>
<SLOB>

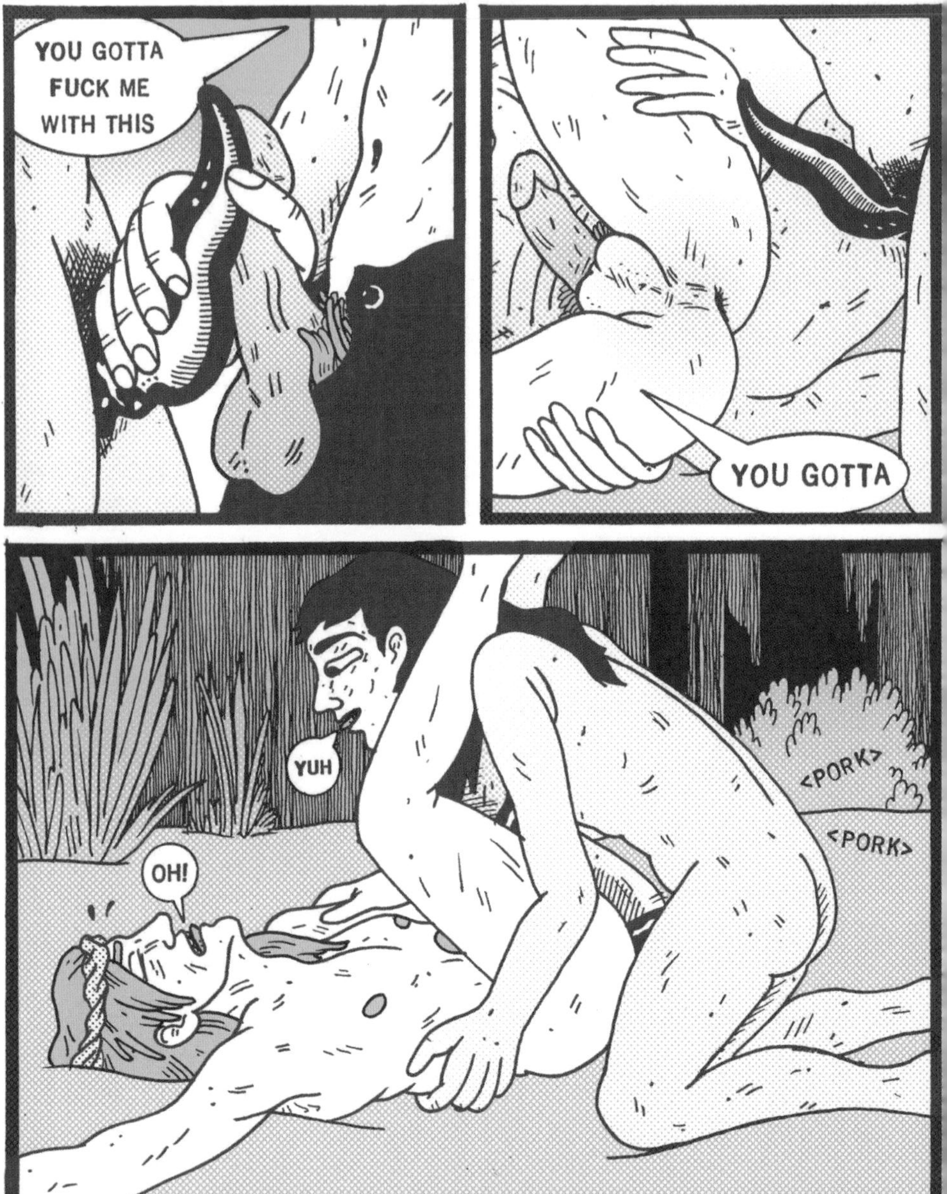
YOU GOTTA FUCK ME WITH THIS
YOU GOTTA
YUH
<PORK>
<PORK>
OH!

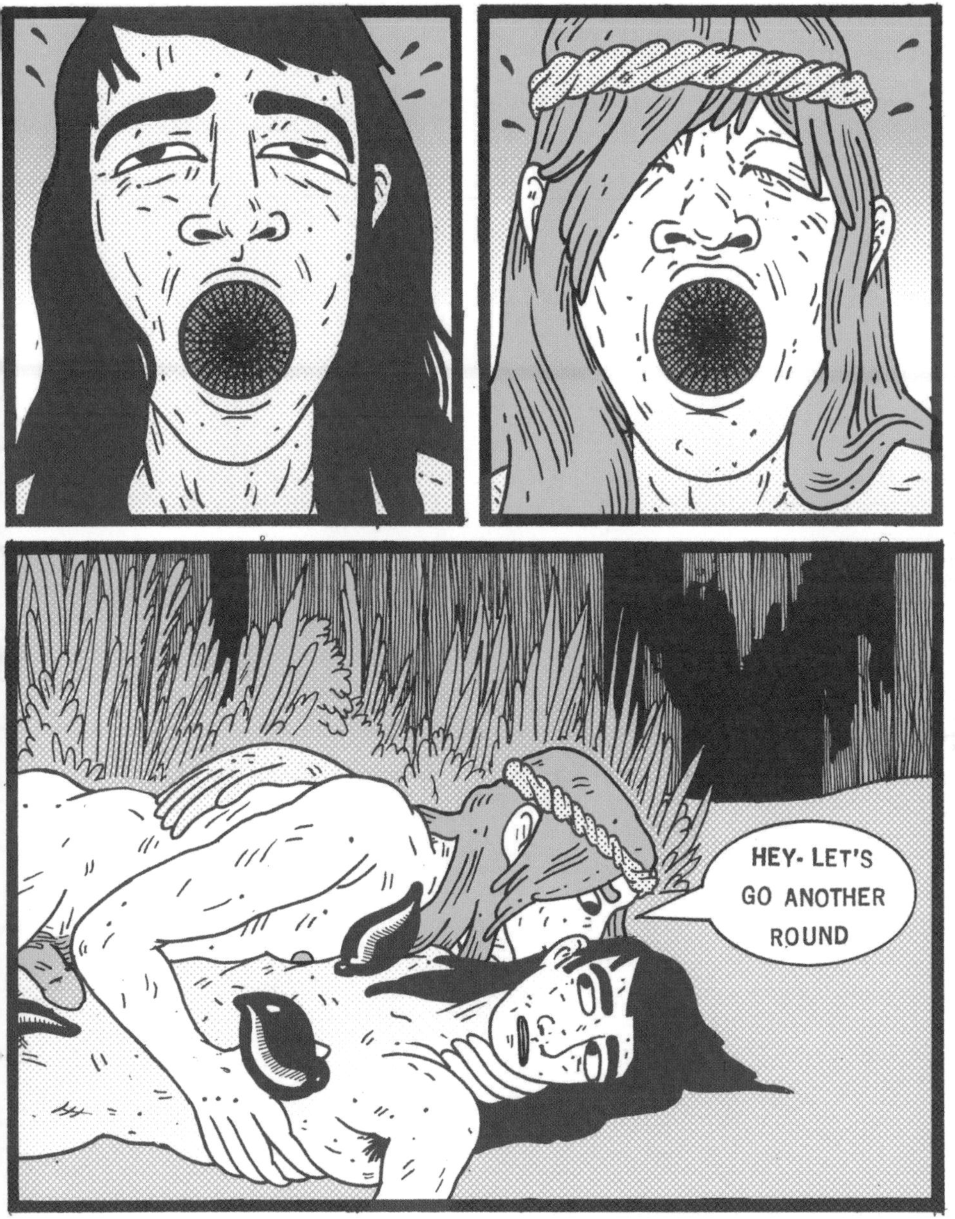
HEY- LET'S GO ANOTHER ROUND

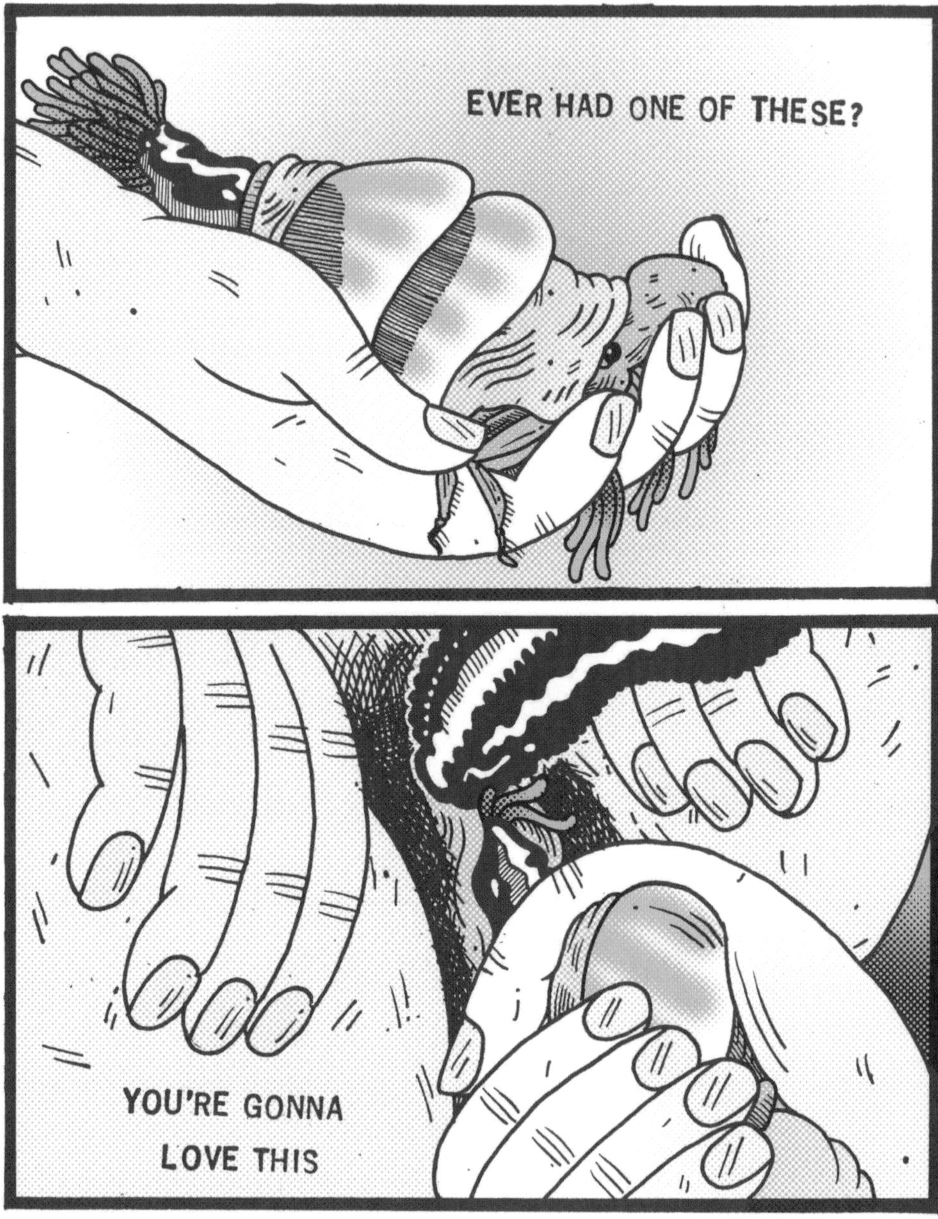
EVER HAD ONE OF THESE?
YOU'RE GONNA LOVE THIS

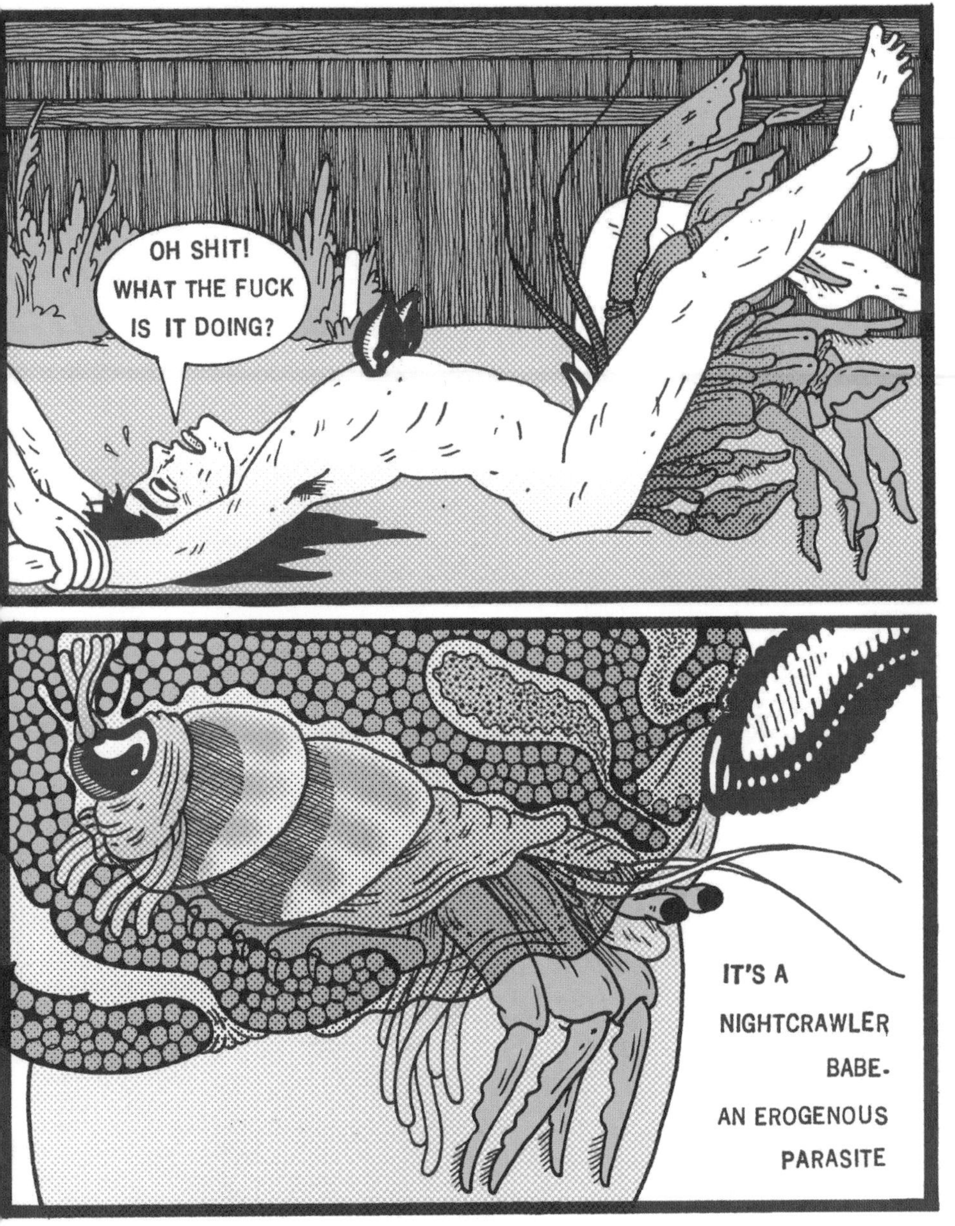
OH SHIT!
WHAT THE FUCK
IS IT DOING?
IT'S A
NIGHTCRAWLER
BABE-
AN EROGENOUS
PARASITE

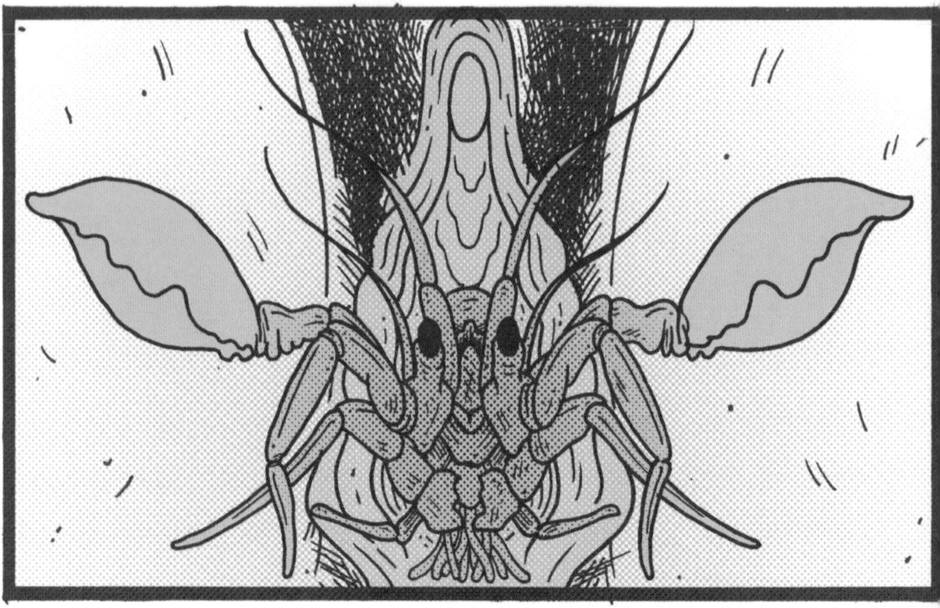

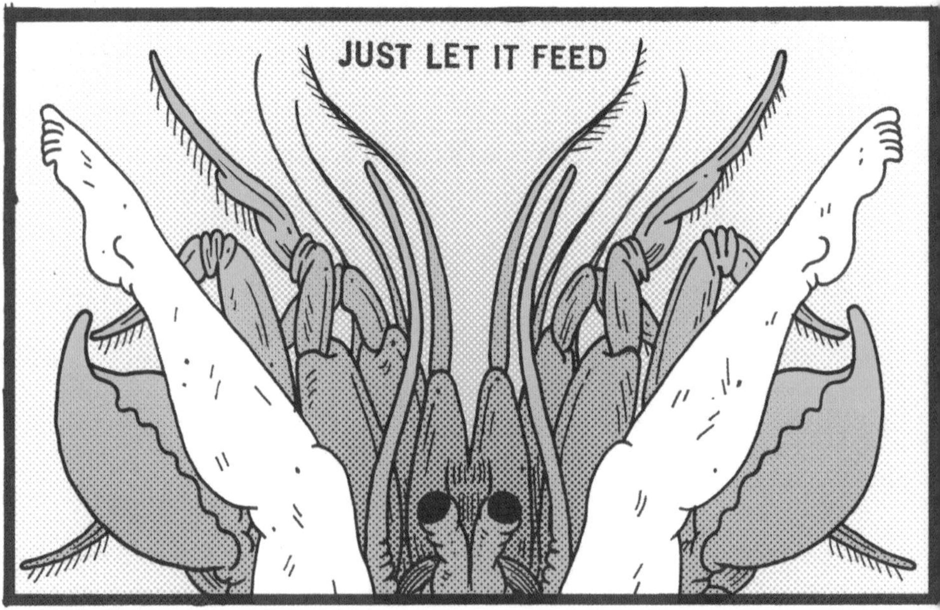
JUST LET IT FEED

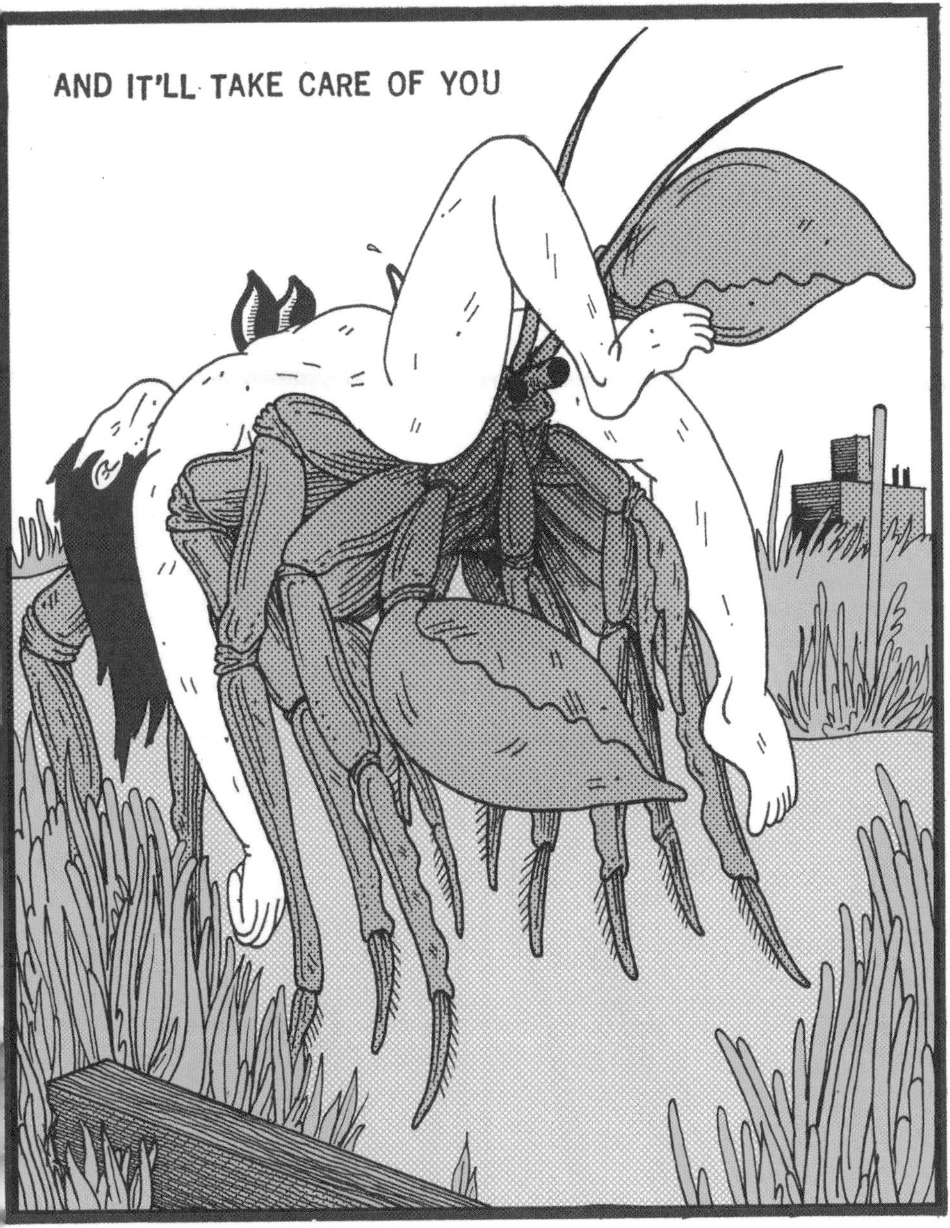
AND IT'LL TAKE CARE OF YOU

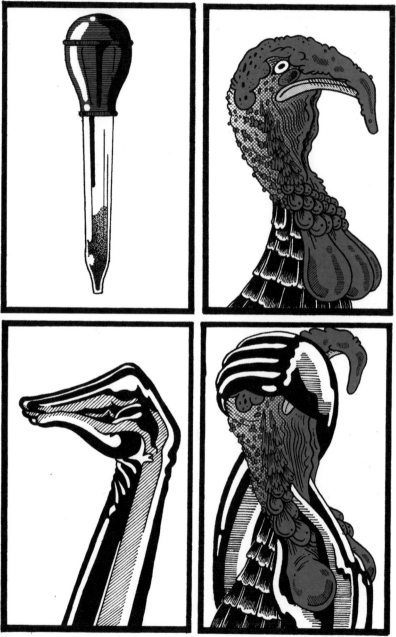

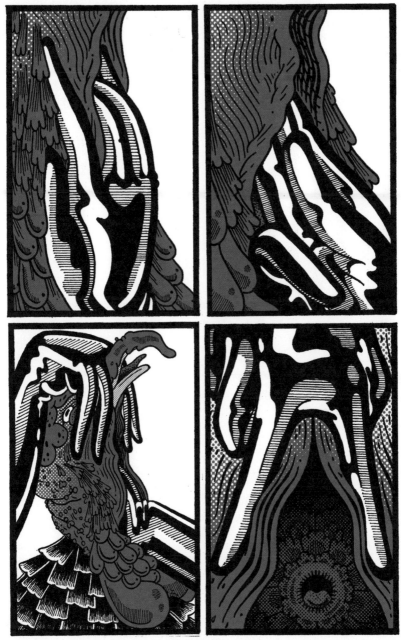

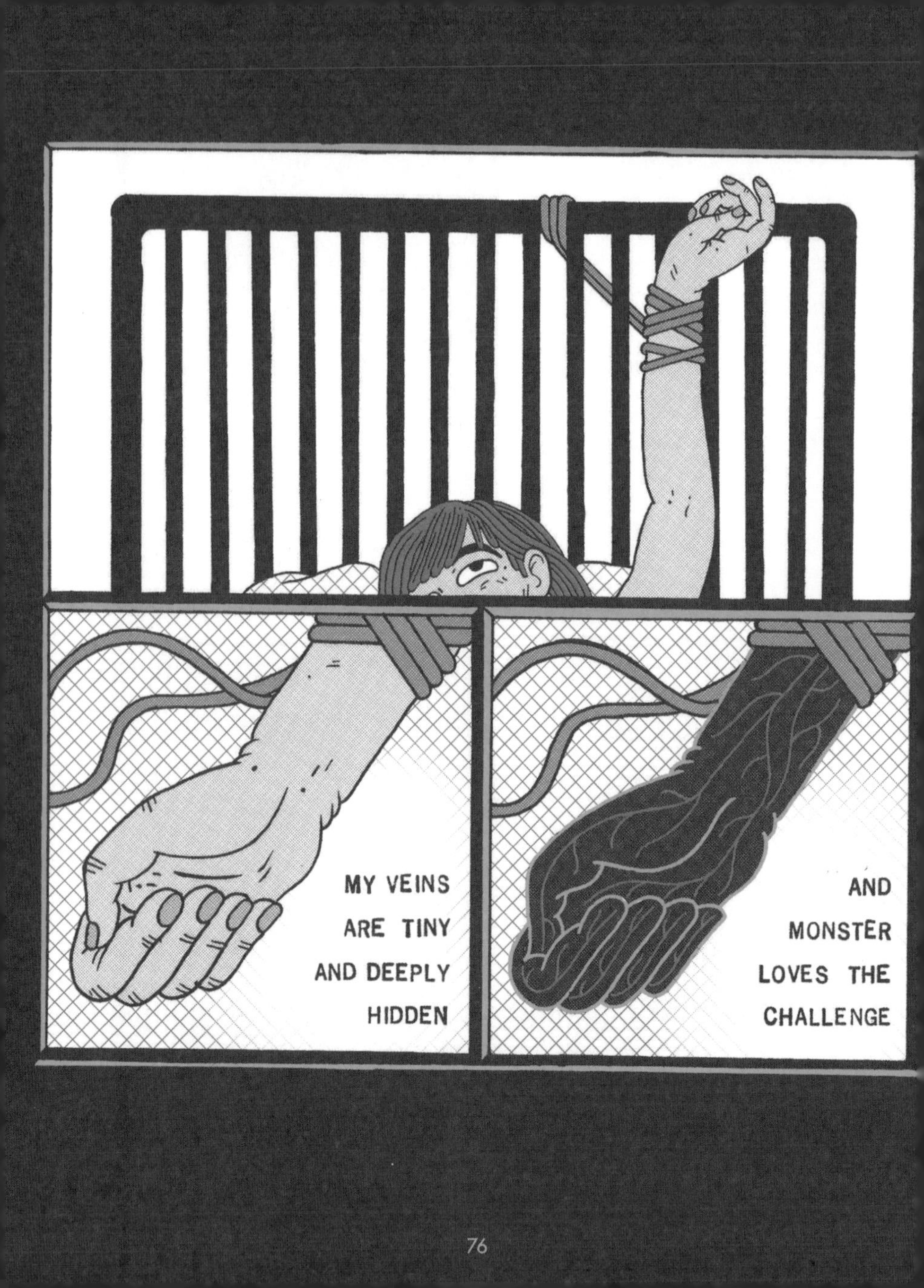
MY VEINS
ARE TINY
AND DEEPLY
HIDDEN
AND
MONSTER
LOVES THE
CHALLENGE

I HATE SEEING THE NEEDLES GO IN
BUT SHE MAKES ME WATCH
YOU'LL GET IT ALL BACK SOON ENOUGH

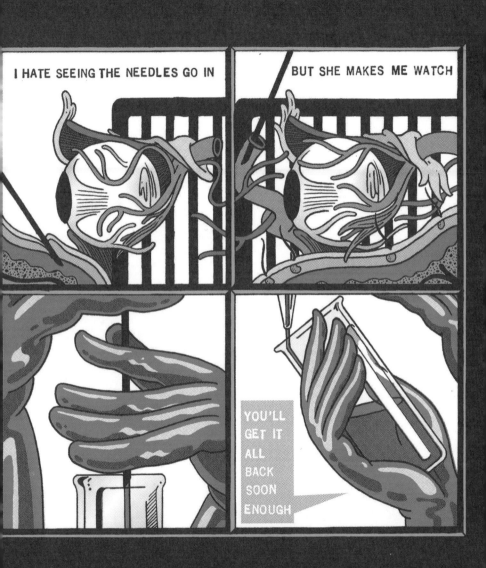

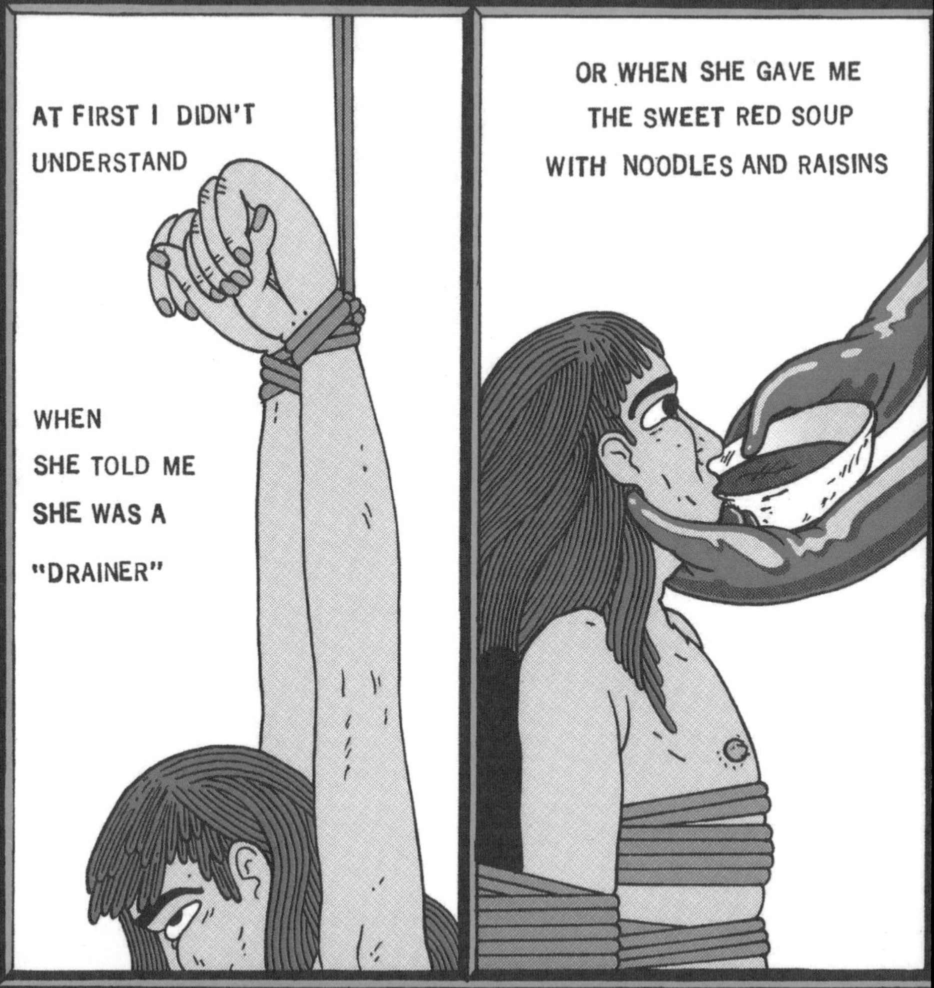
AT FIRST I DIDN'T UNDERSTAND
WHEN SHE TOLD ME SHE WAS A "DRAINER"
OR WHEN SHE GAVE ME THE SWEET RED SOUP WITH NOODLES AND RAISINS

IT WAS
MY OWN
BLOOD
BEING
FED TO ME

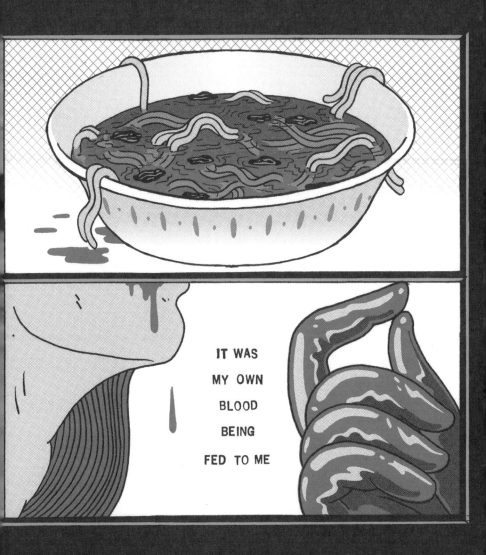

THOUGH LATELY
I'VE HAD LESS
AND LESS
TO GIVE
YOU CALL THIS A
PERIOD, FAGGOT?

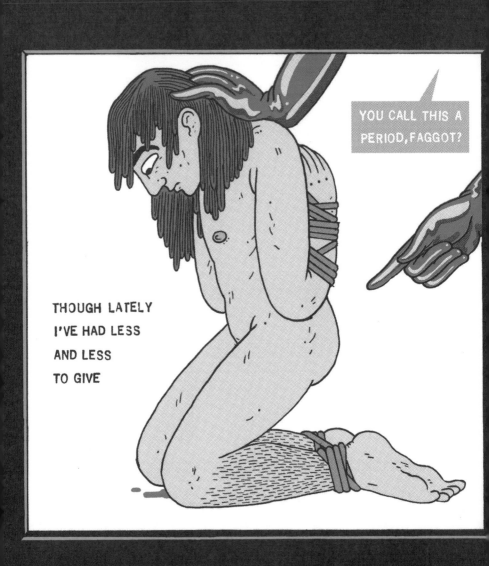

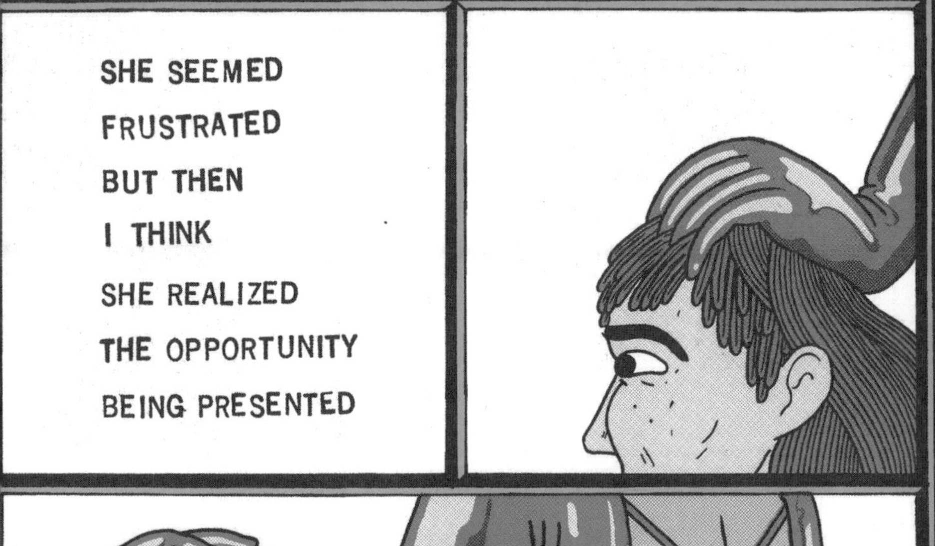

SHE SEEMED
FRUSTRATED
BUT THEN
I THINK
SHE REALIZED
THE OPPORTUNITY
BEING PRESENTED

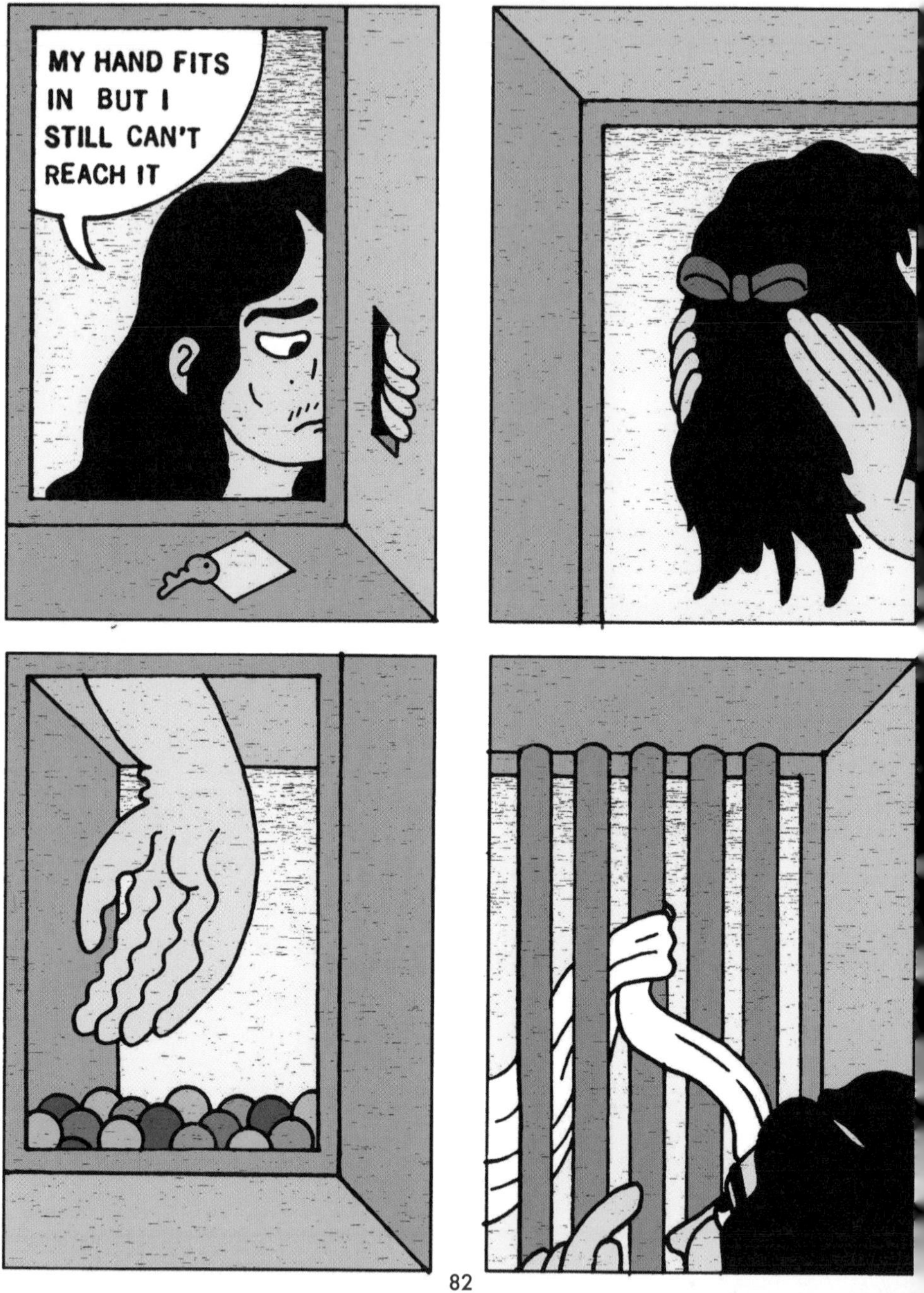
MY HAND FITS IN BUT I STILL CAN'T REACH IT

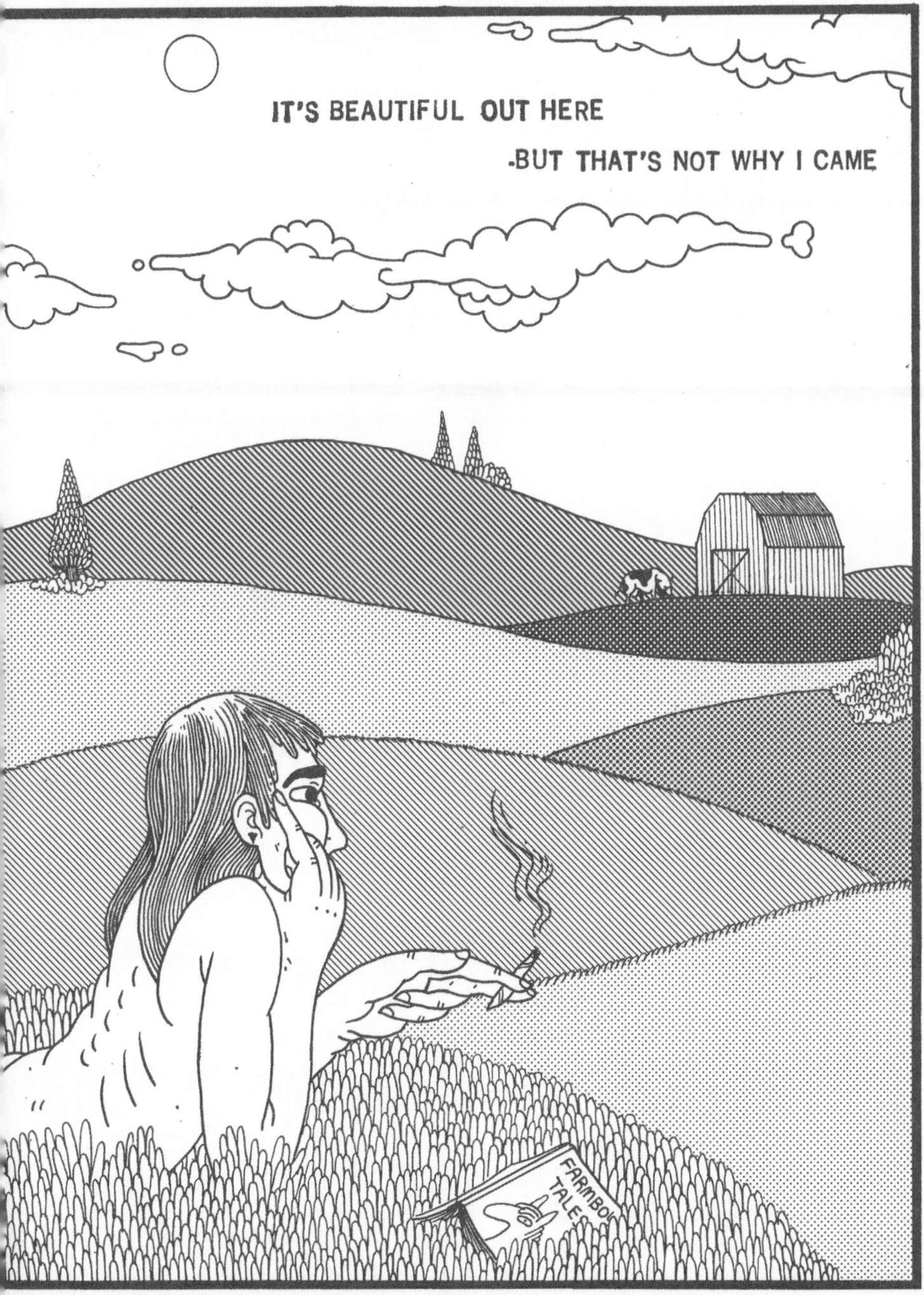
IT'S BEAUTIFUL OUT HERE
-BUT THAT'S NOT WHY I CAME
FARMBOY TALES

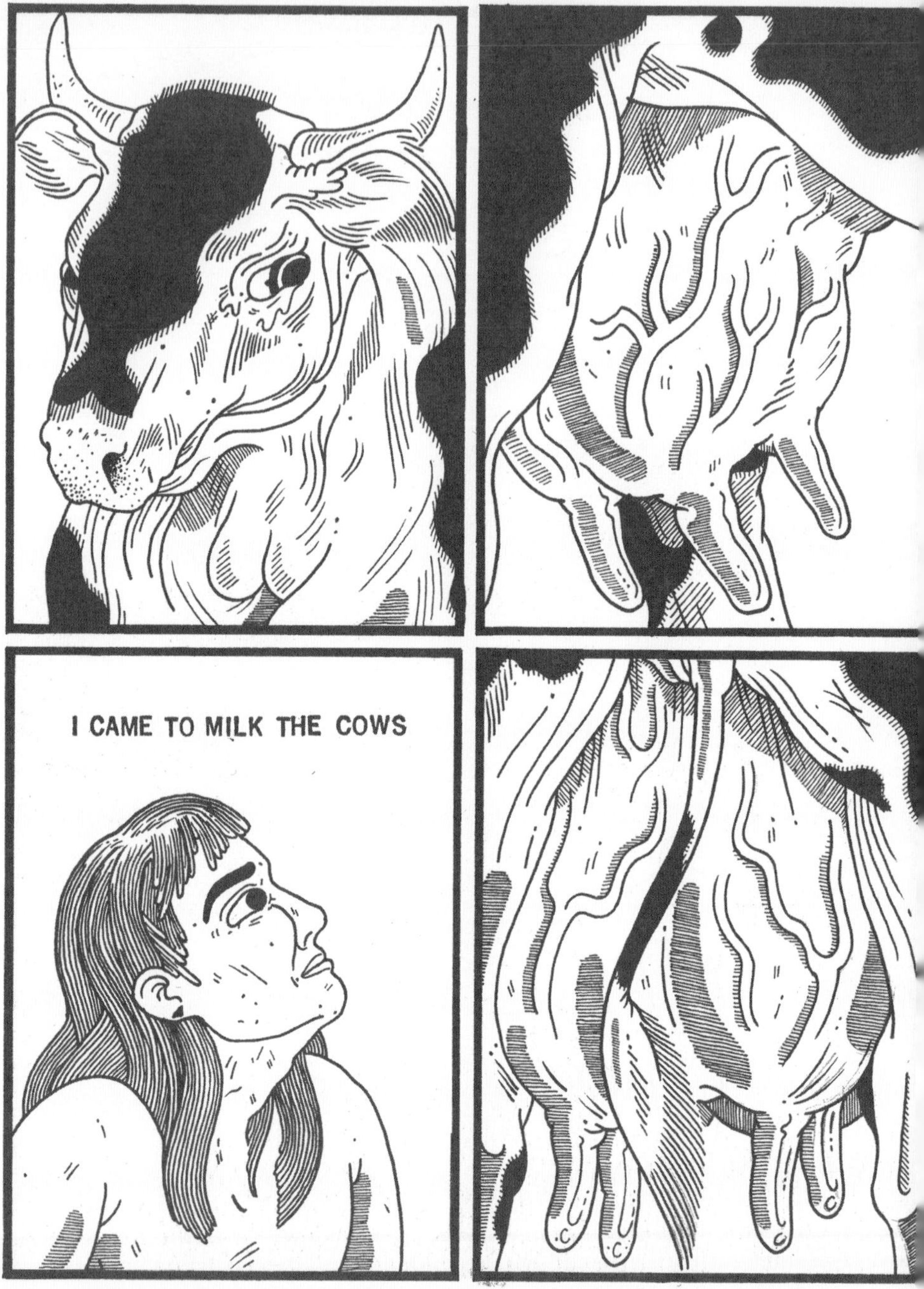
I CAME TO MILK THE COWS

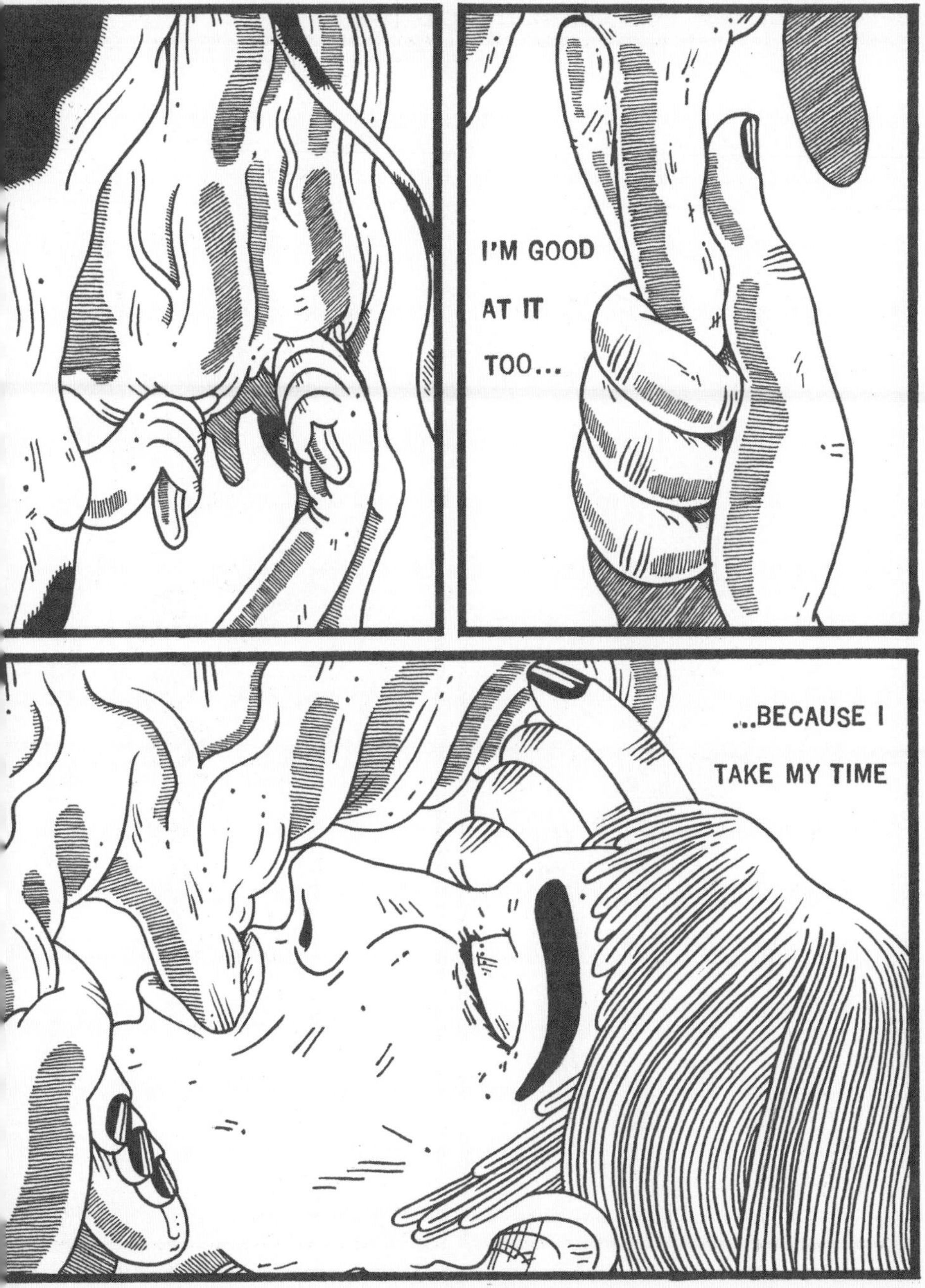
I'M GOOD AT IT TOO...
...BECAUSE I TAKE MY TIME

GRIP THEIR LONG, SWOLLEN TEETS AND TUG...

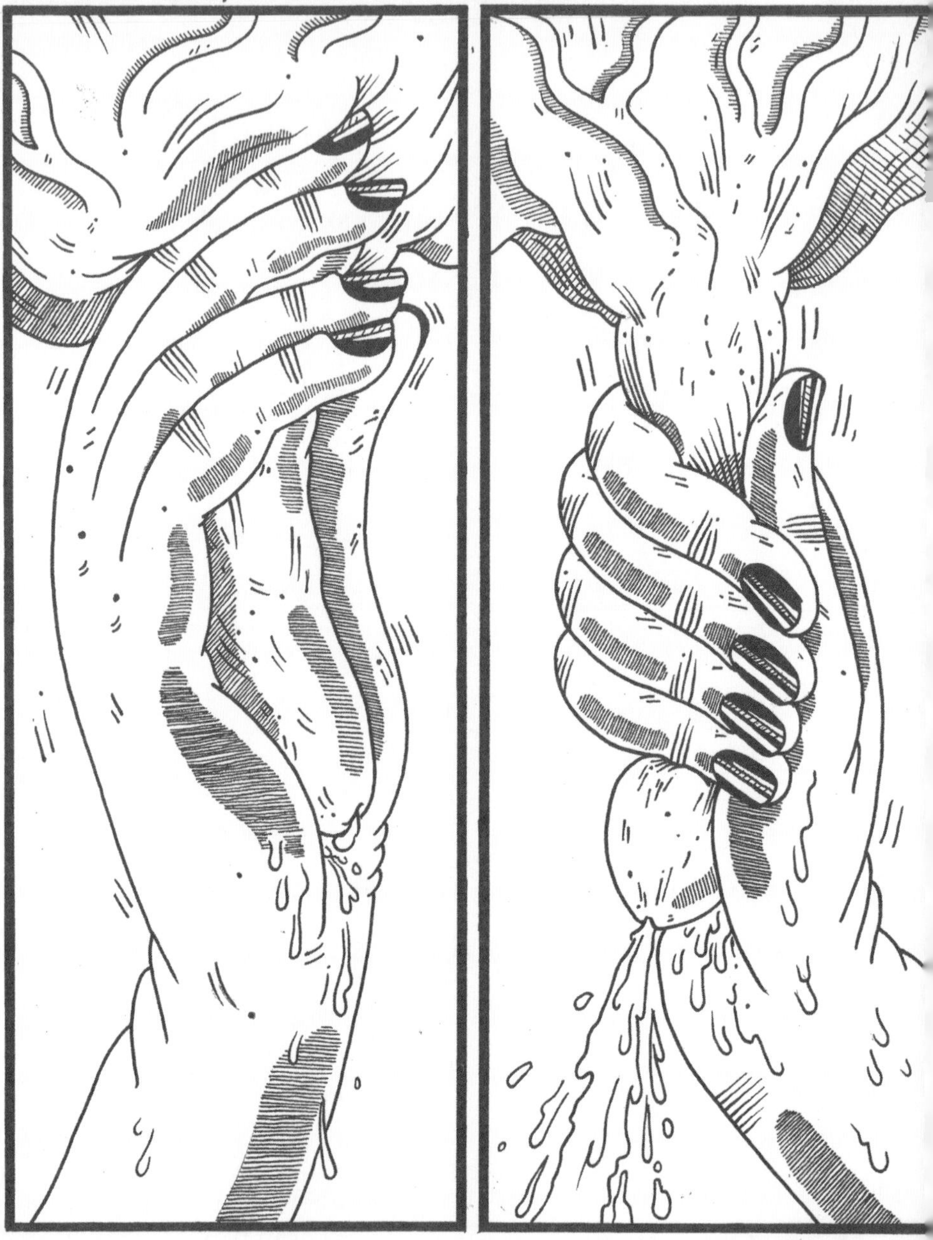

...IT'S A DYING AR

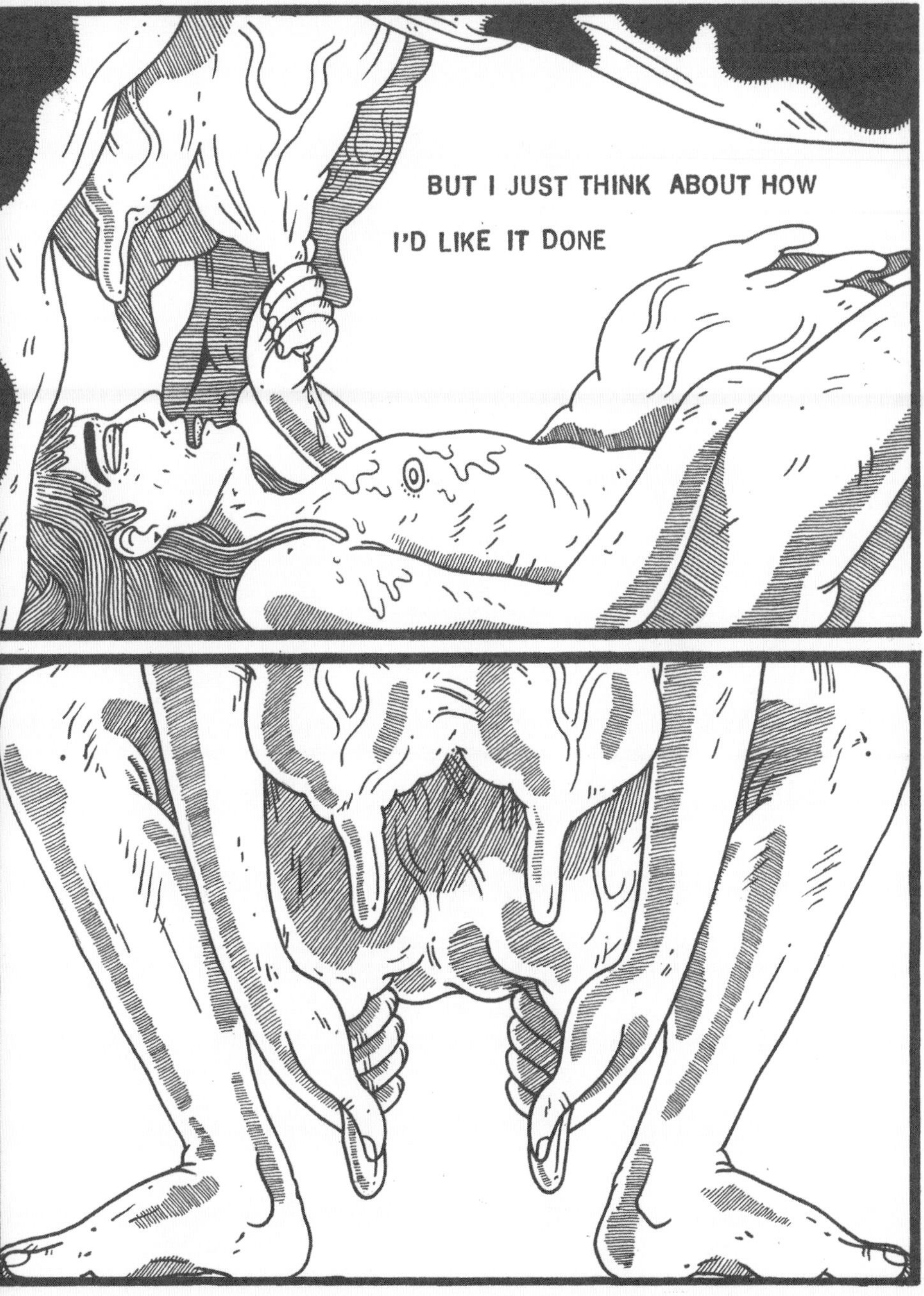
BUT I JUST THINK ABOUT HOW
I'D LIKE IT DONE

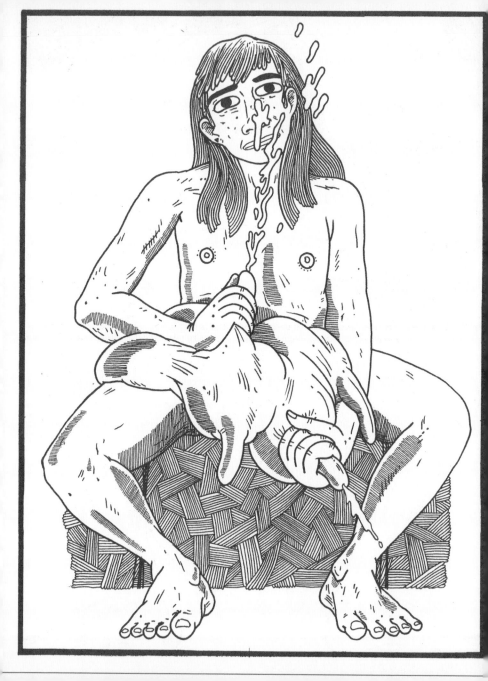

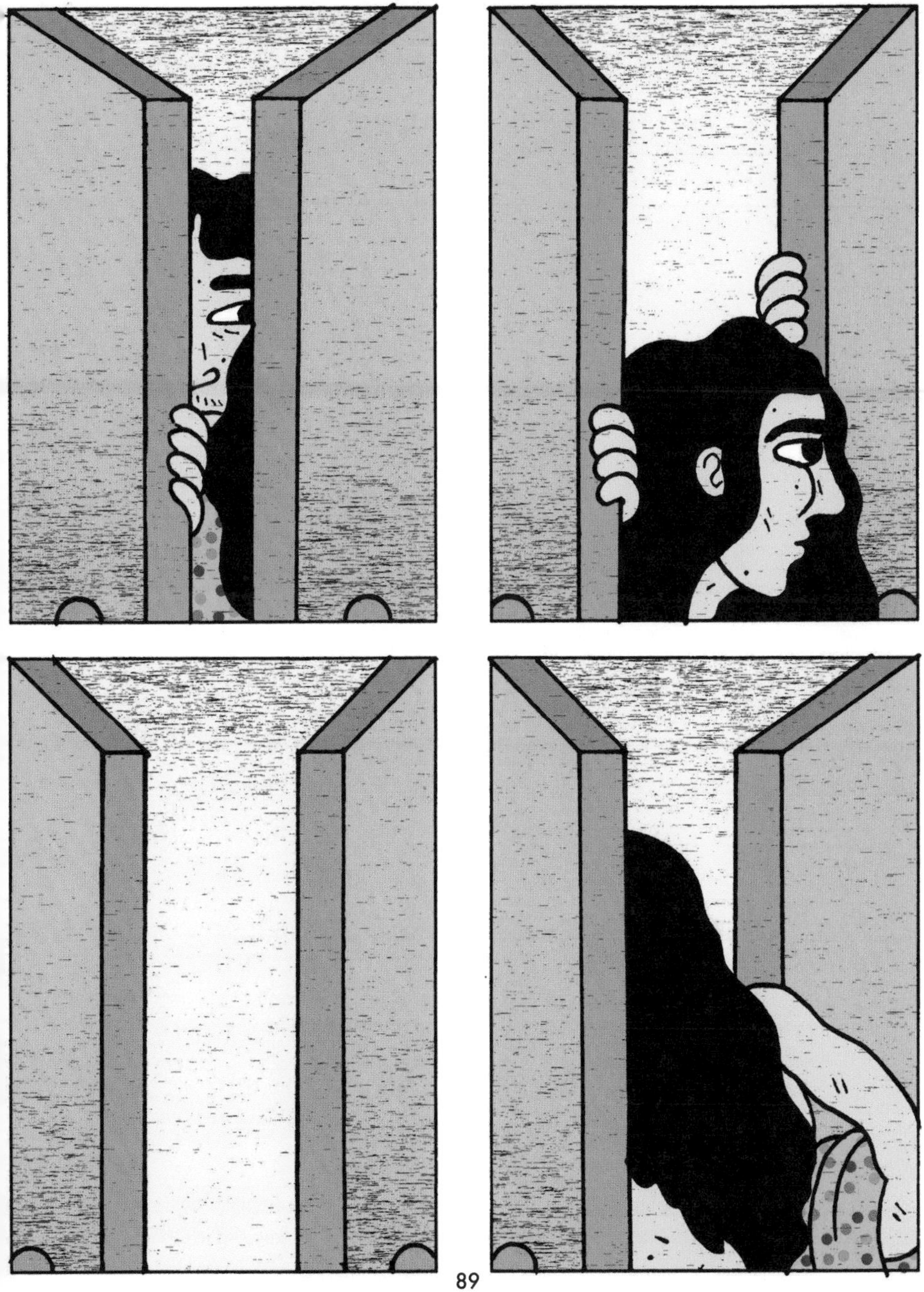

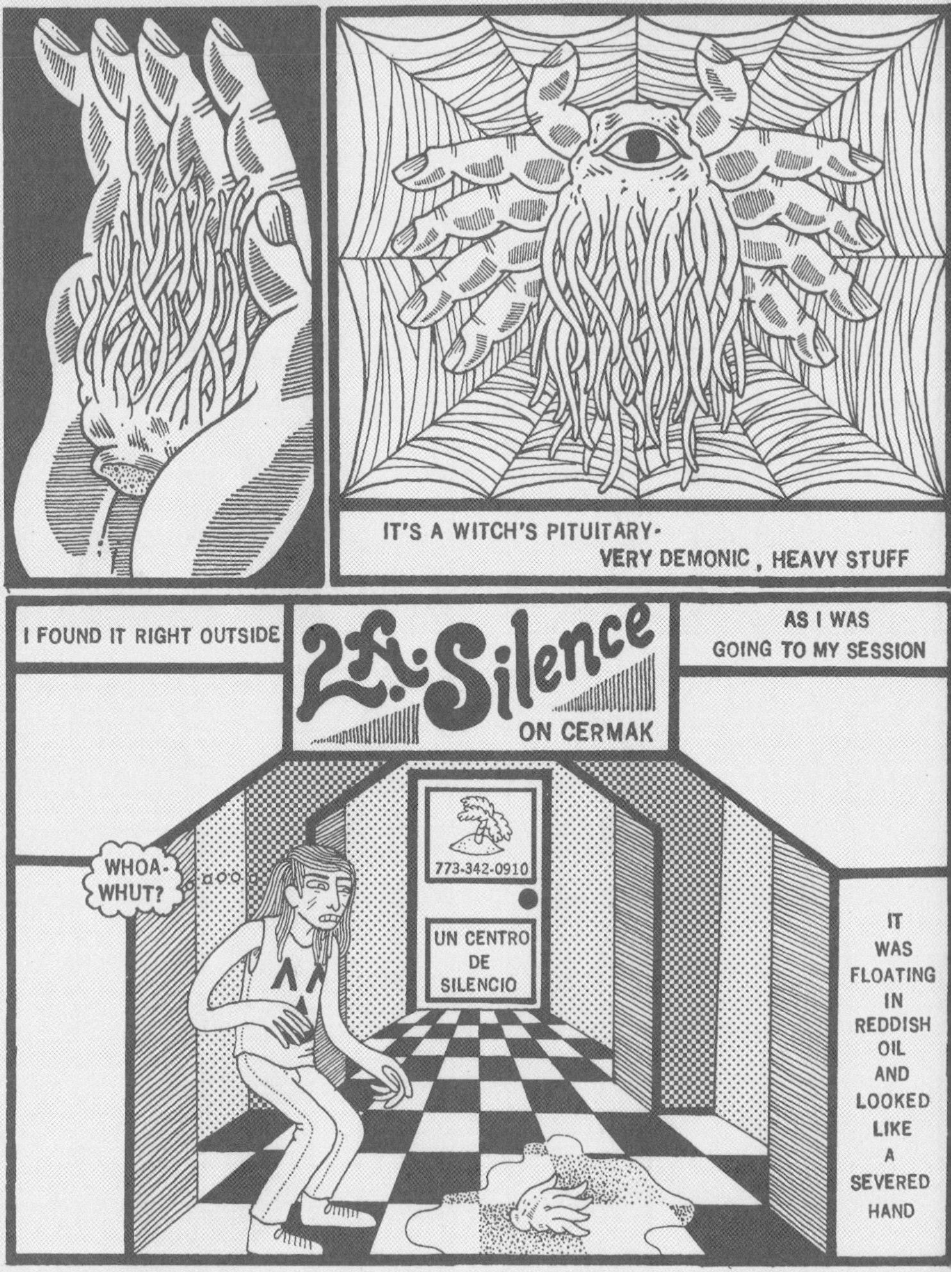
IT'S A WITCH'S PITUITARY-
VERY DEMONIC, HEAVY STUFF
I FOUND IT RIGHT OUTSIDE
2A. Silence
ON CERMAK
AS I WAS
GOING TO MY SESSION
773-342-0910
UN CENTRO
DE
SILENCIO
WHOA-
WHUT?
IT
WAS
FLOATING
IN
REDDISH
OIL
AND
LOOKED
LIKE
A
SEVERED
HAND

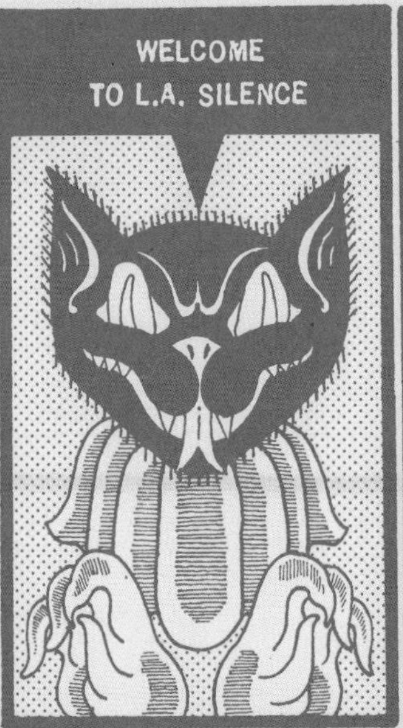
WELCOME
TO L.A. SILENCE

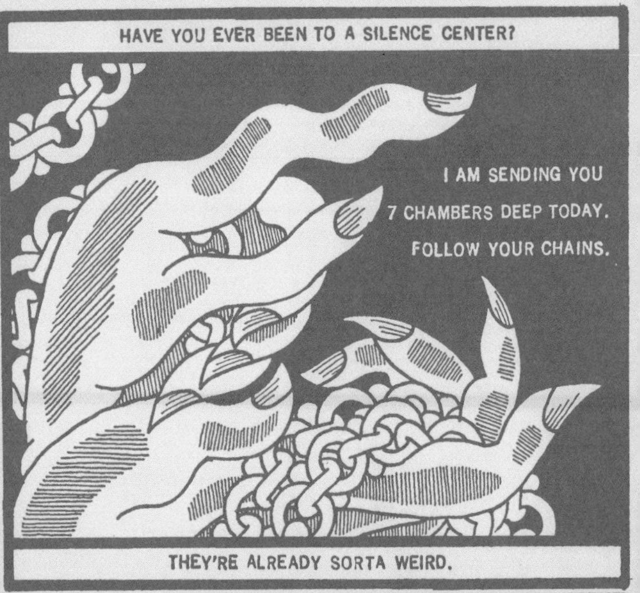
HAVE YOU EVER BEEN TO A SILENCE CENTER?
I AM SENDING YOU
7 CHAMBERS DEEP TODAY.
FOLLOW YOUR CHAINS.
THEY'RE ALREADY SORTA WEIRD.

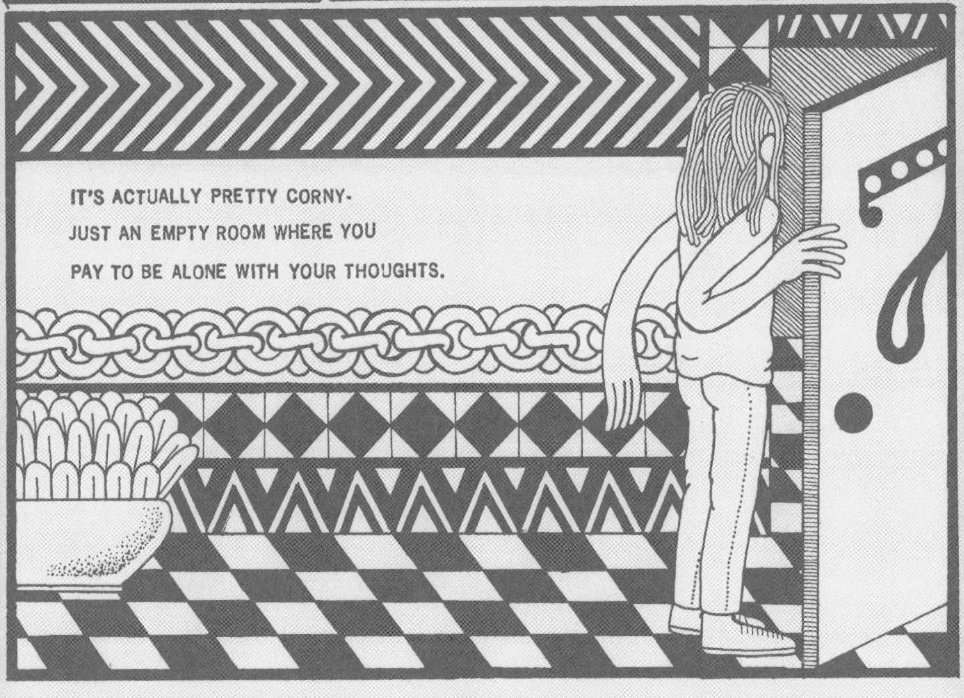
IT'S ACTUALLY PRETTY CORNY-
JUST AN EMPTY ROOM WHERE YOU
PAY TO BE ALONE WITH YOUR THOUGHTS.

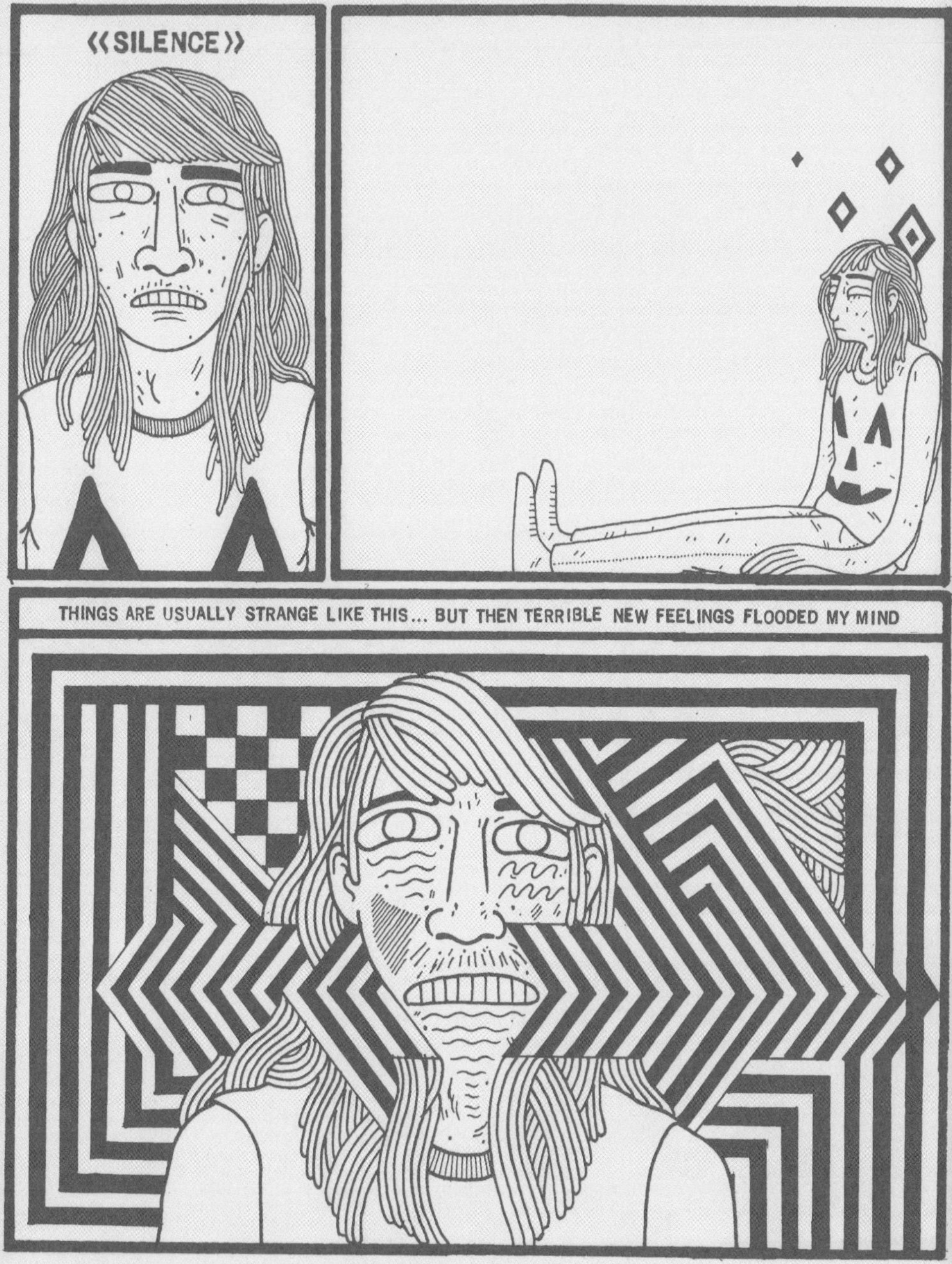
«SILENCE»
THINGS ARE USUALLY STRANGE LIKE THIS... BUT THEN TERRIBLE NEW FEELINGS FLOODED MY MIND

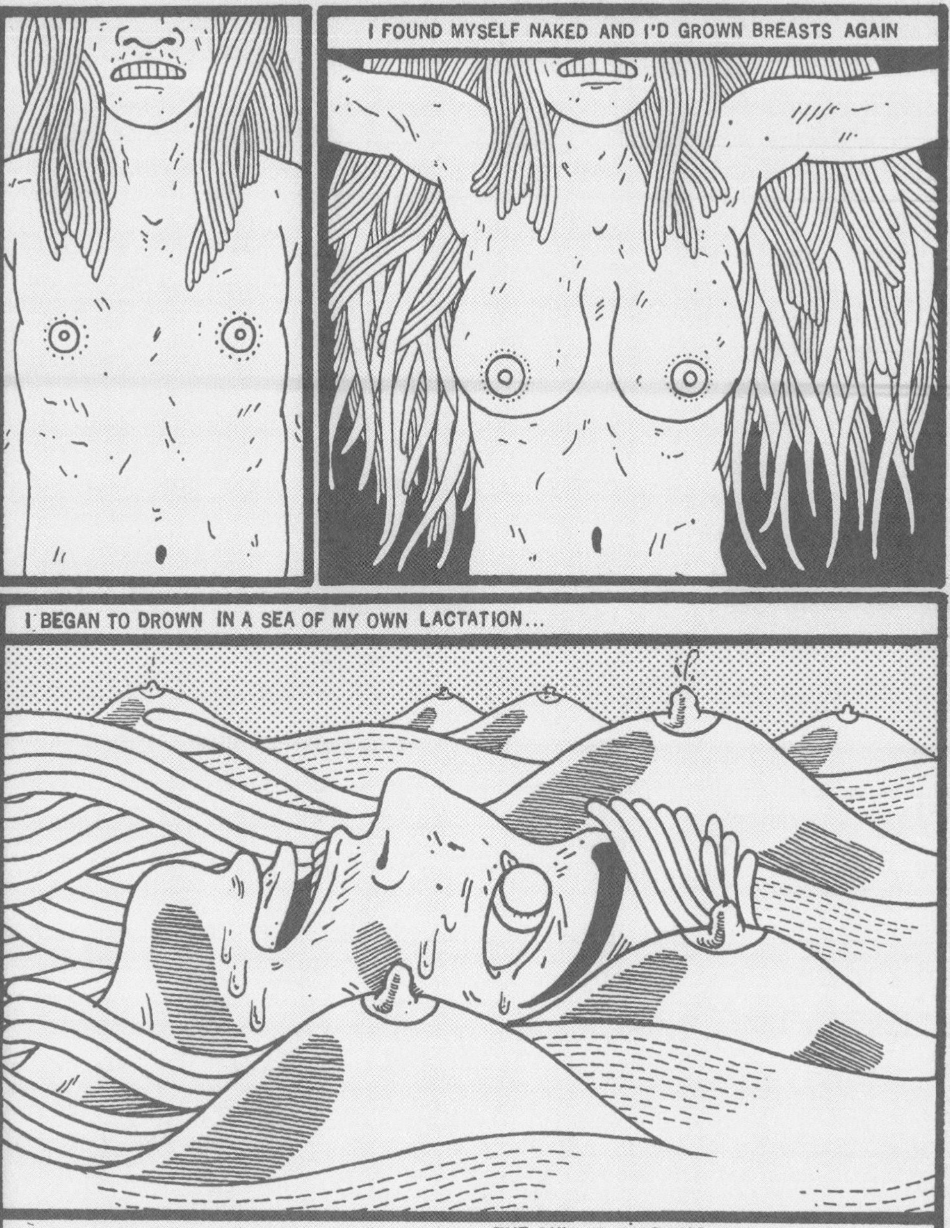
I FOUND MYSELF NAKED AND I'D GROWN BREASTS AGAIN
I BEGAN TO DROWN IN A SEA OF MY OWN LACTATION...
...THE ONLY ESCAPE WAS TO SWALLOW IT ALL.

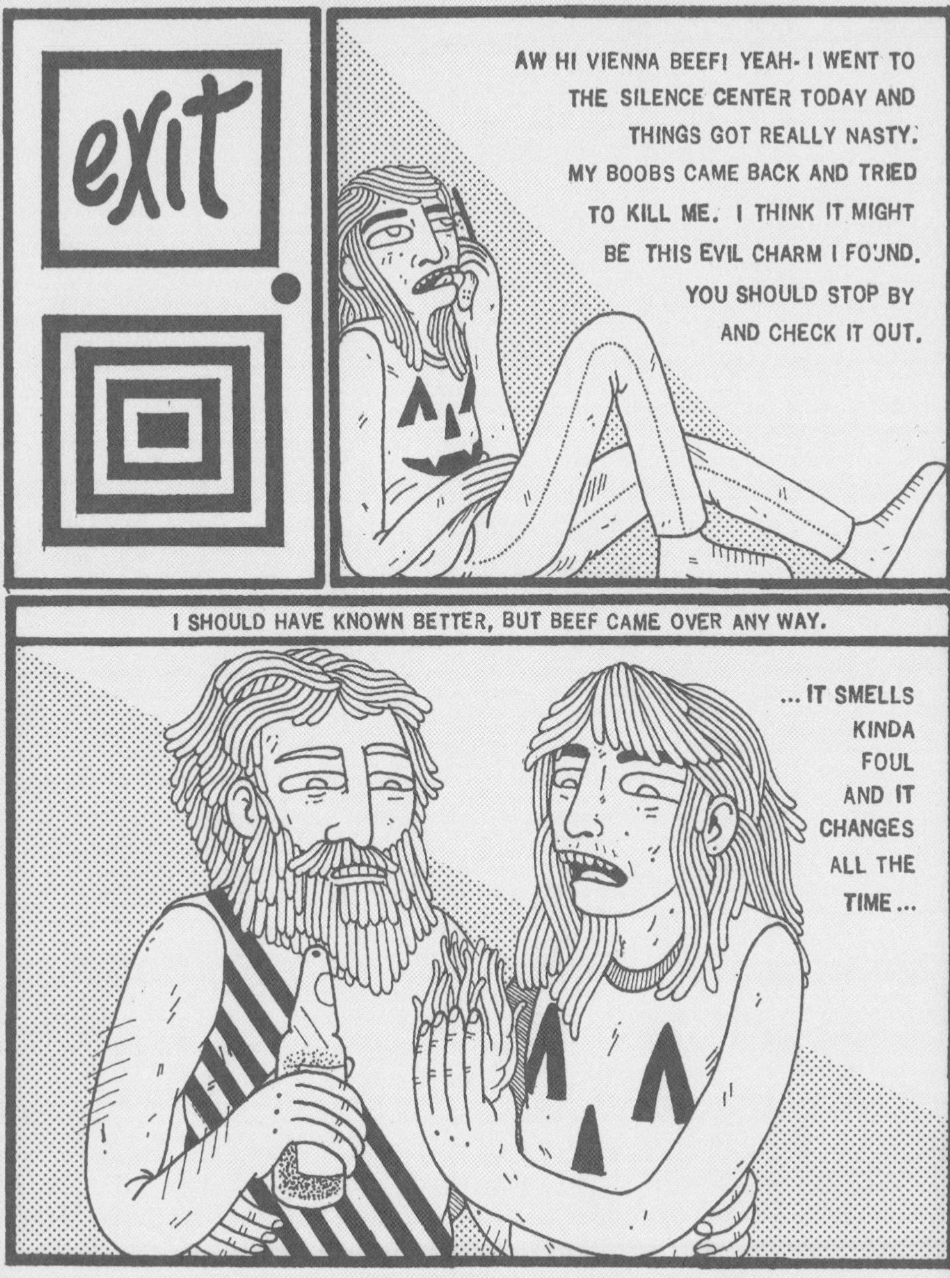
exit
AW HI VIENNA BEEF! YEAH- I WENT TO THE SILENCE CENTER TODAY AND THINGS GOT REALLY NASTY. MY BOOBS CAME BACK AND TRIED TO KILL ME. I THINK IT MIGHT BE THIS EVIL CHARM I FOUND. YOU SHOULD STOP BY AND CHECK IT OUT.
I SHOULD HAVE KNOWN BETTER, BUT BEEF CAME OVER ANY WAY.
... IT SMELLS KINDA FOUL AND IT CHANGES ALL THE TIME ...

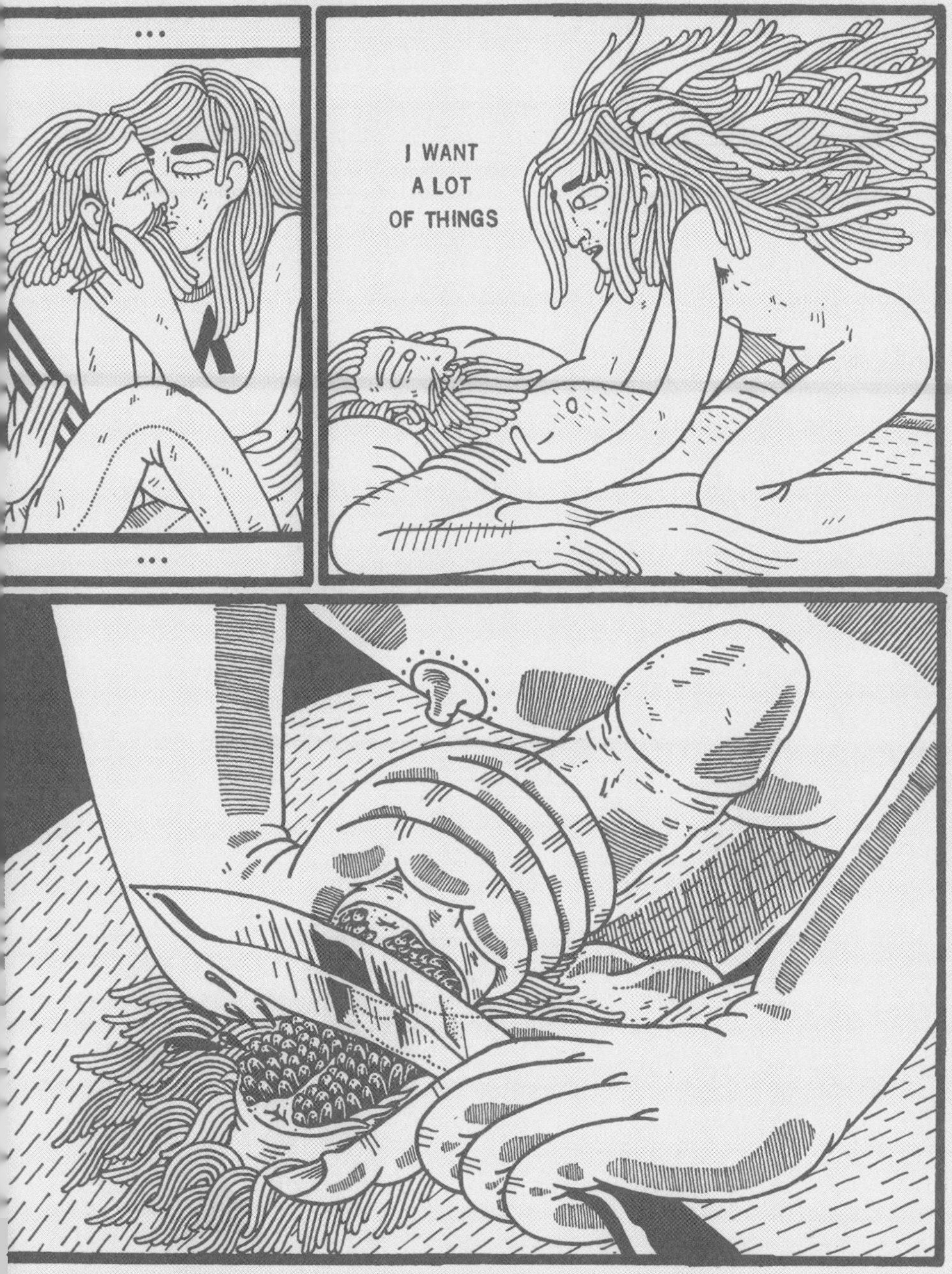
...
I WANT
A LOT
OF THINGS
...

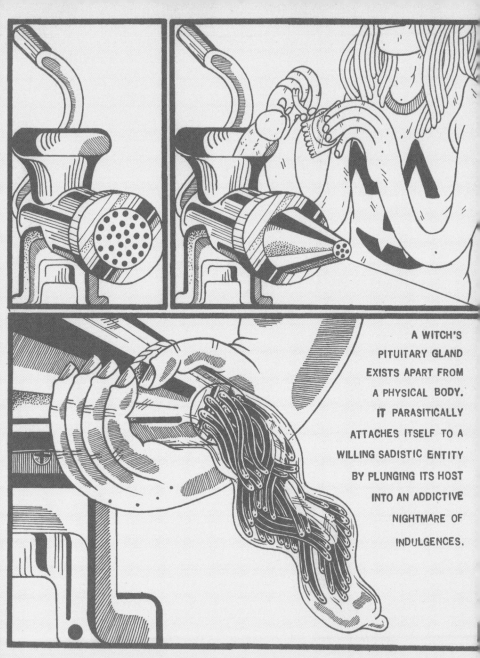

A WITCH'S PITUITARY GLAND EXISTS APART FROM A PHYSICAL BODY. IT PARASITICALLY ATTACHES ITSELF TO A WILLING SADISTIC ENTITY BY PLUNGING ITS HOST INTO AN ADDICTIVE NIGHTMARE OF INDULGENCES.

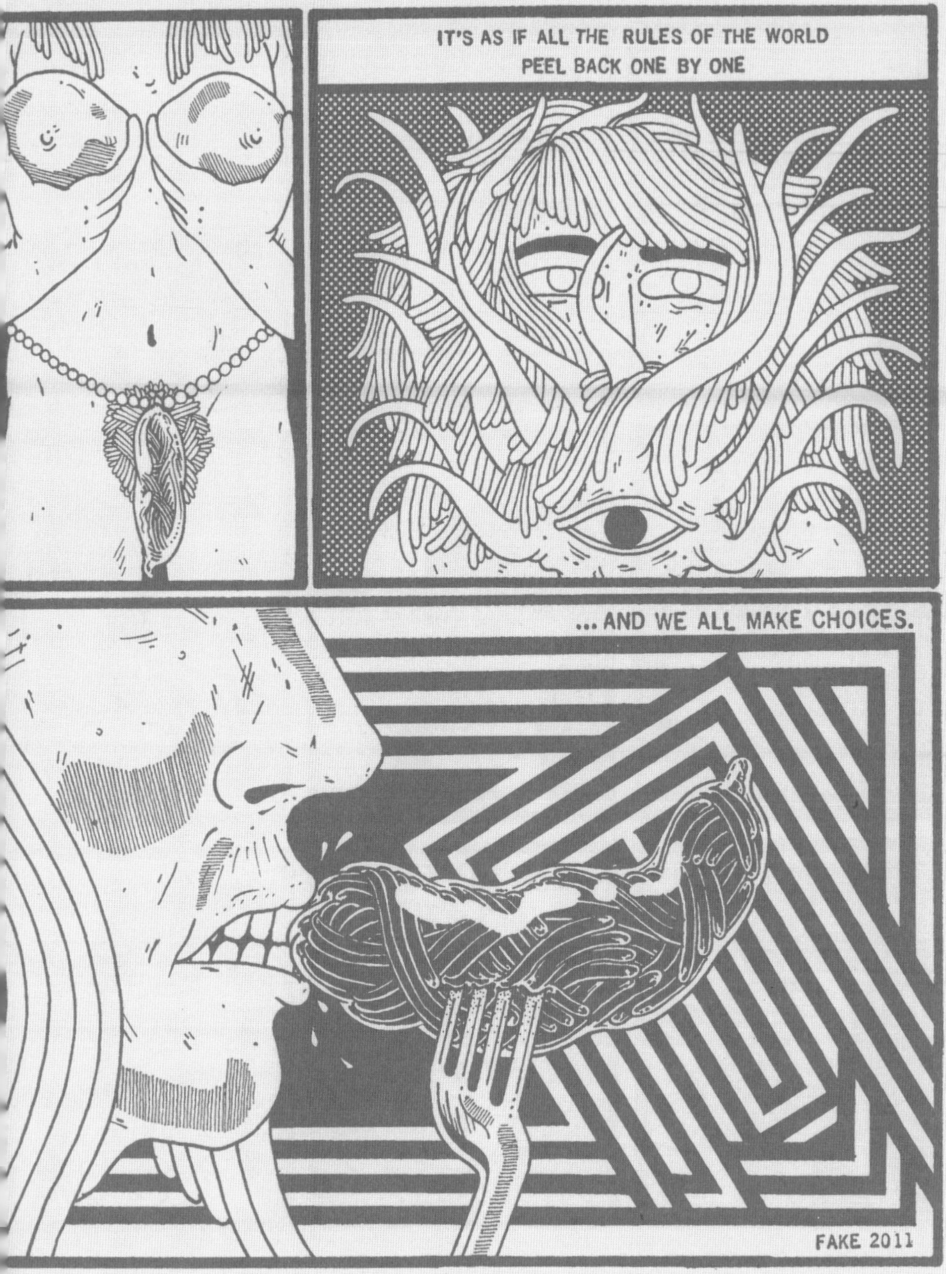
IT'S AS IF ALL THE RULES OF THE WORLD
PEEL BACK ONE BY ONE
...AND WE ALL MAKE CHOICES.
FAKE 2011

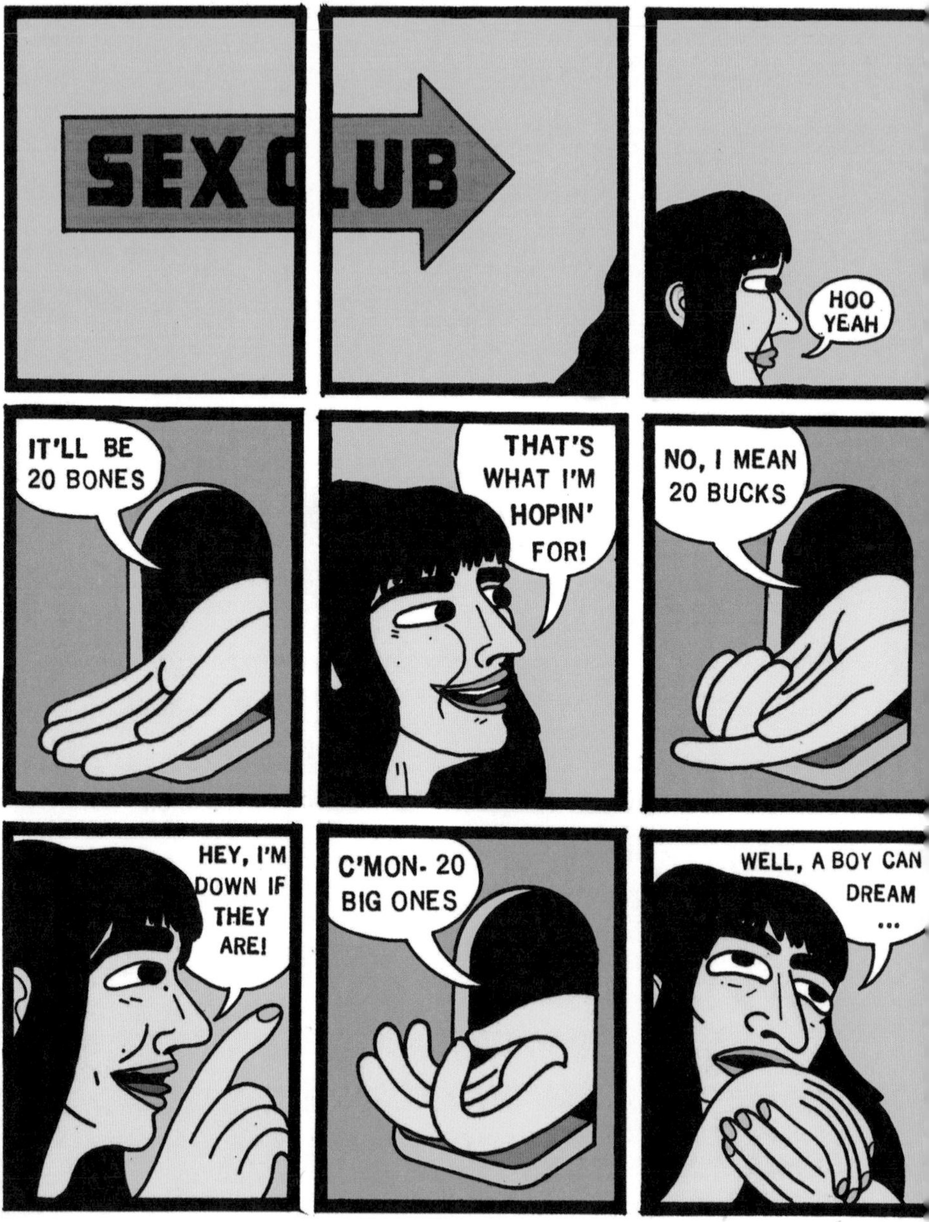
SEX CLUB
HOO YEAH
IT'LL BE 20 BONES
THAT'S WHAT I'M HOPIN' FOR!
NO, I MEAN 20 BUCKS
HEY, I'M DOWN IF THEY ARE!
C'MON- 20 BIG ONES
WELL, A BOY CAN DREAM ...

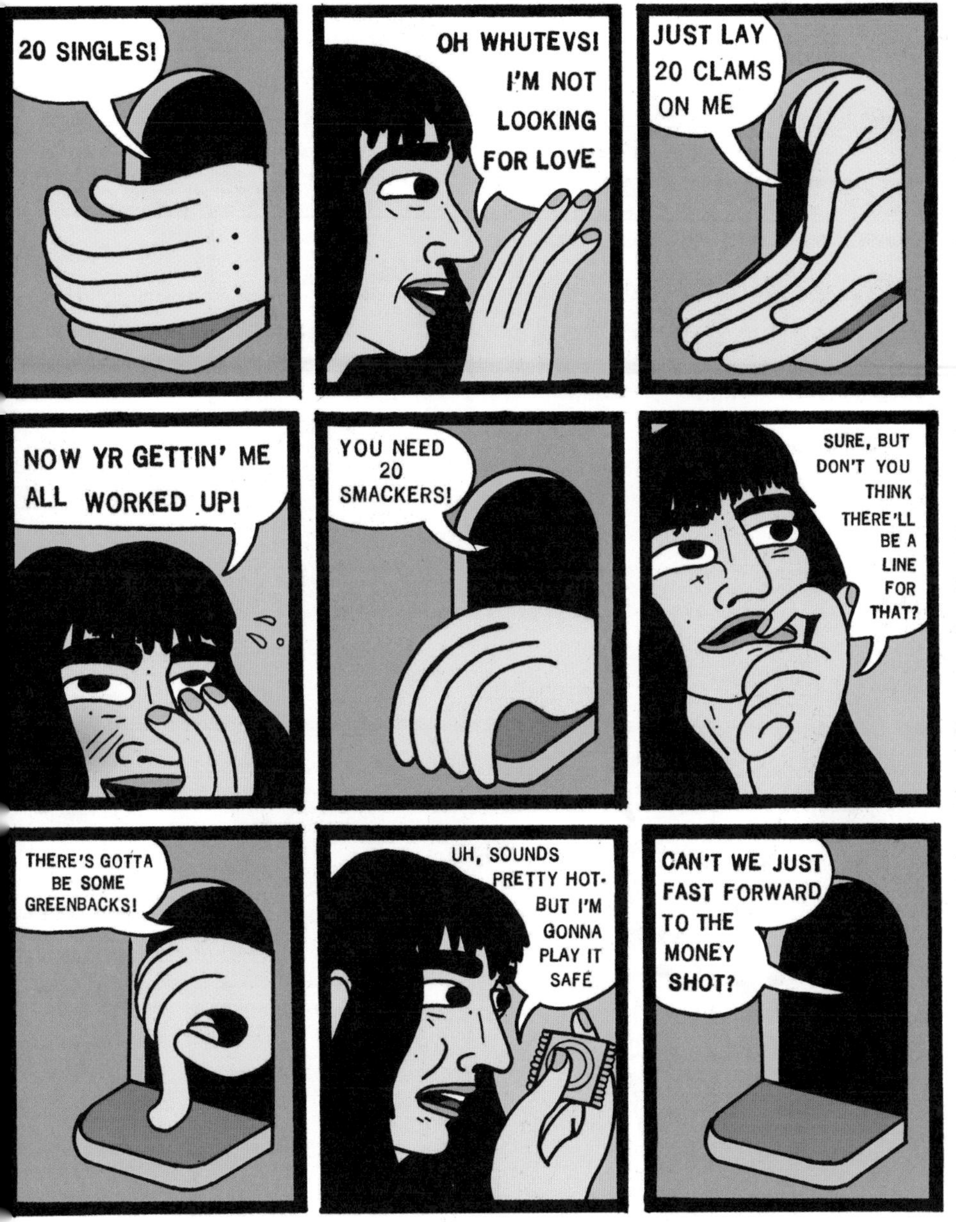
20 SINGLES!
OH WHUTEVS! I'M NOT LOOKING FOR LOVE
JUST LAY 20 CLAMS ON ME
NOW YR GETTIN' ME ALL WORKED UP!
YOU NEED 20 SMACKERS!
SURE, BUT DON'T YOU THINK THERE'LL BE A LINE FOR THAT?
THERE'S GOTTA BE SOME GREENBACKS!
UH, SOUNDS PRETTY HOT- BUT I'M GONNA PLAY IT SAFE
CAN'T WE JUST FAST FORWARD TO THE MONEY SHOT?

This is a new kind of Color-by-Number book.

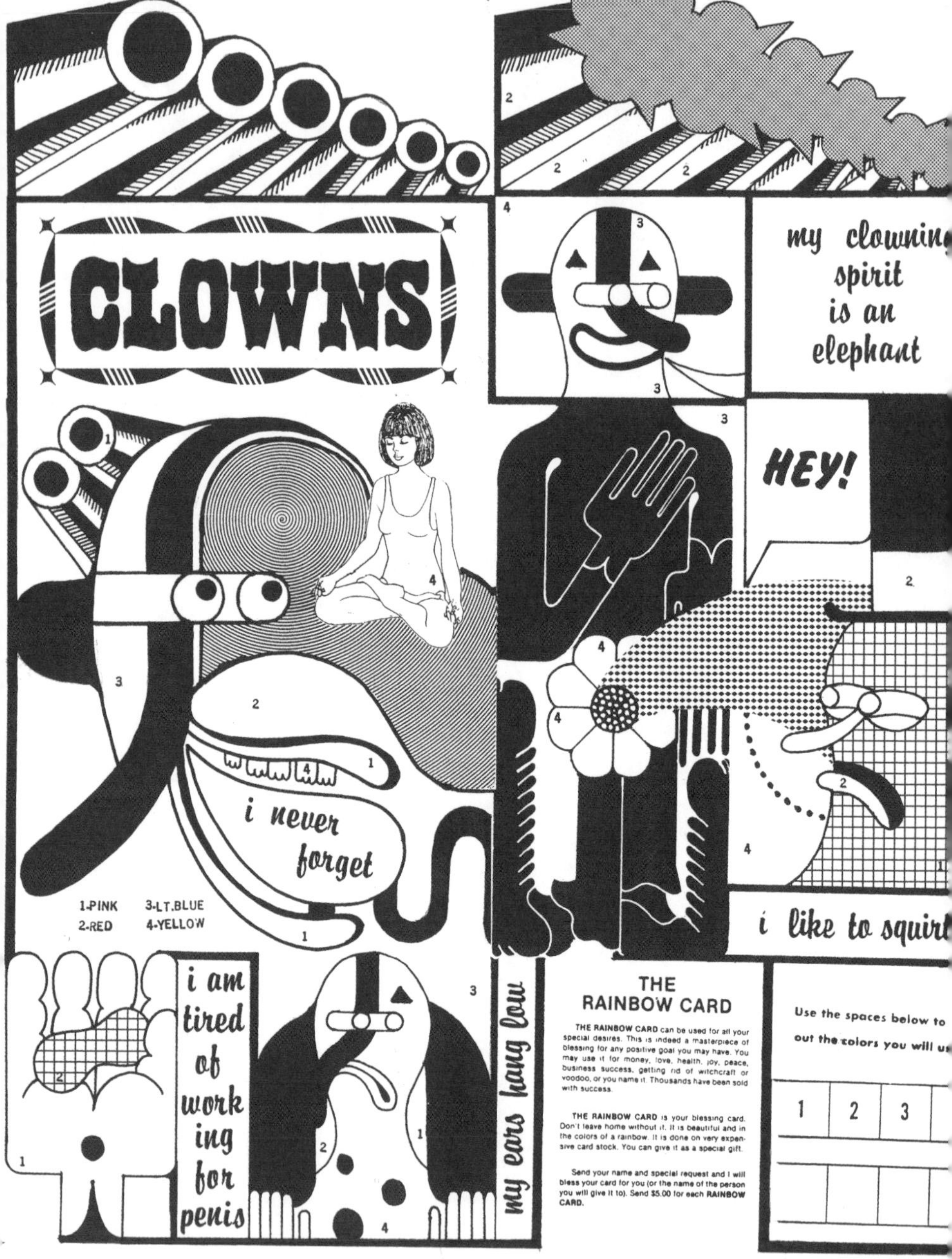
CLOWNS
my clowning spirit is an elephant
HEY!
i never forget
1-PINK 3-LT.BLUE
2-RED 4-YELLOW
i like to squirt
i am tired of working for penis
my ears hang low
THE RAINBOW CARD
THE RAINBOW CARD can be used for all your special desires. This is indeed a masterpiece of blessing for any positive goal you may have. You may use it for money, love, health, joy, peace, business success, getting rid of witchcraft or voodoo, or you name it. Thousands have been sold with success.
THE RAINBOW CARD is your blessing card. Don't leave home without it. It is beautiful and in the colors of a rainbow. It is done on very expensive card stock. You can give it as a special gift.
Send your name and special request and I will bless your card for you (or the name of the person you will give it to). Send $5.00 for each RAINBOW CARD.
Use the spaces below to
out the colors you will u
1 2 3

BEFORE I ASK
SAY YES

COMB MY CYBERSKIN DILDO

SOME BRUTAL SHIT HAPPENED

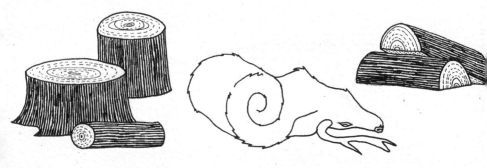

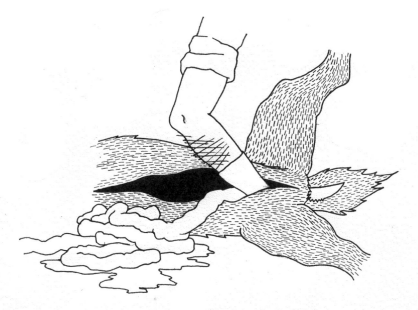

LOVE AND  UNDERSTANDING

MOUSTACHIO

PISTACHIO

PASTICHE

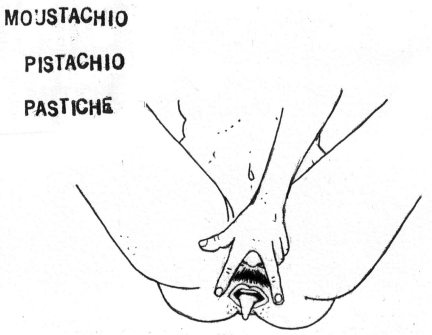

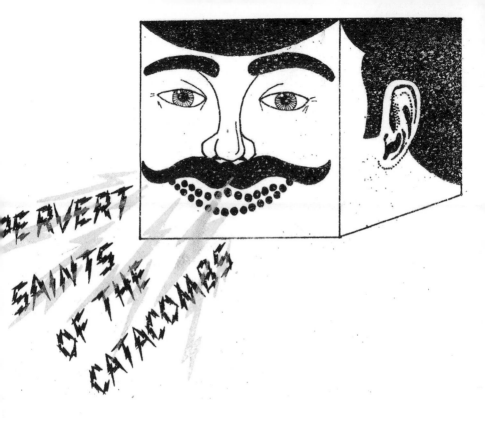

PERVERT SAINTS OF THE CATACOMBS

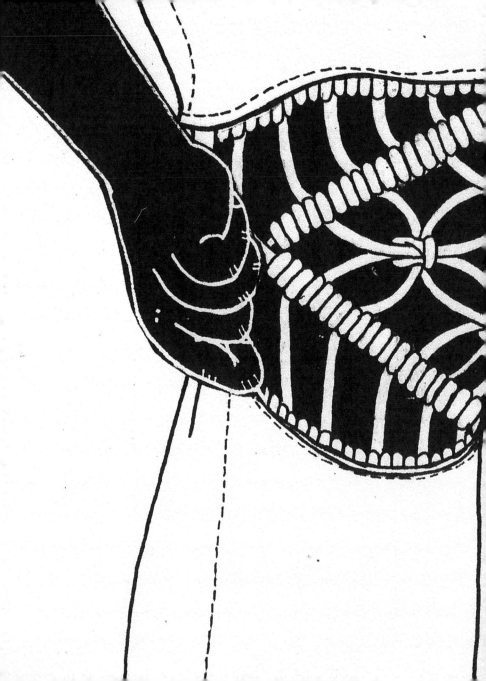

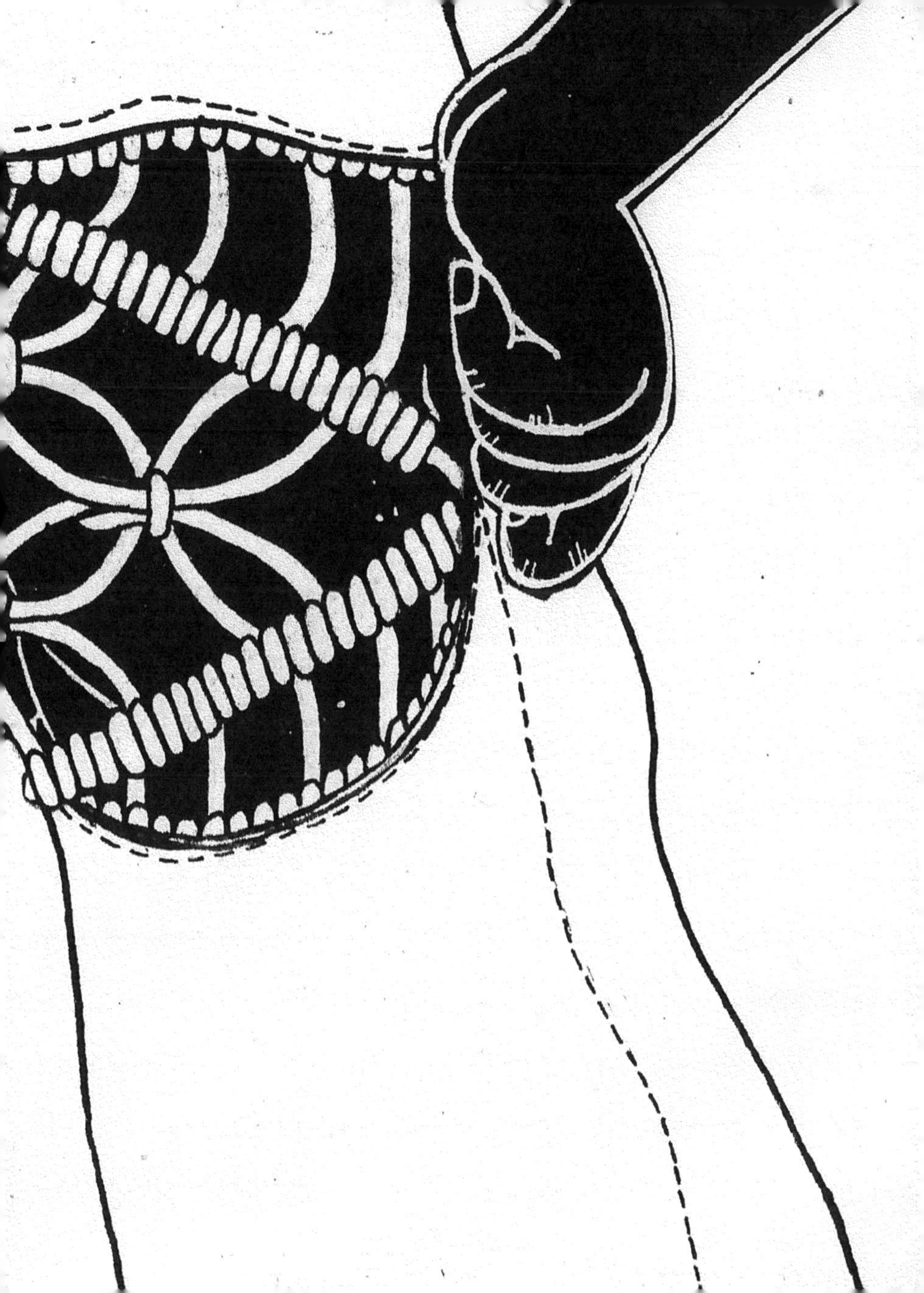

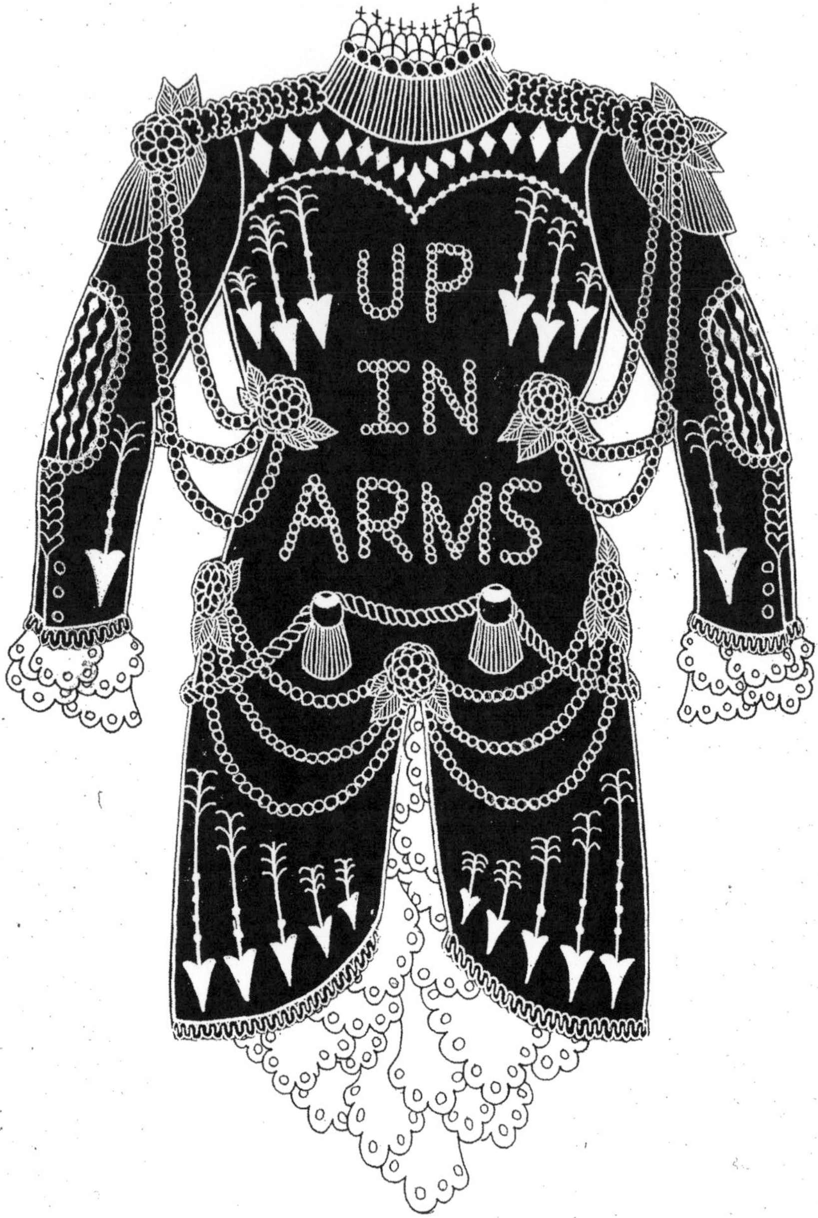
UP
IN
ARMS

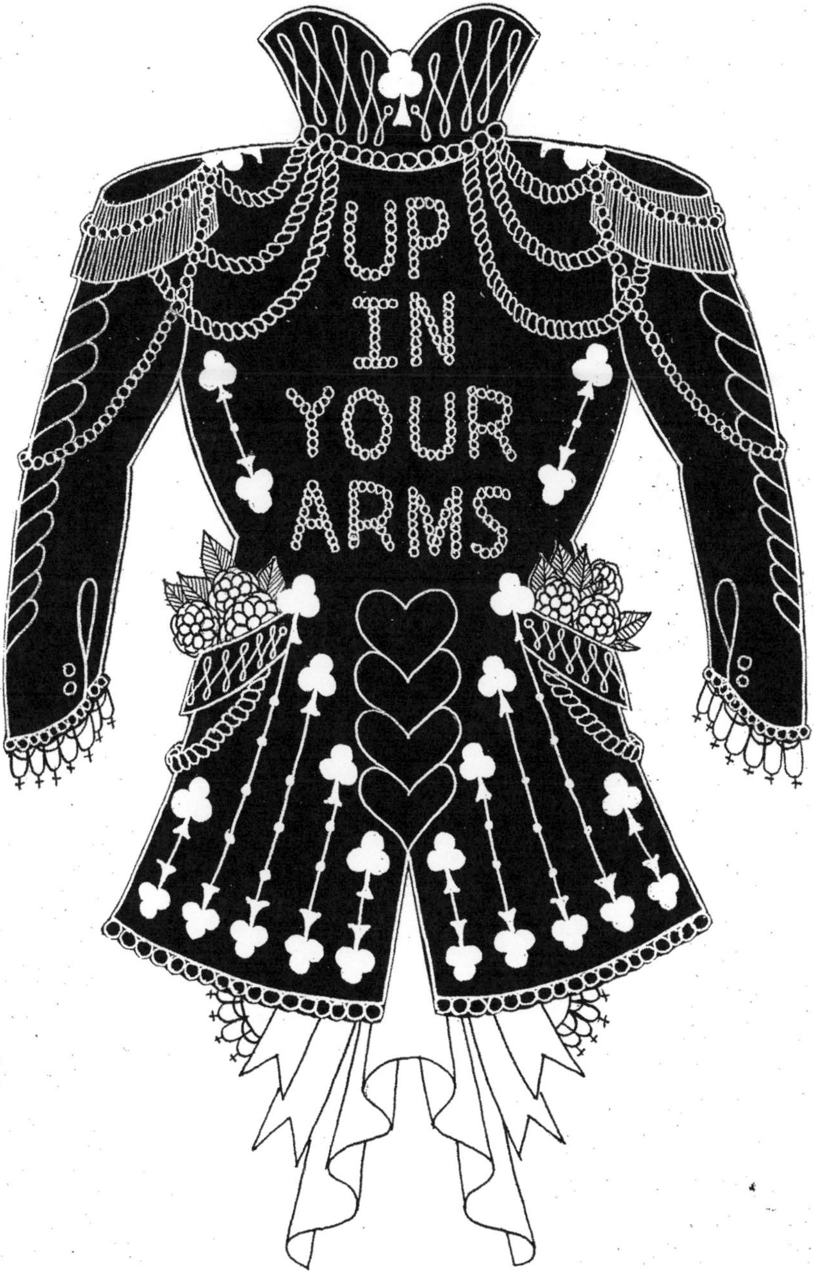
UP
IN
YOUR
ARMS

THISISNO
TAPLACEF
ORLOVER
S

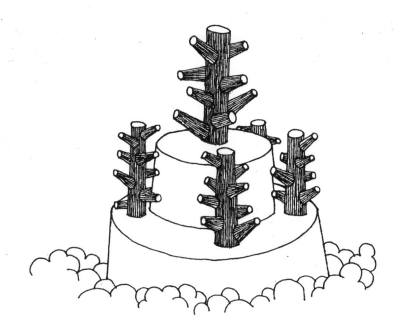

RETREAT

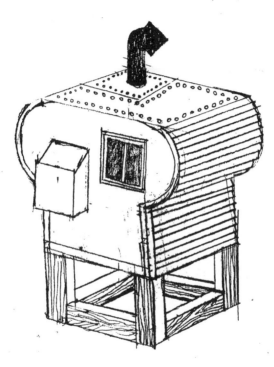

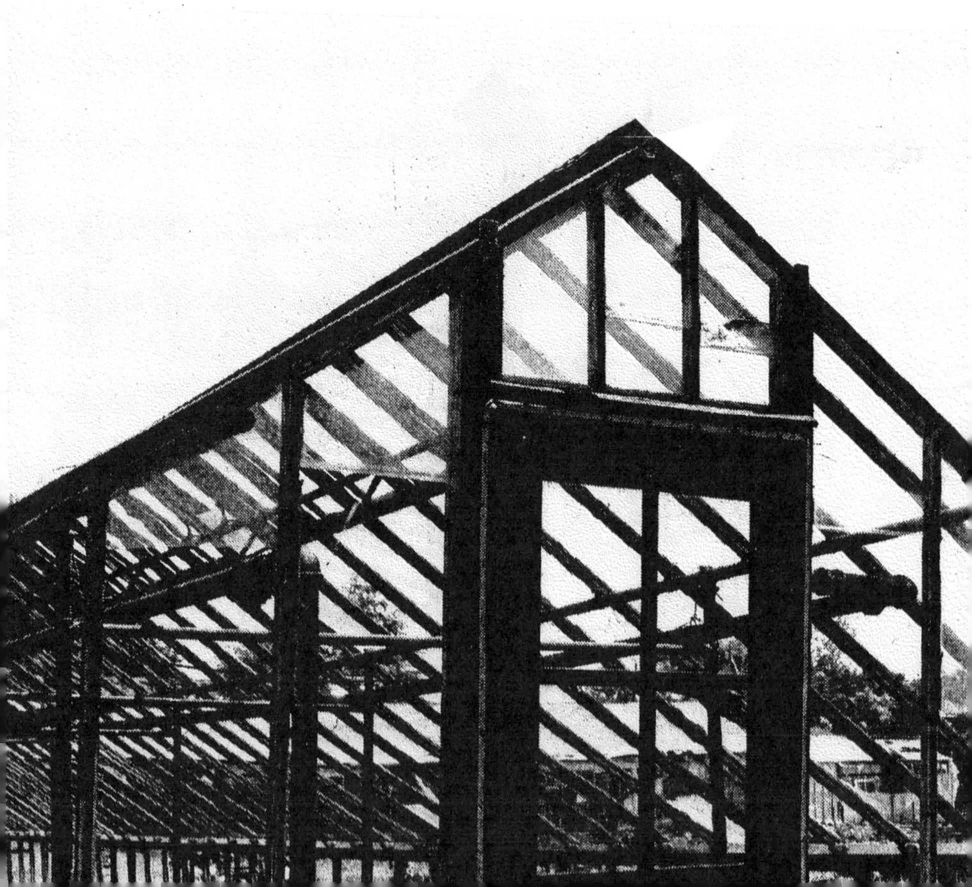

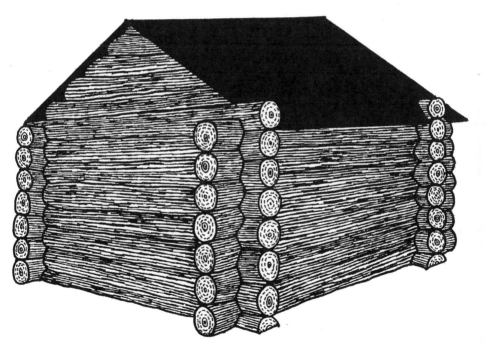

WARP ZONE

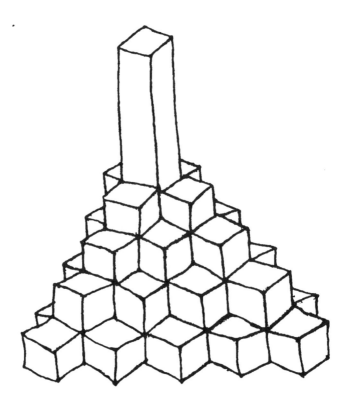

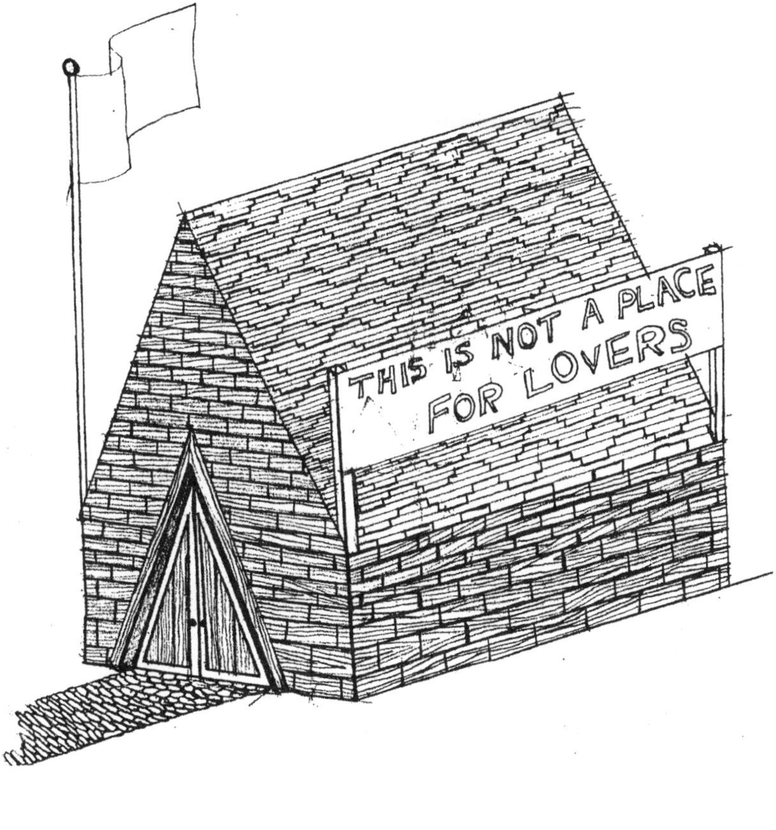
THIS IS NOT A PLACE
FOR LOVERS

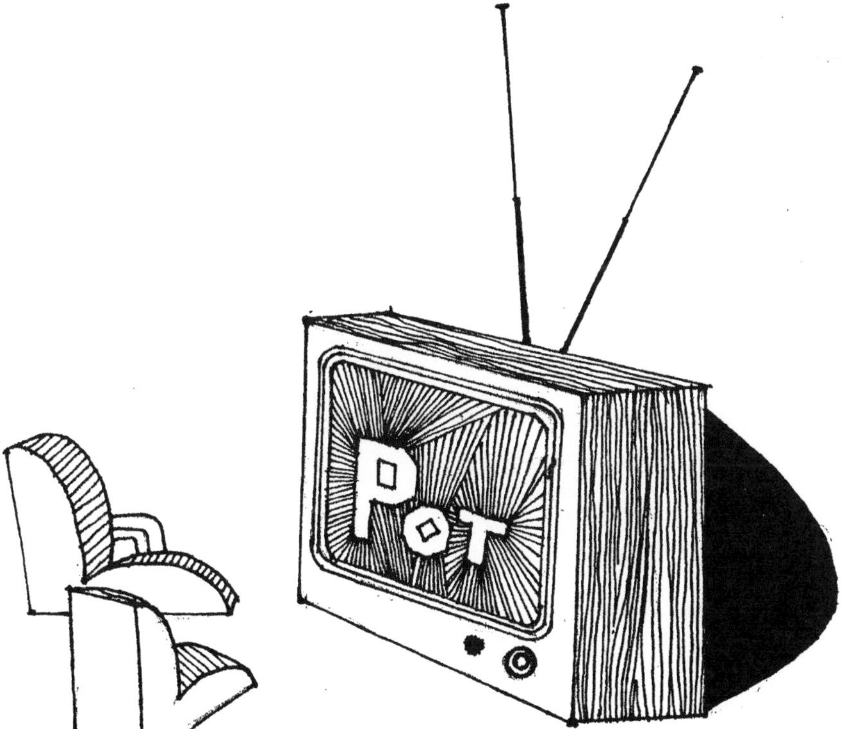
Pot

DEEP
INTO
MY
EYES

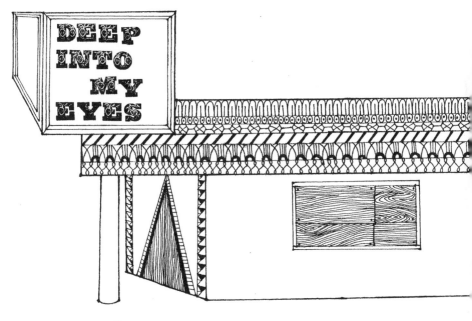

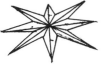

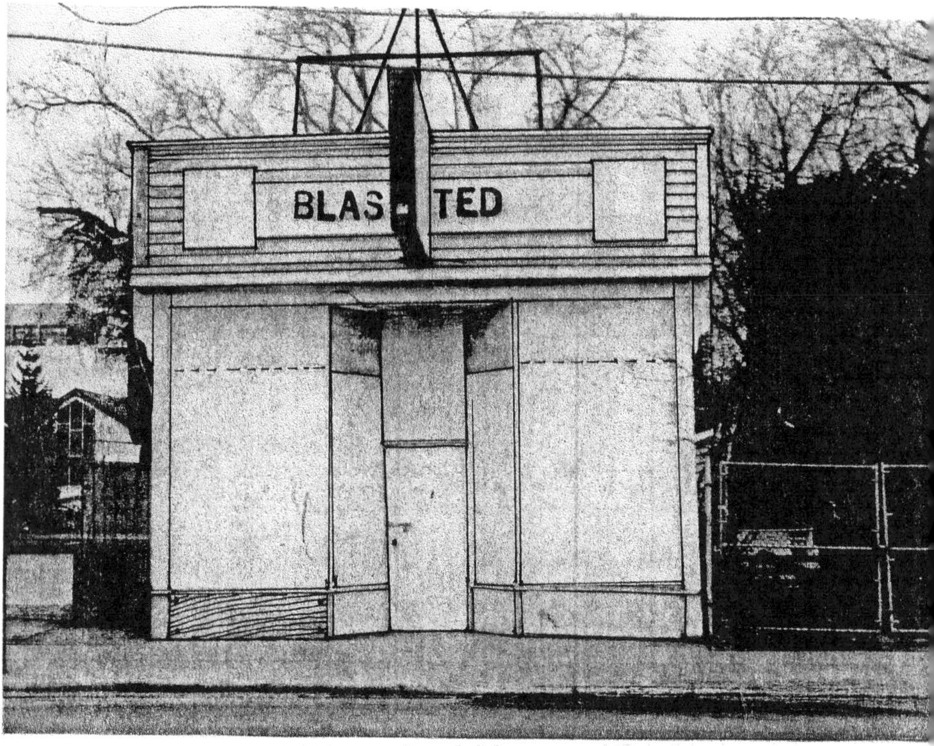
BLAS TED

INSULT
ED

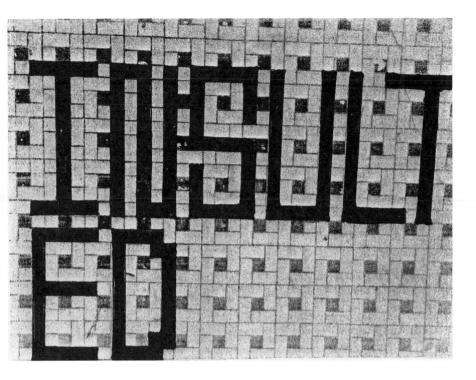

HELD

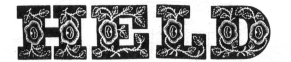

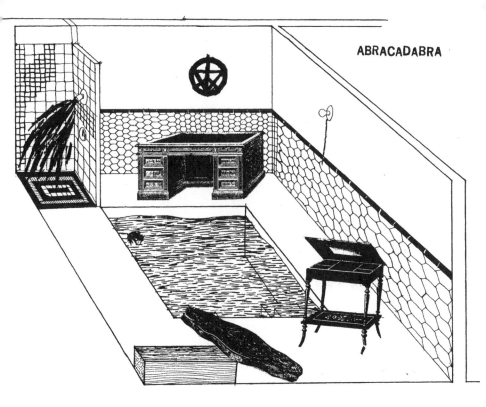

ABRACADABRA

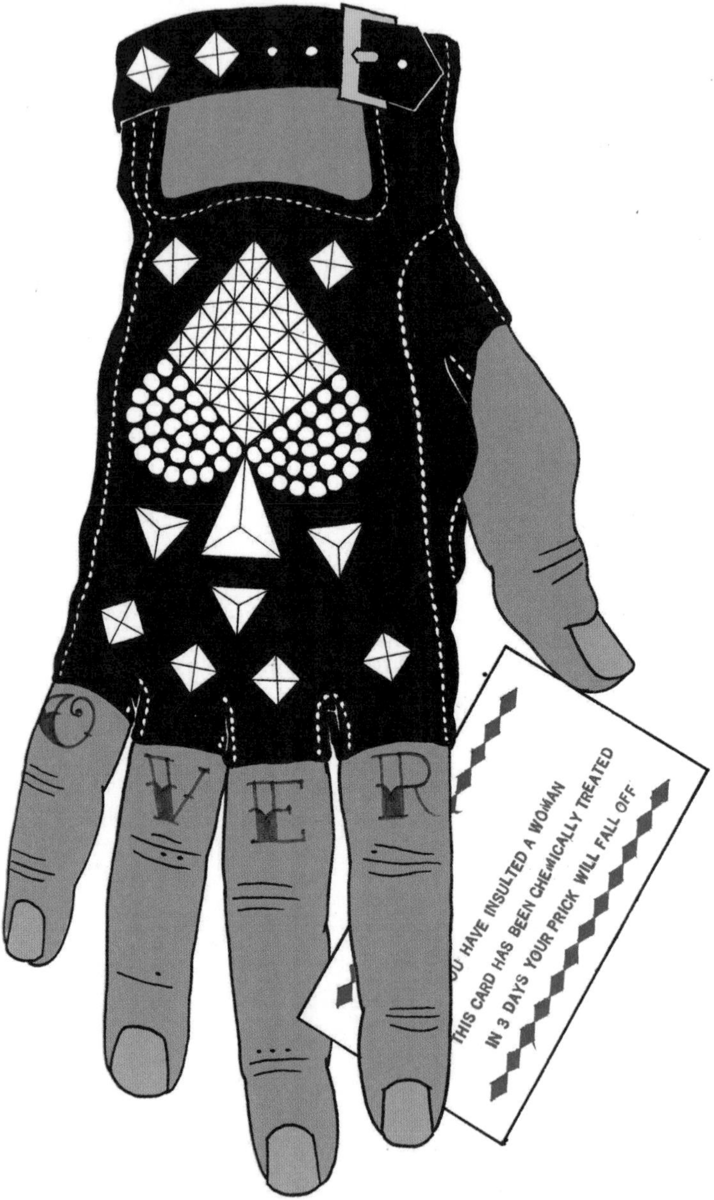
OU HAVE INSULTED A WOMAN
THIS CARD HAS BEEN CHEMICALLY TREATED
IN 3 DAYS YOUR PRICK WILL FALL OFF

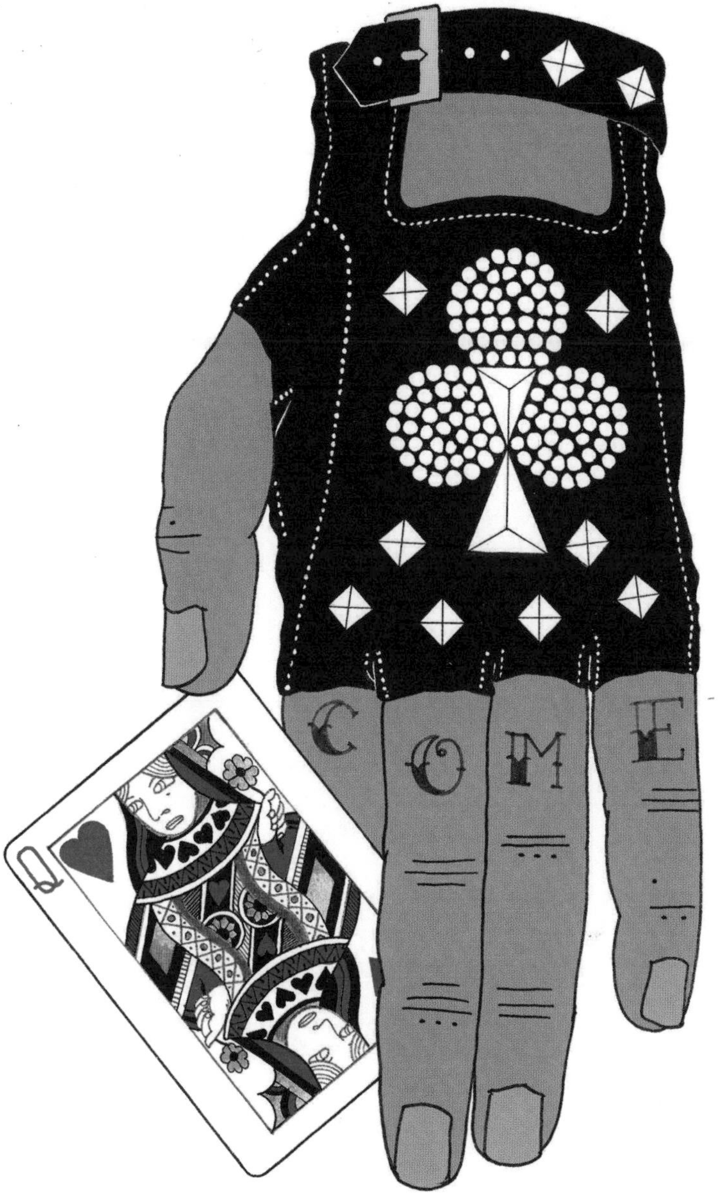
COME

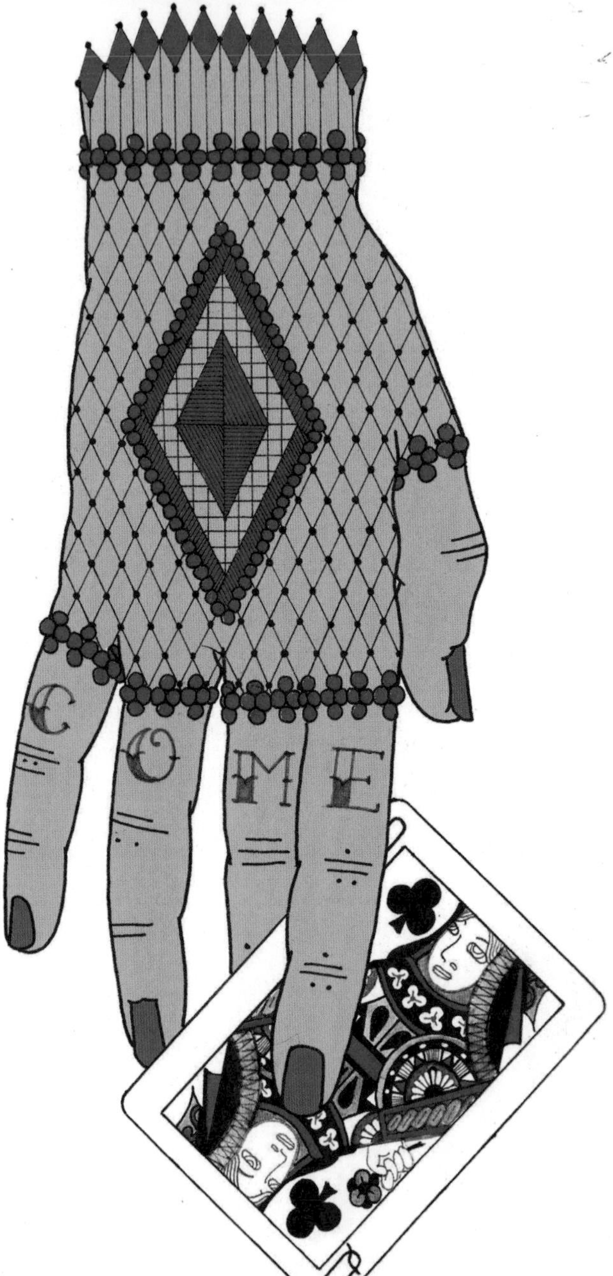
COME

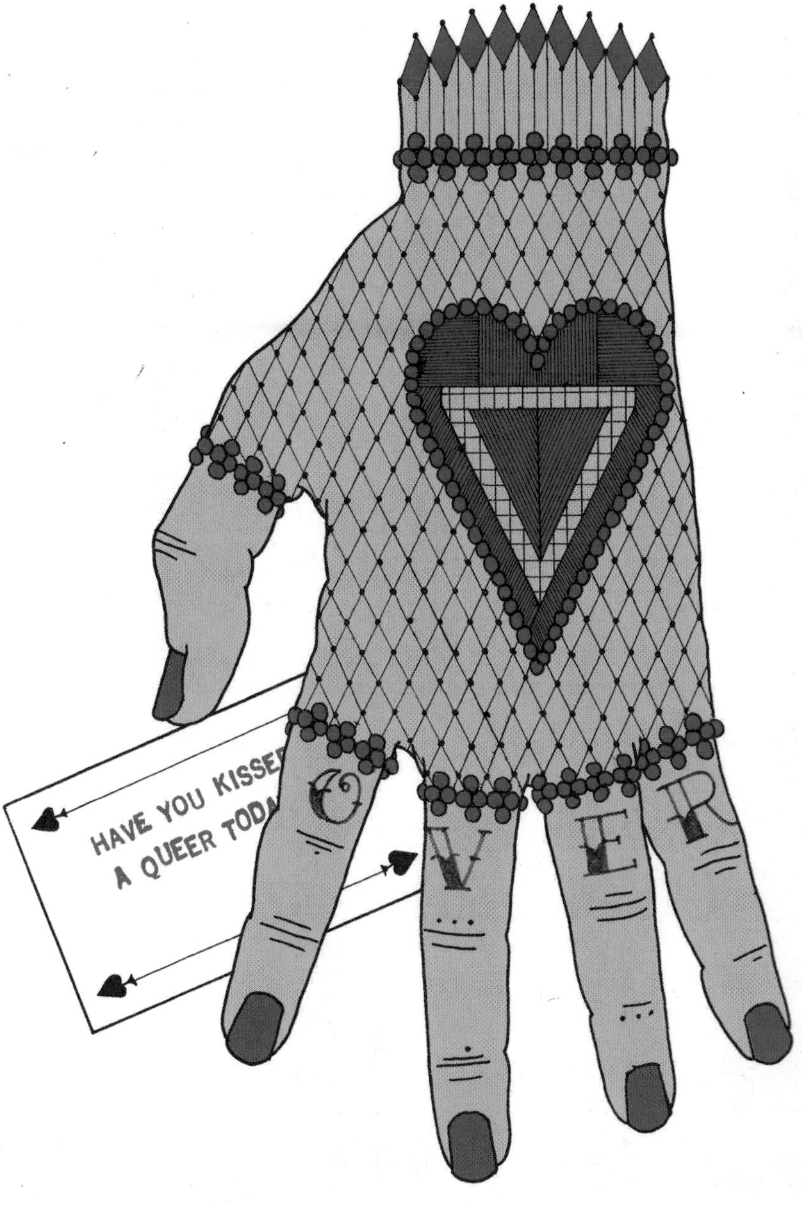
HAVE YOU KISSE
A QUEER TODA
OVER

CLOWNS

MANY CLOWNS RELY ON THE ART OF CAMOUFLAGE TO AVOID BEING SPOTTED BY PREDATORS

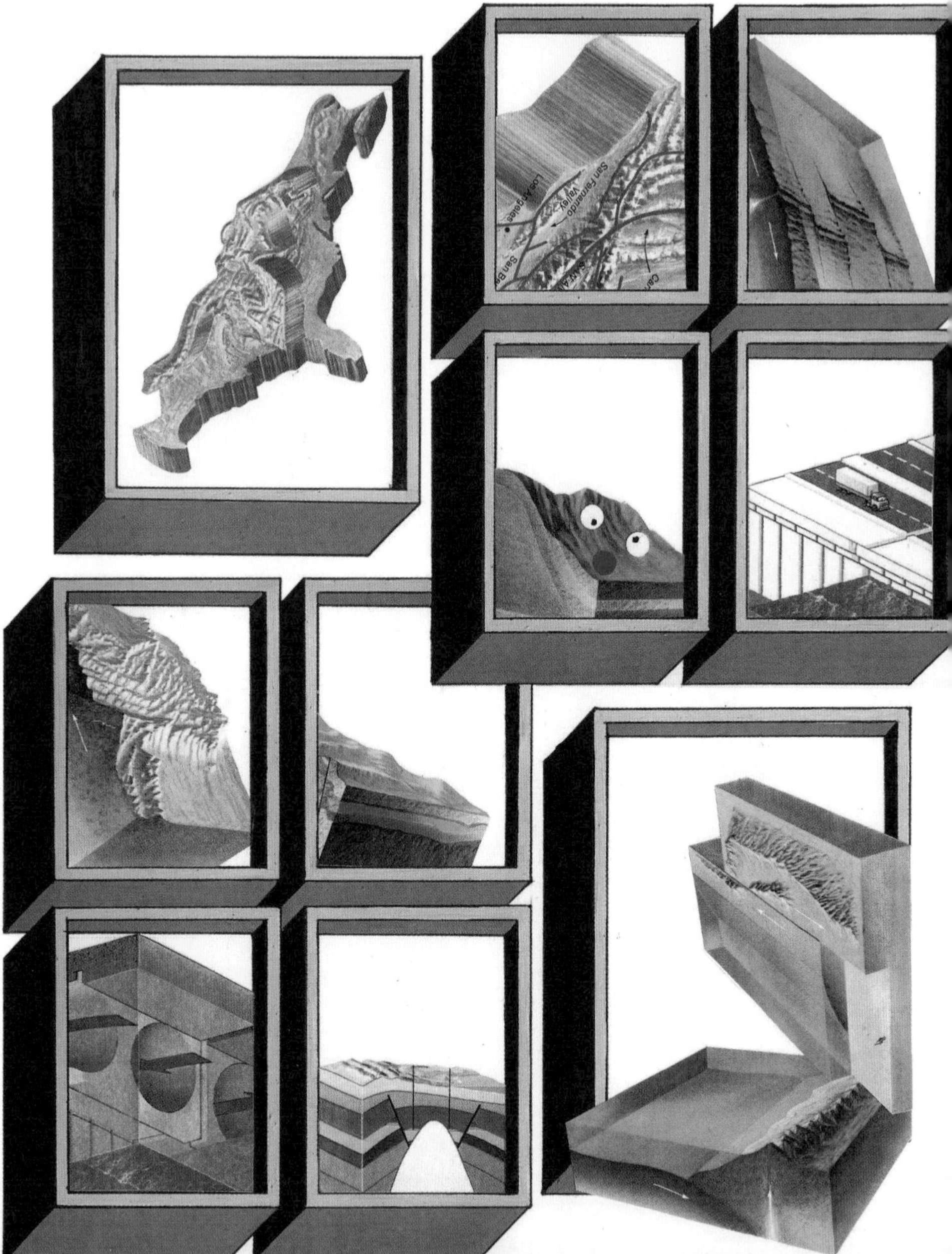
Los Angeles
San Fernando Valley

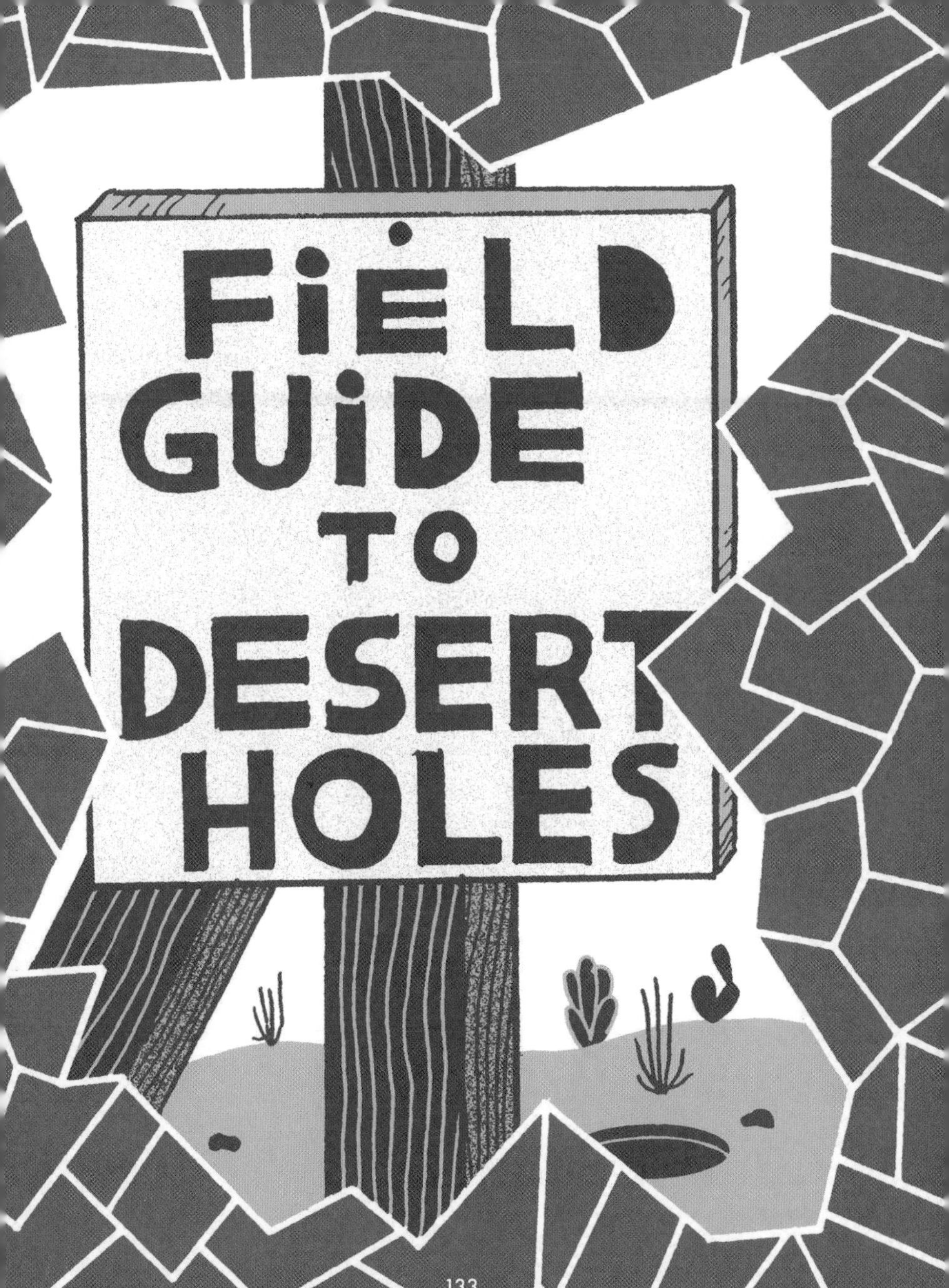
FiELD
GUiDE
TO
DESERT
HOLES

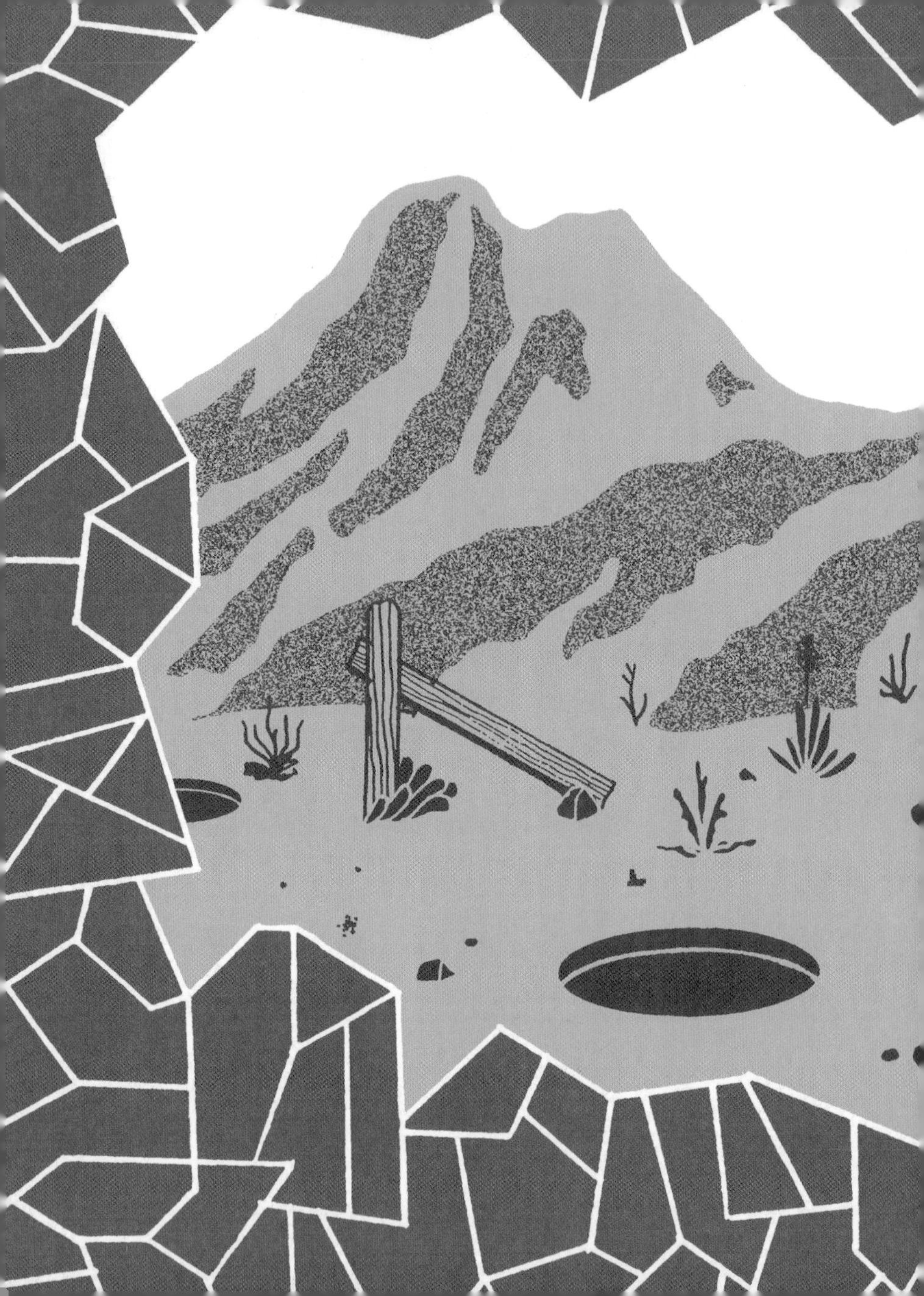

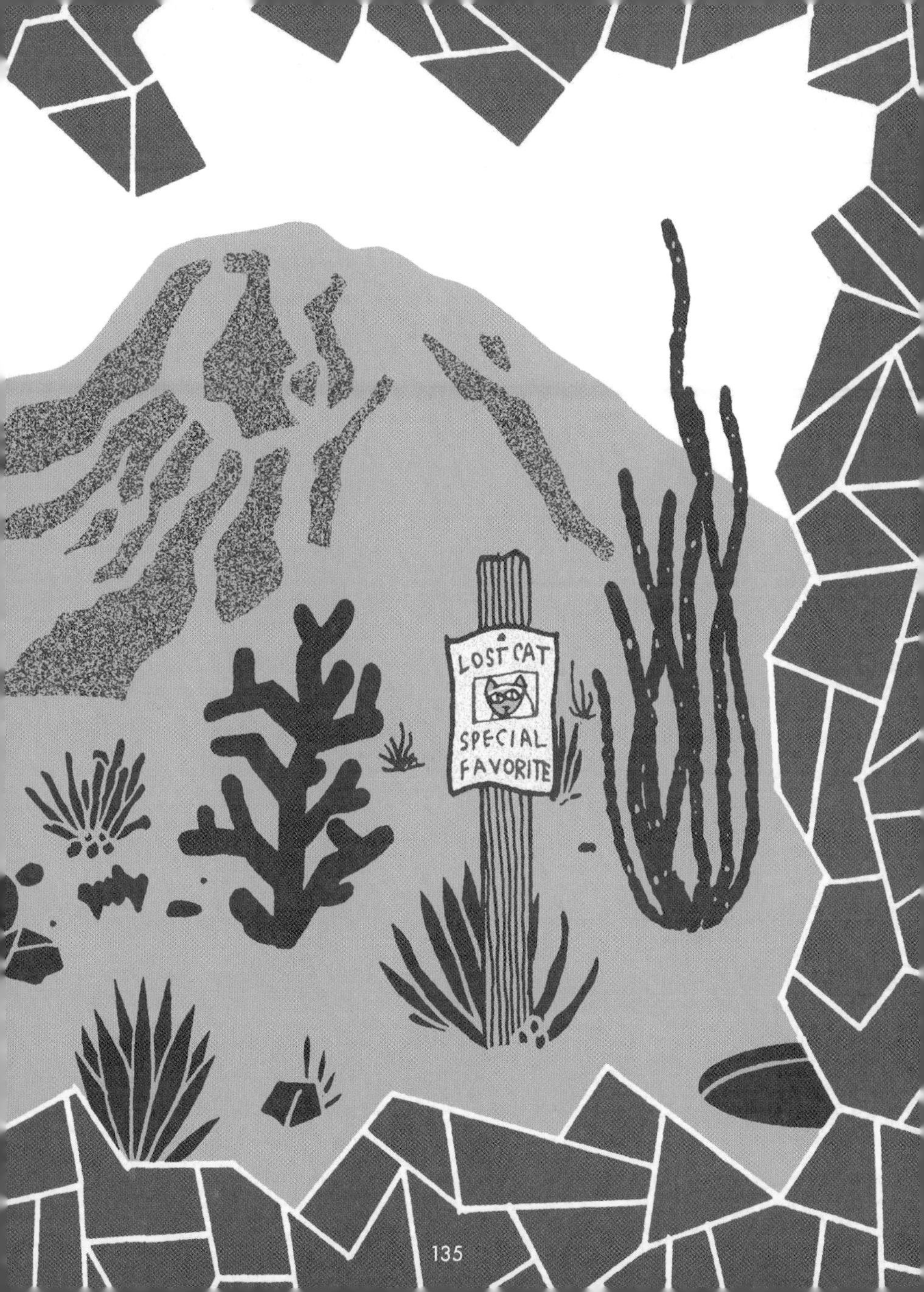
LOST CAT
SPECIAL FAVORITE

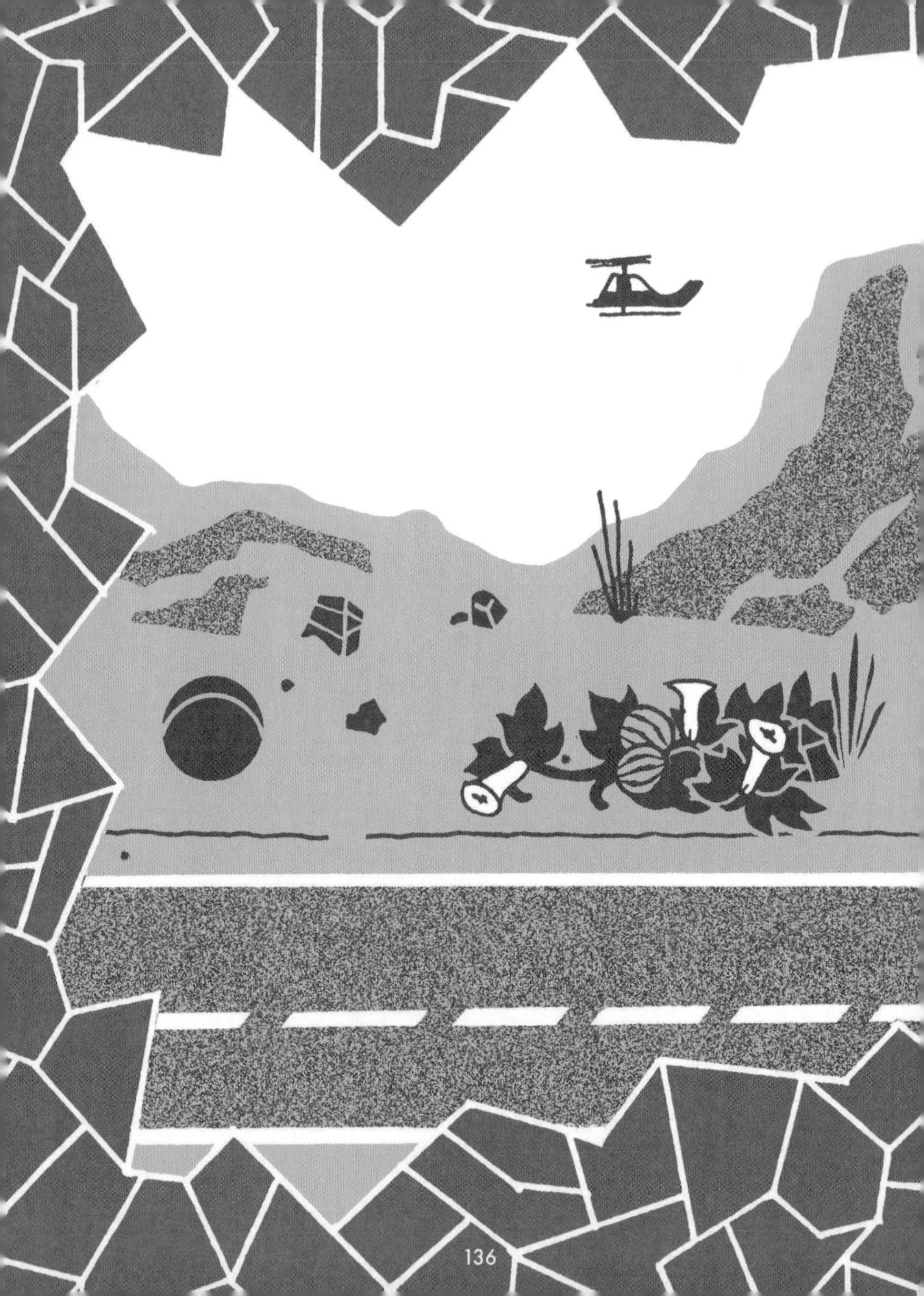

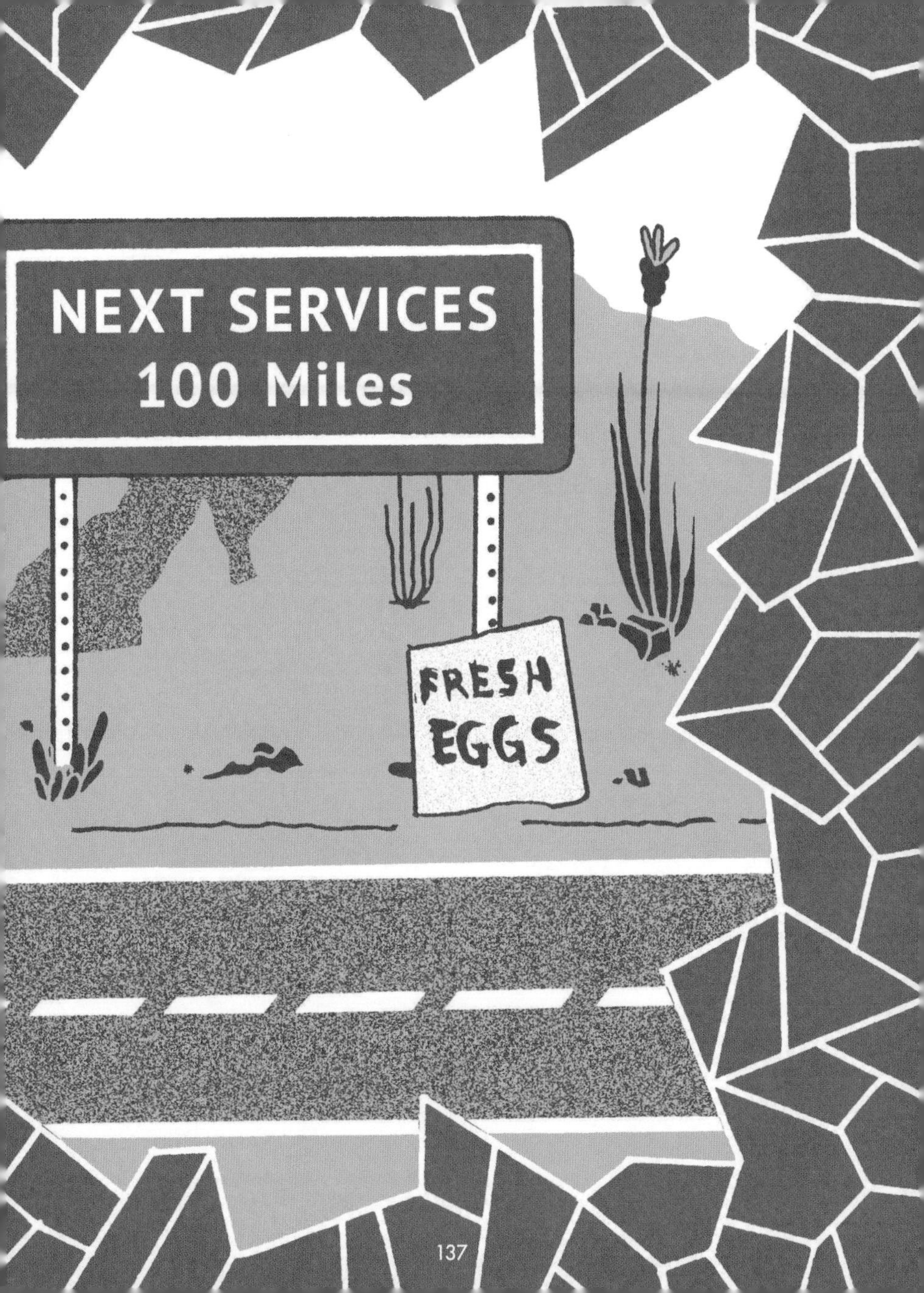
NEXT SERVICES
100 Miles
FRESH
EGGS

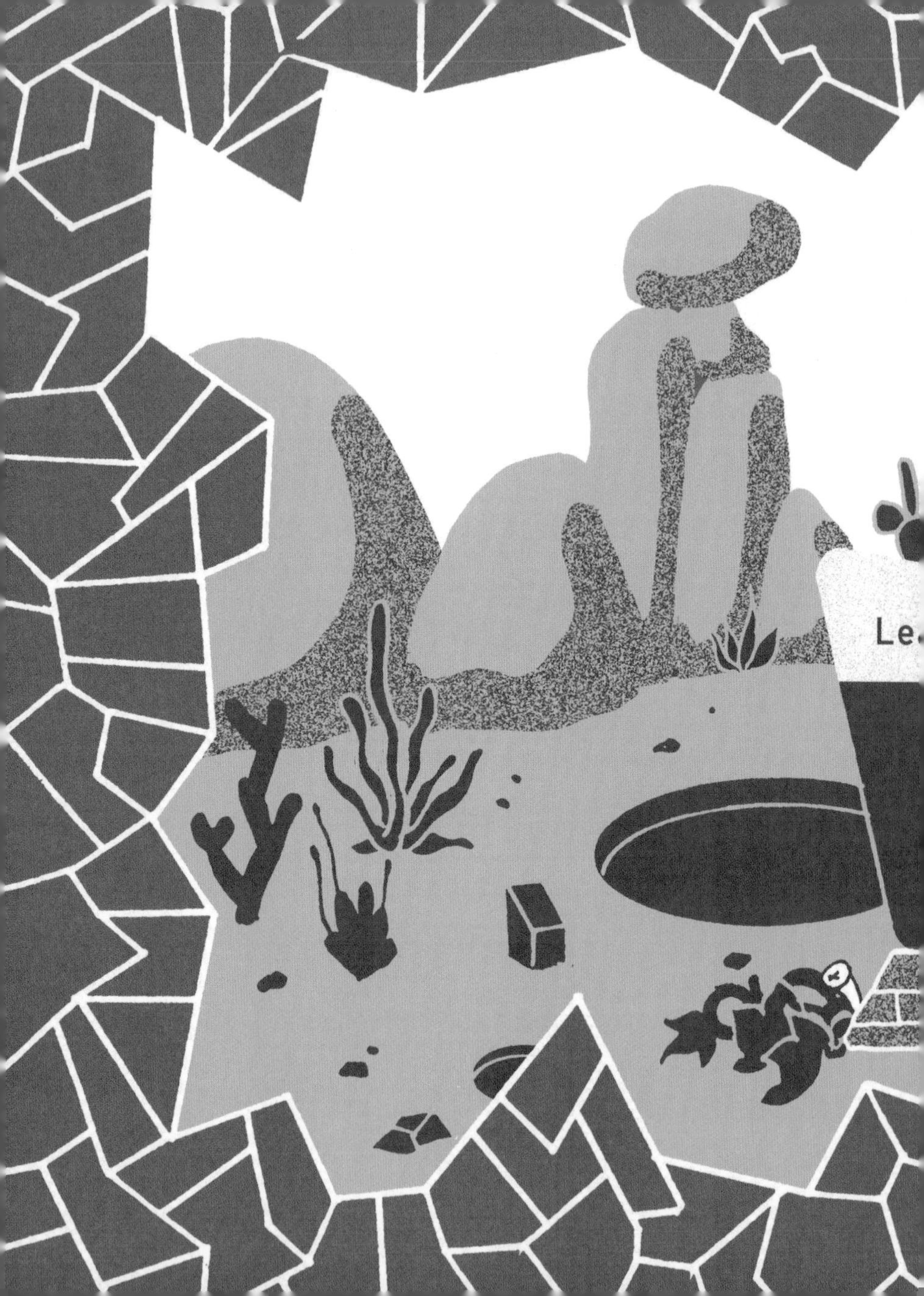

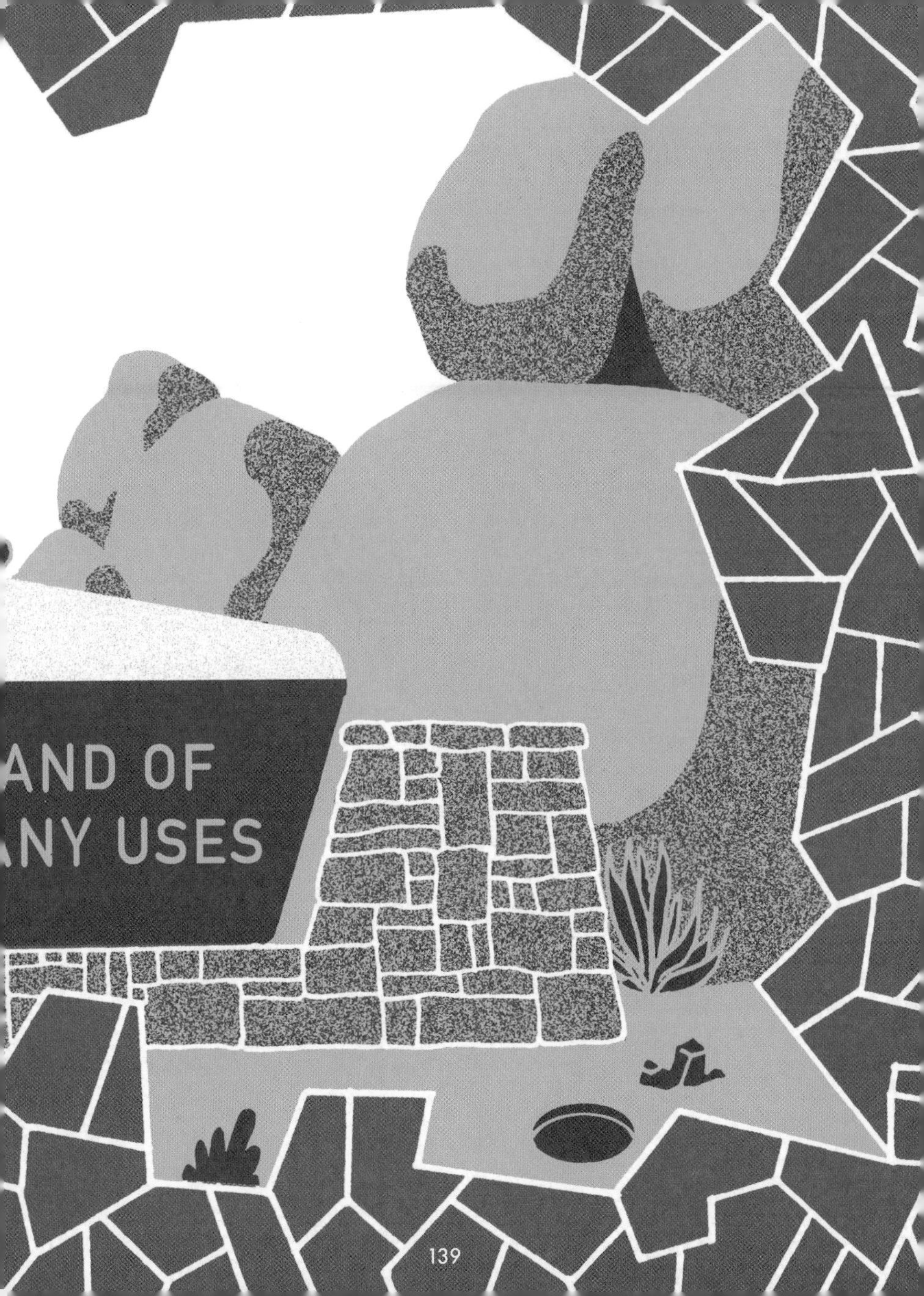
AND OF
ANY USES

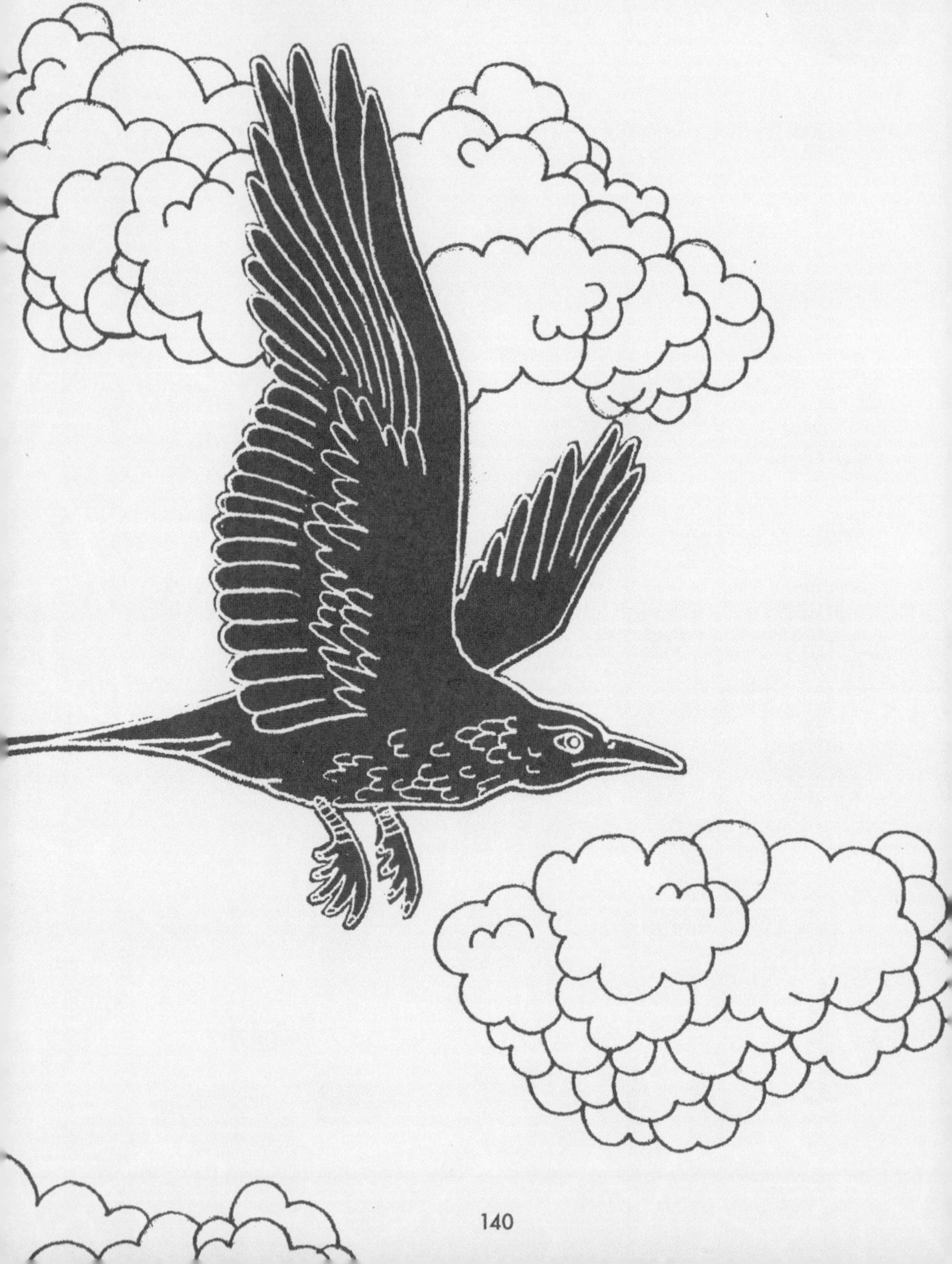

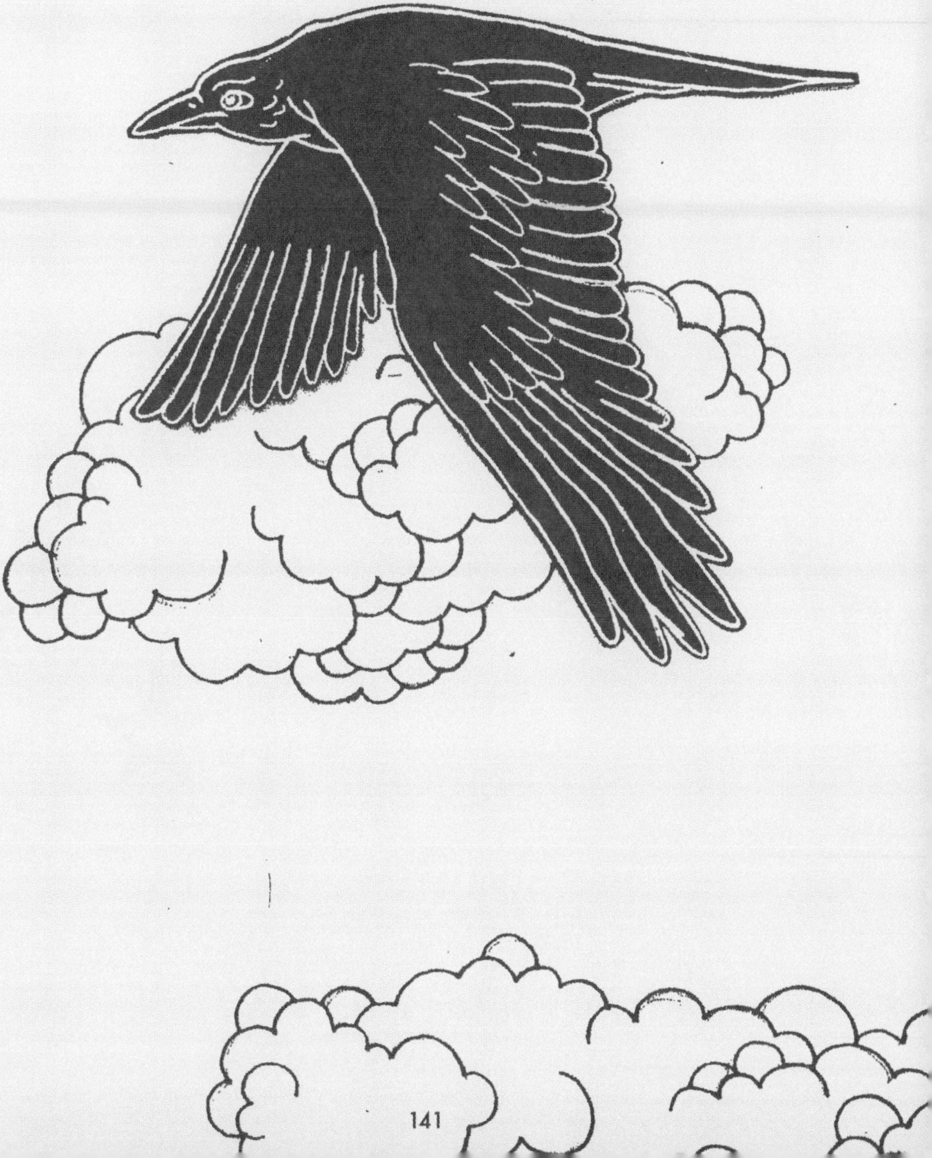

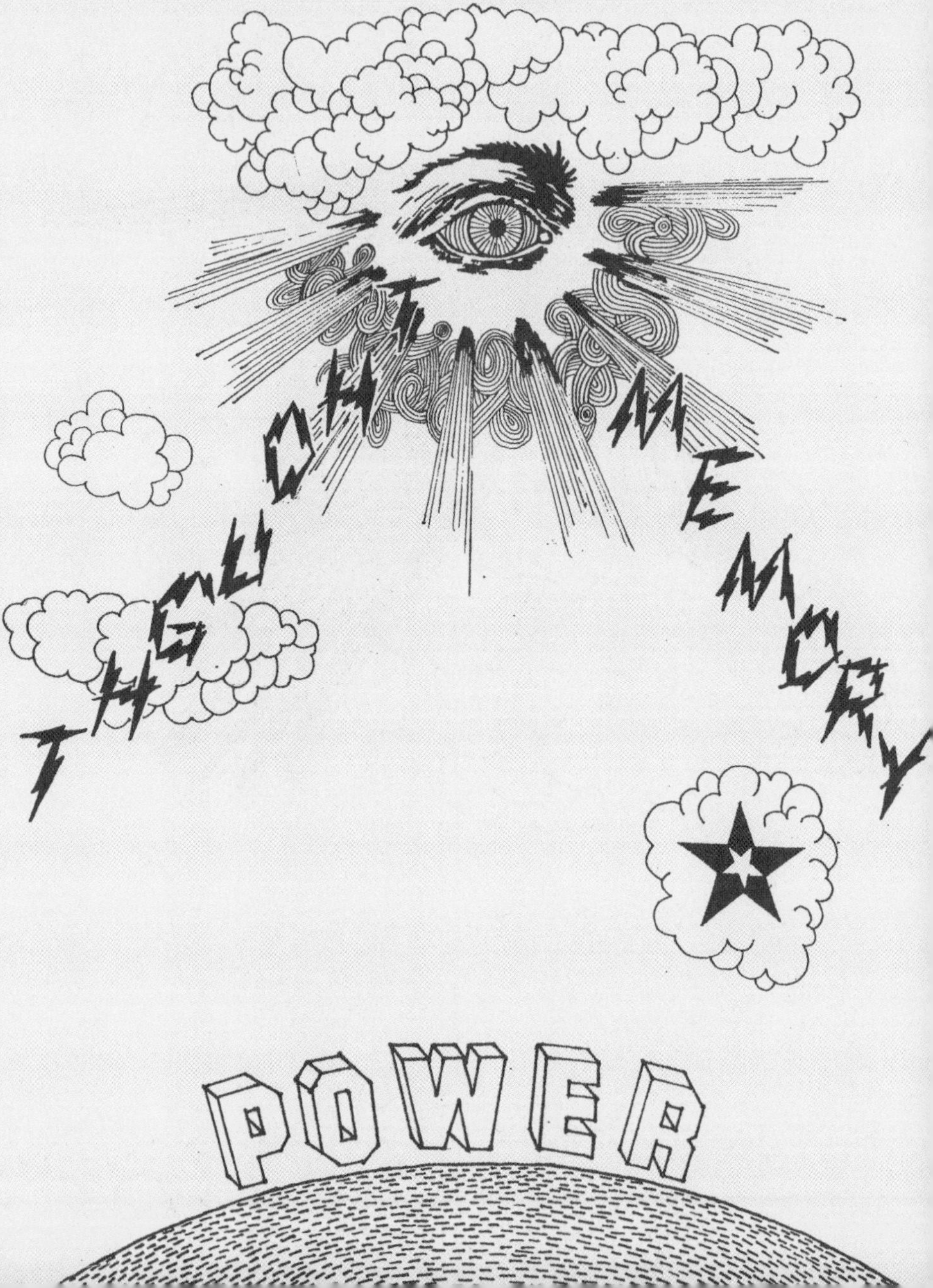
MEMORY
POWER

VALHALLA

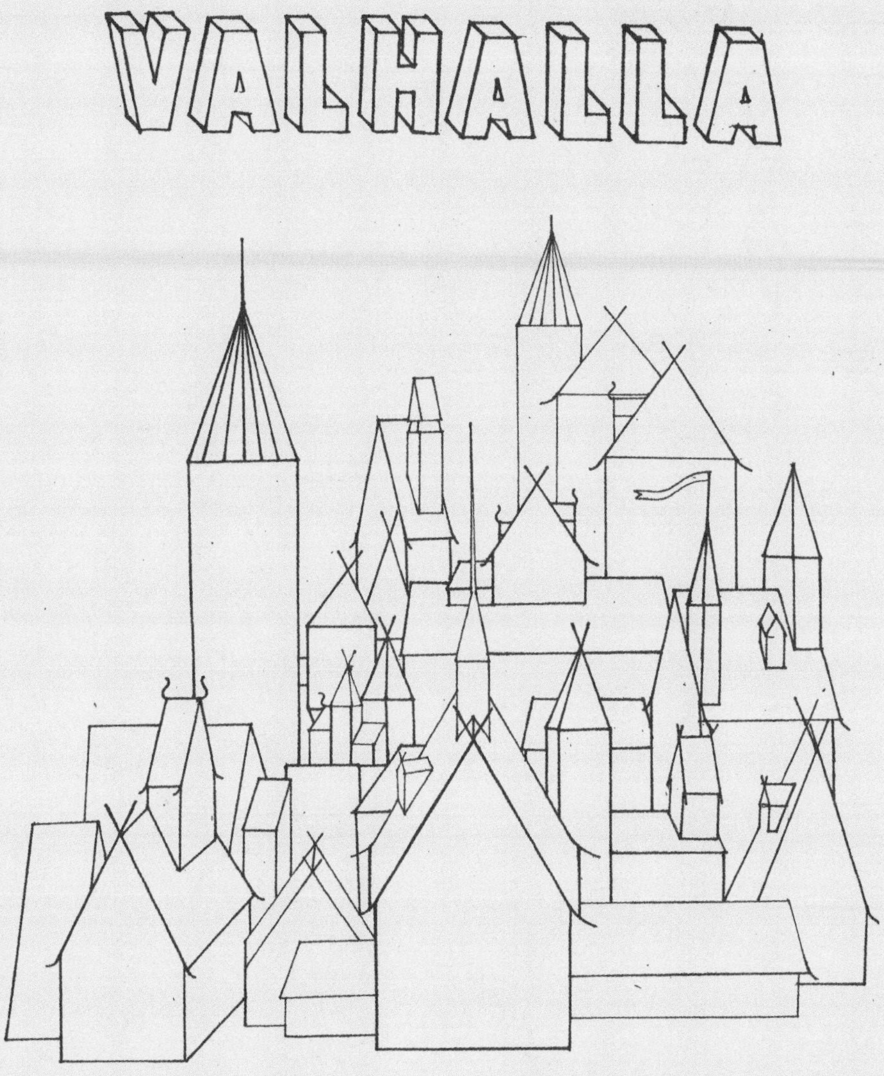

YOU SHALL RESIDE AT MY MANOR?

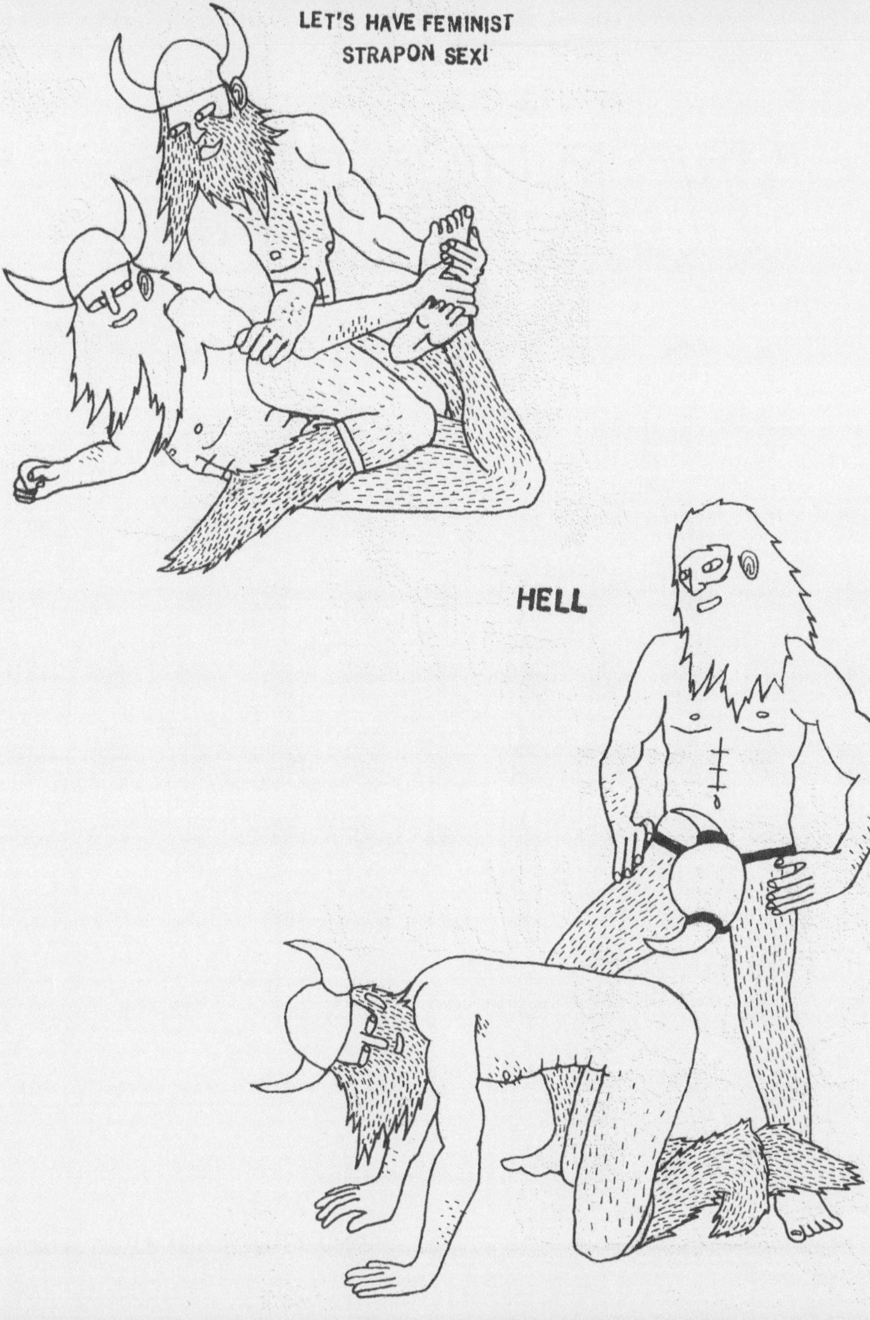
LET'S HAVE FEMINIST STRAPON SEX!
HELL

RICO MCTACO IS A DYKE

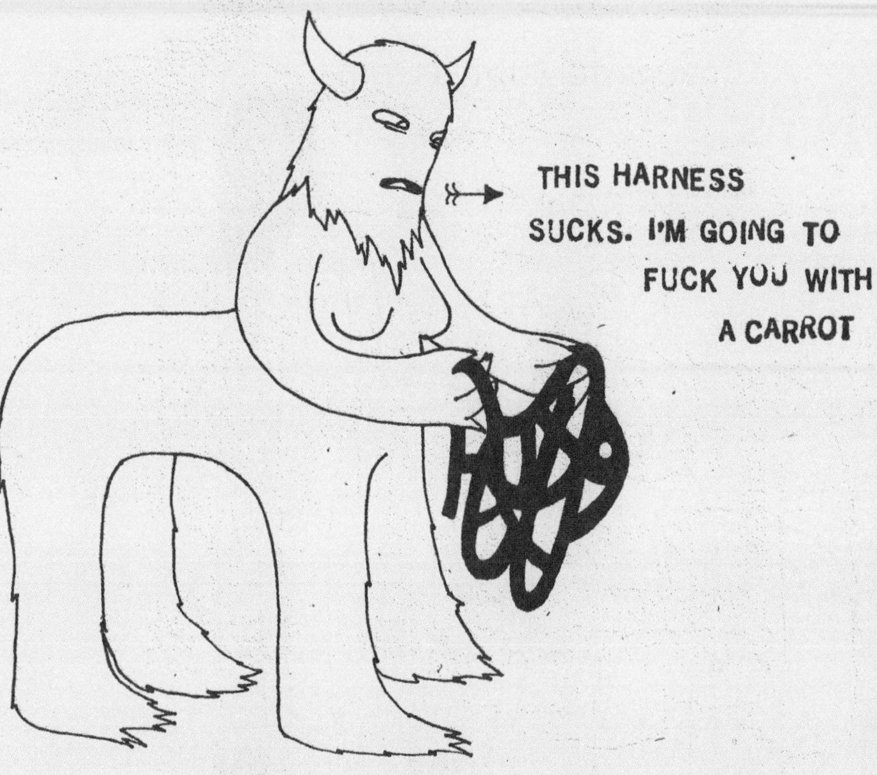
THIS HARNESS SUCKS. I'M GOING TO FUCK YOU WITH A CARROT

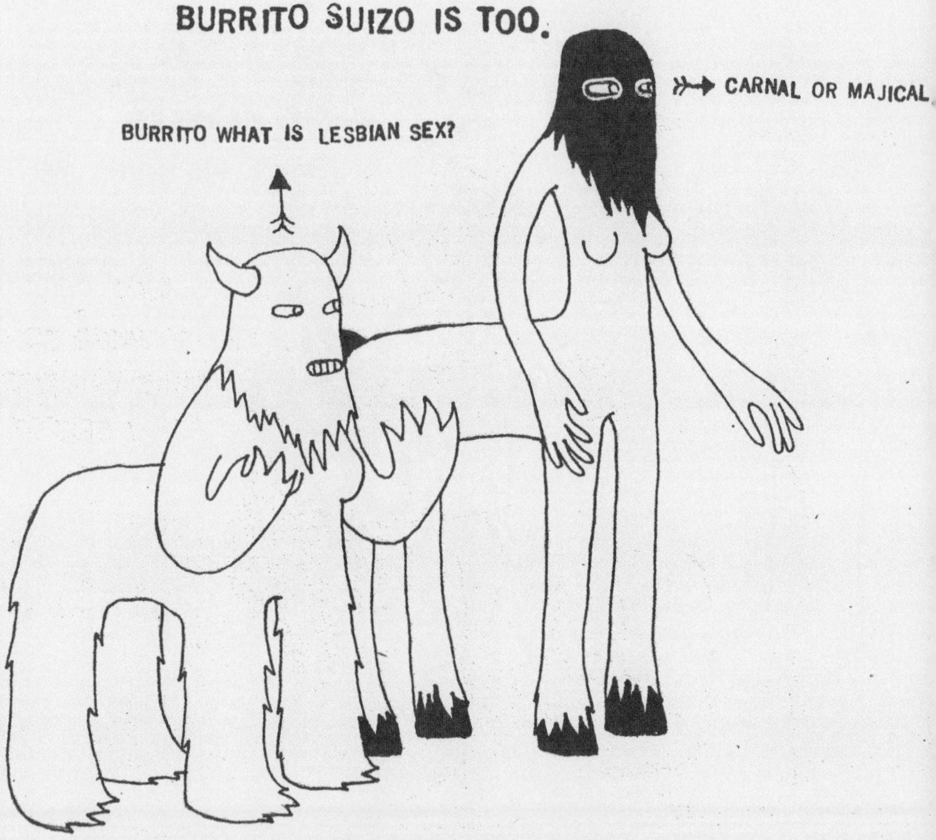
BURRITO SUIZO IS TOO.
CARNAL OR MAJICAL
BURRITO WHAT IS LESBIAN SEX?

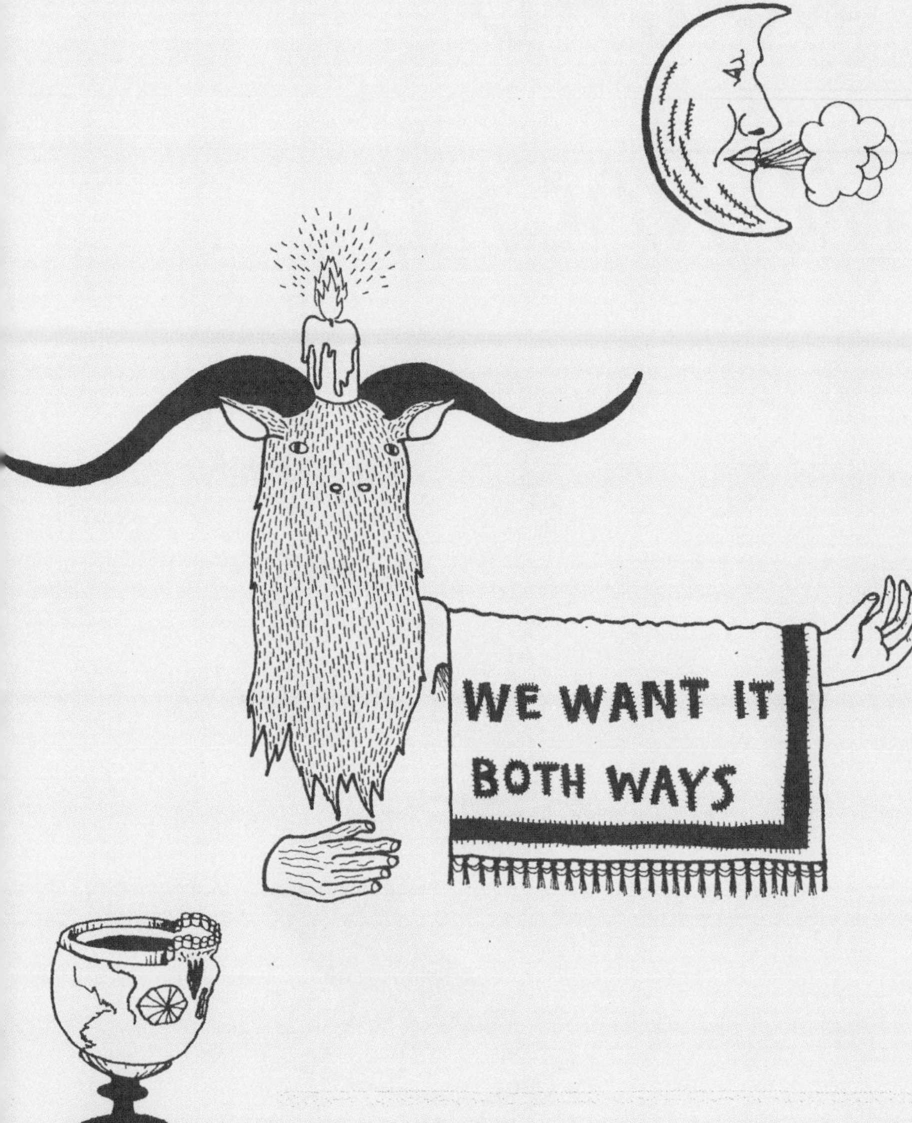
WE WANT IT
BOTH WAYS

MACHO MC NACHO

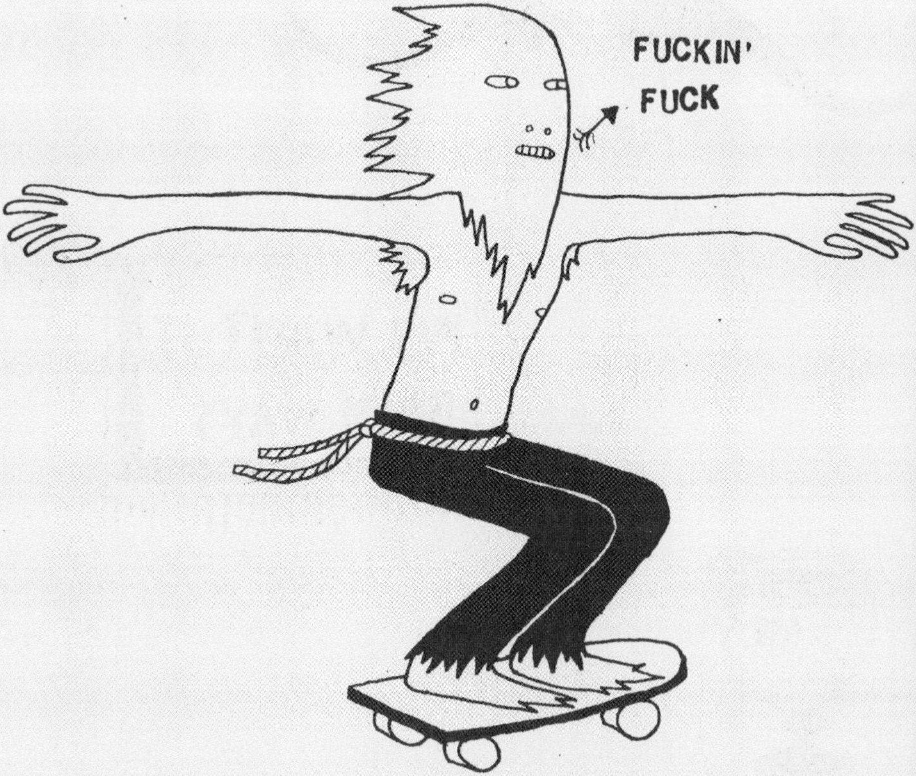
FUCKIN'
FUCK

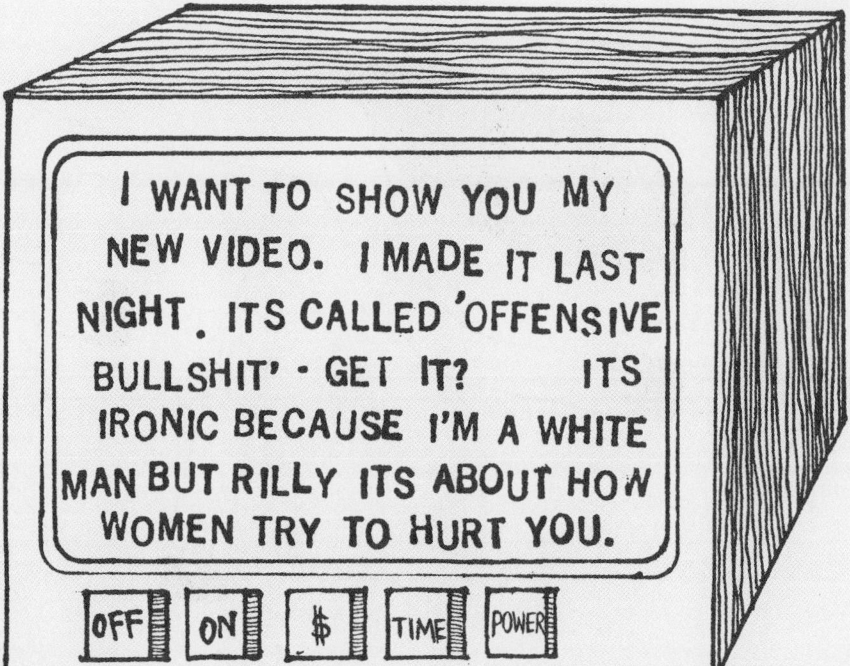
I WANT TO SHOW YOU MY NEW VIDEO. I MADE IT LAST NIGHT. ITS CALLED 'OFFENSIVE BULLSHIT' - GET IT? ITS IRONIC BECAUSE I'M A WHITE MAN BUT RILLY ITS ABOUT HOW WOMEN TRY TO HURT YOU.
OFF
ON
$
TIME
POWER

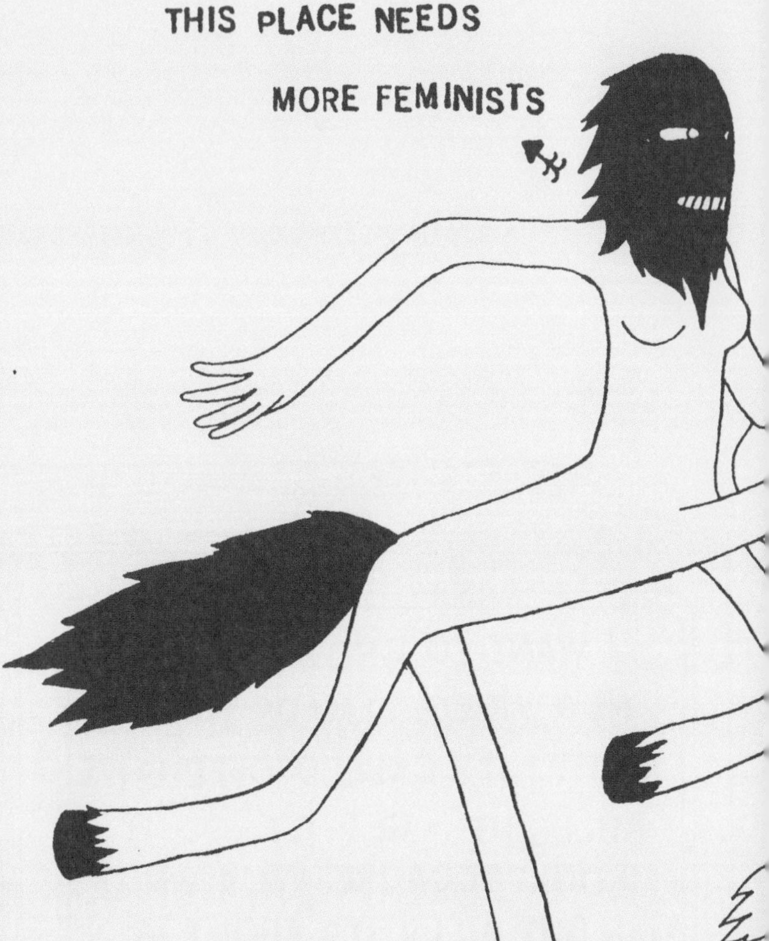
THIS PLACE NEEDS
MORE FEMINISTS

RADICAL FEMINISTS!

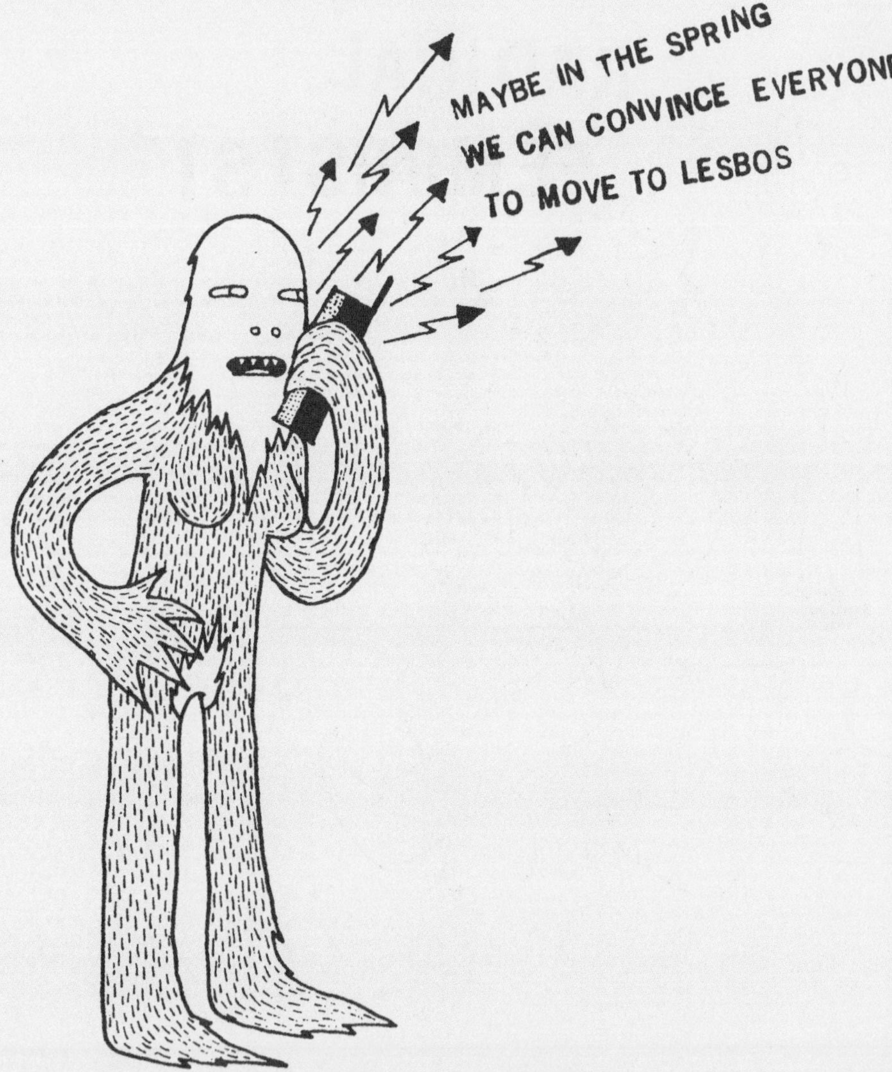
MAYBE IN THE SPRING
WE CAN CONVINCE EVERYONE
TO MOVE TO LESBOS

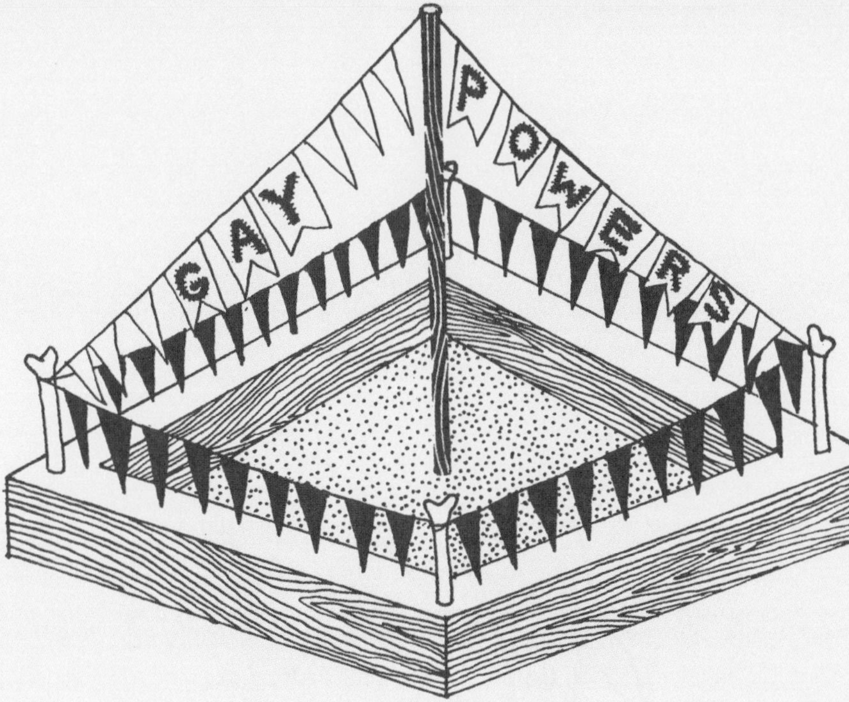
GAY
POWERS

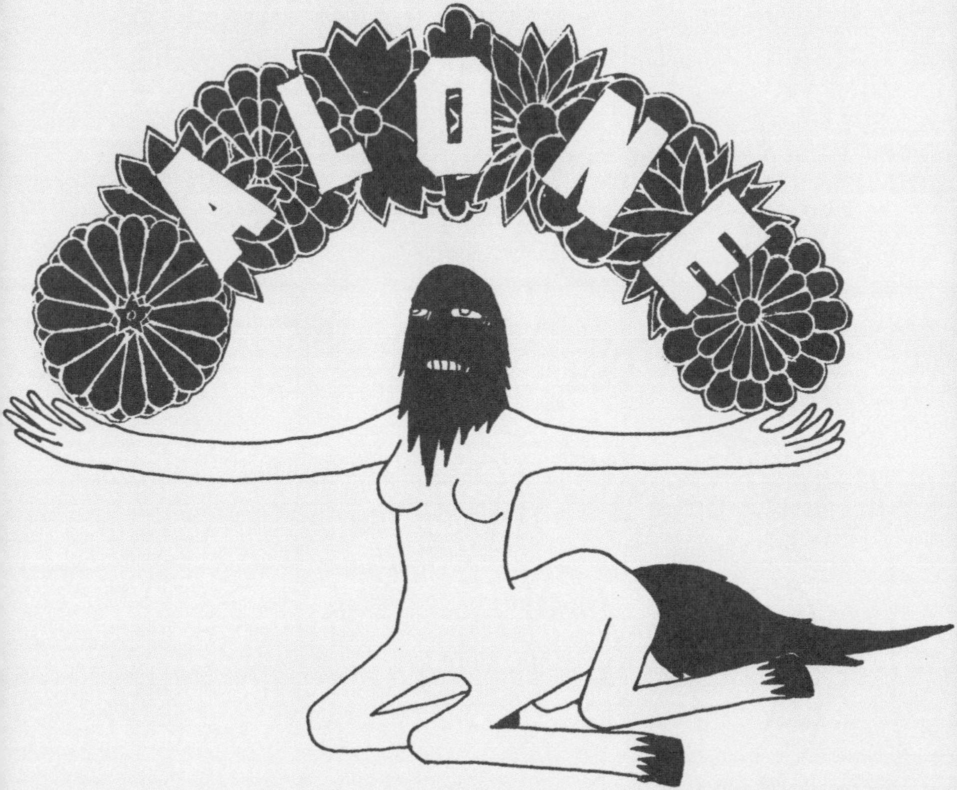
ALONE

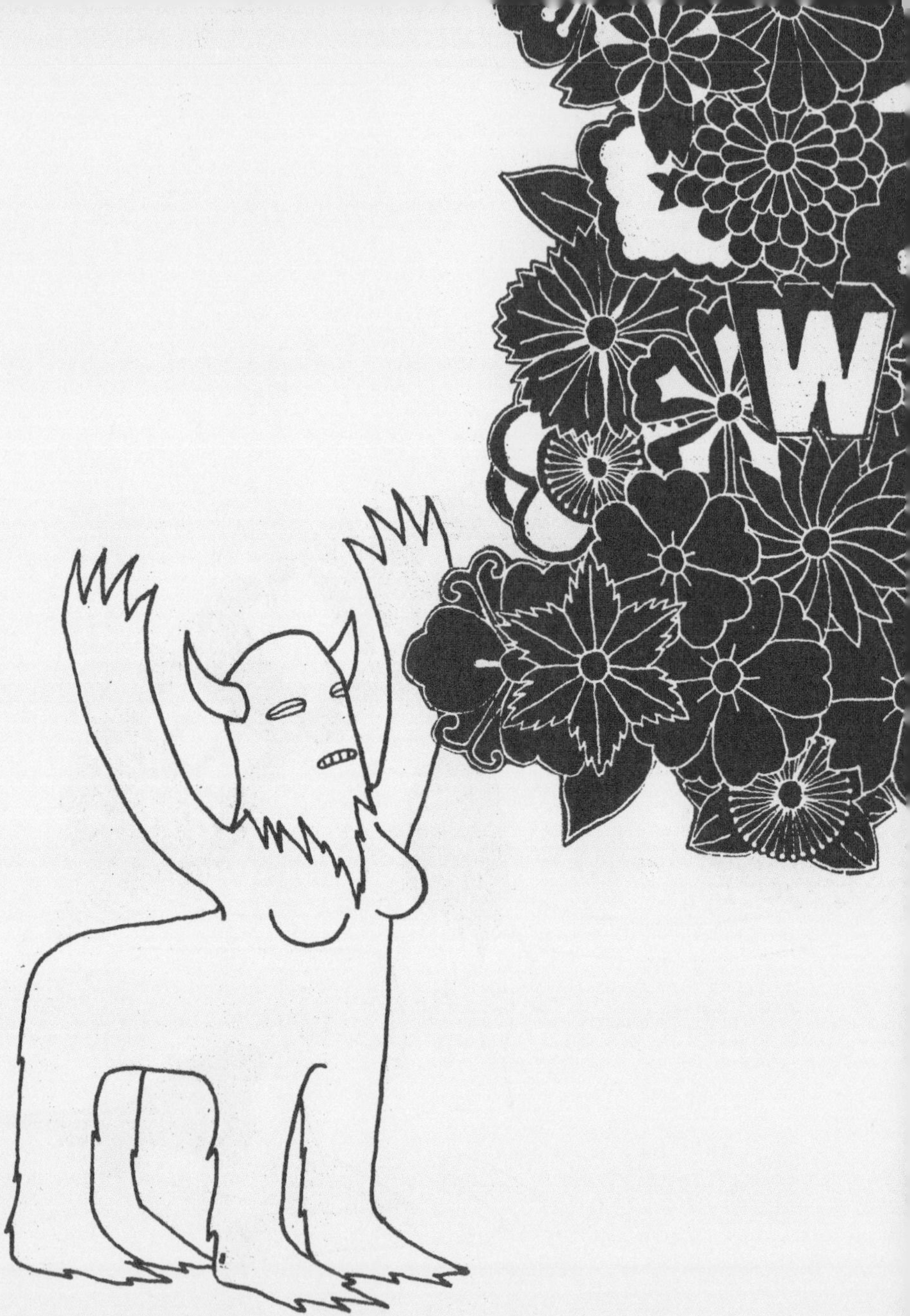
W

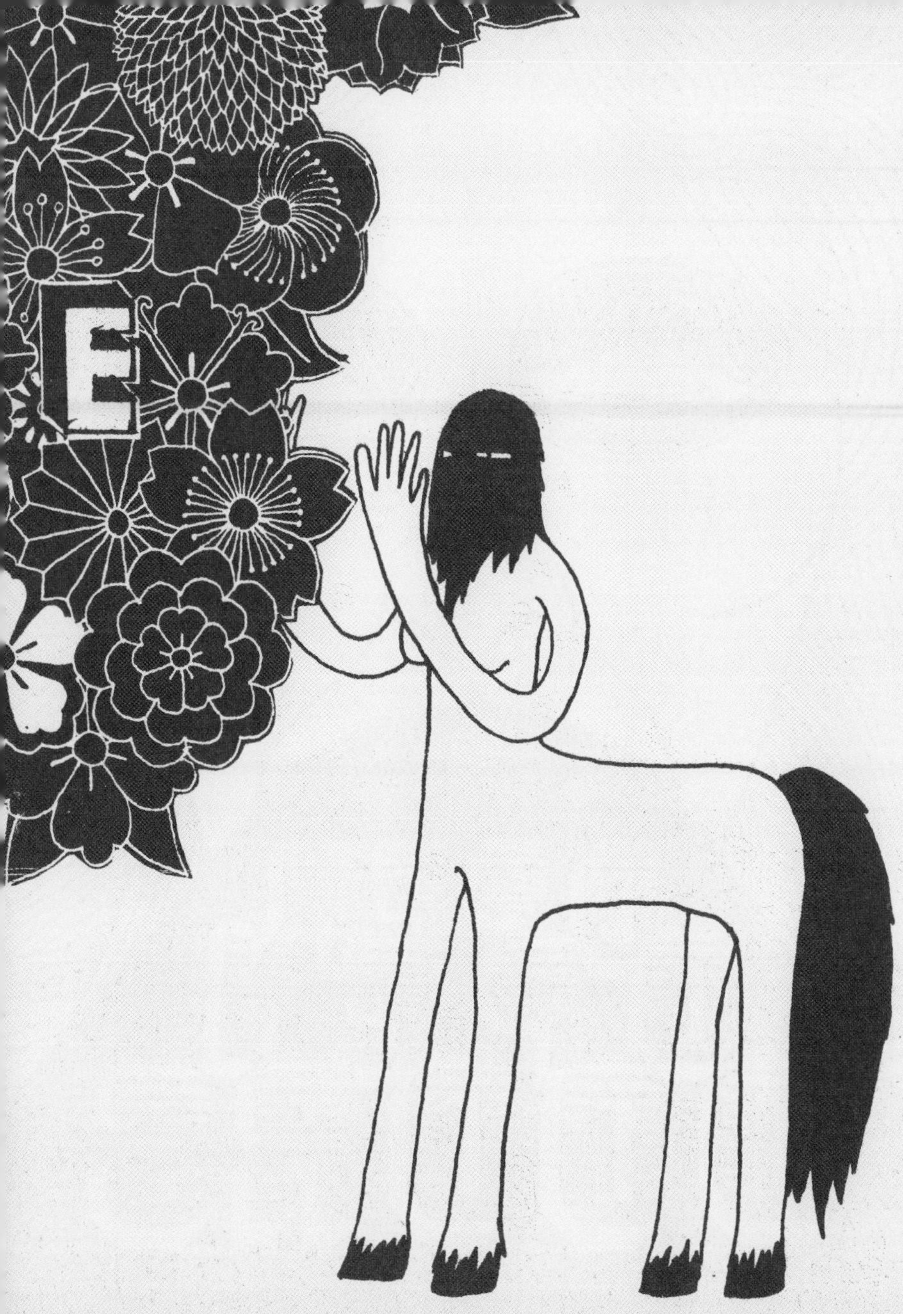
E

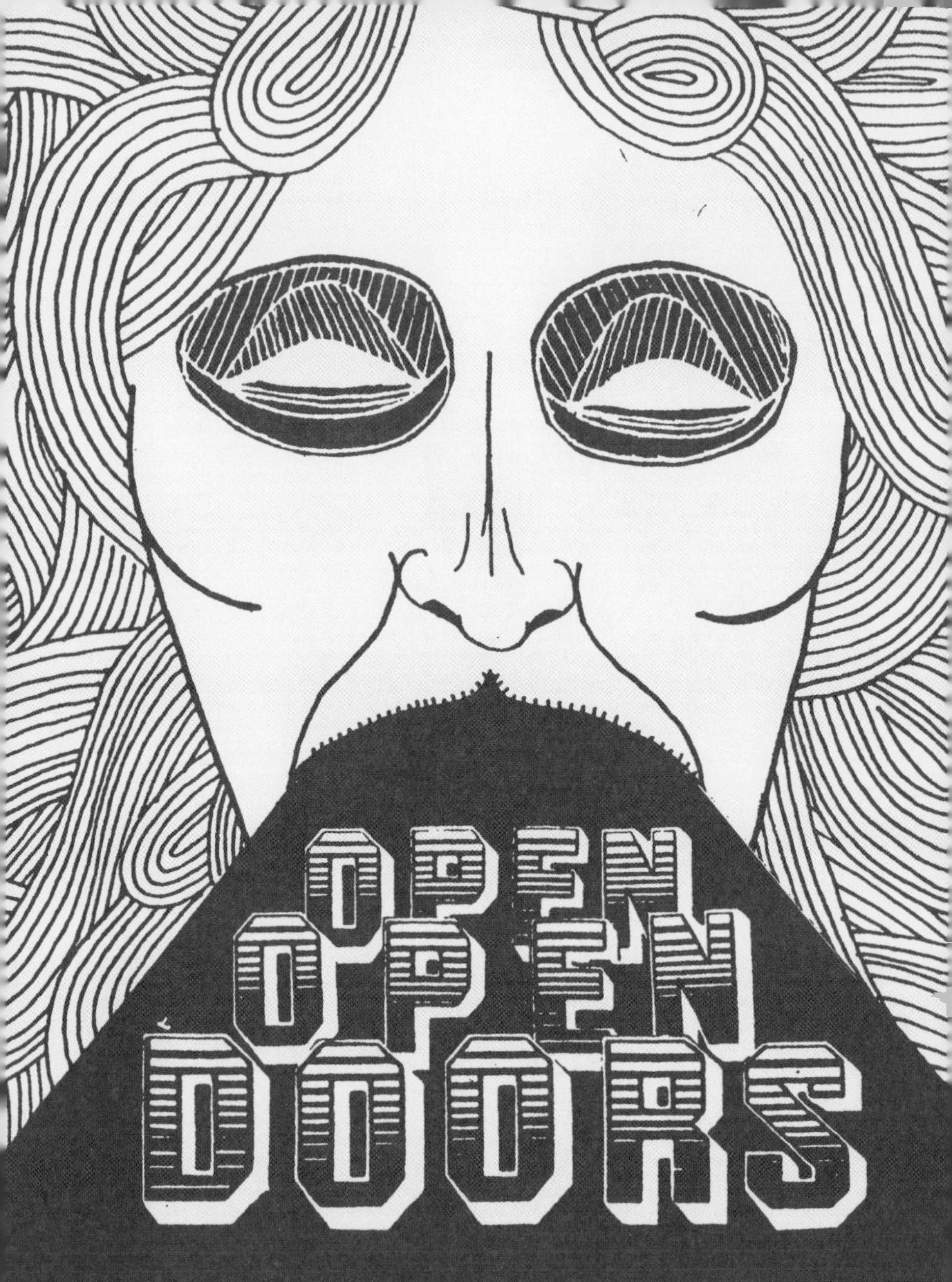
OPEN
OPEN
DOORS

AT THIS POINT

WE ARE ALL VULNERABLE

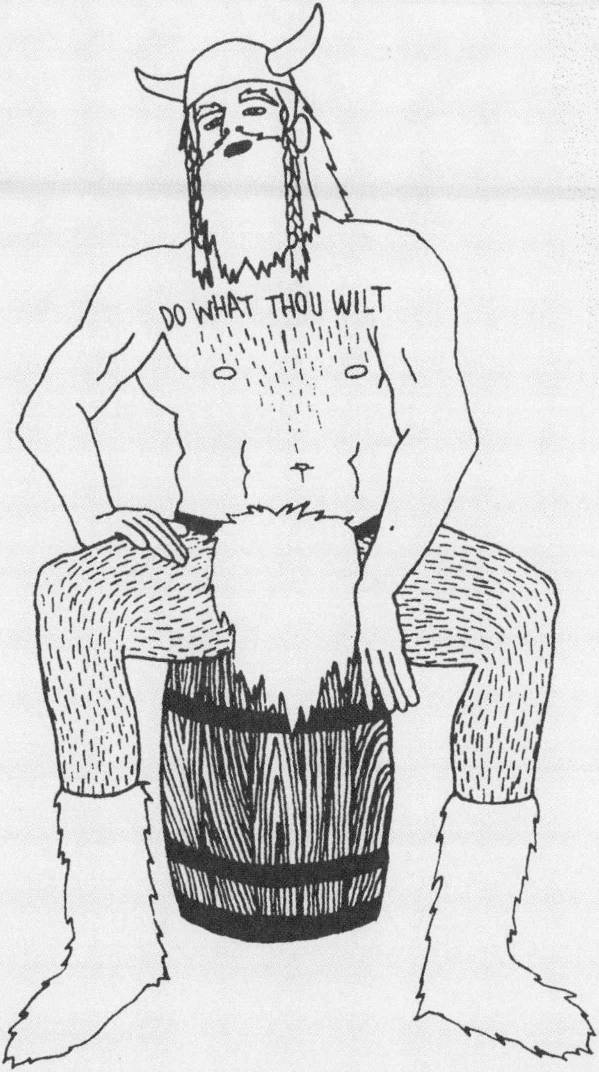
DO WHAT THOU WILT

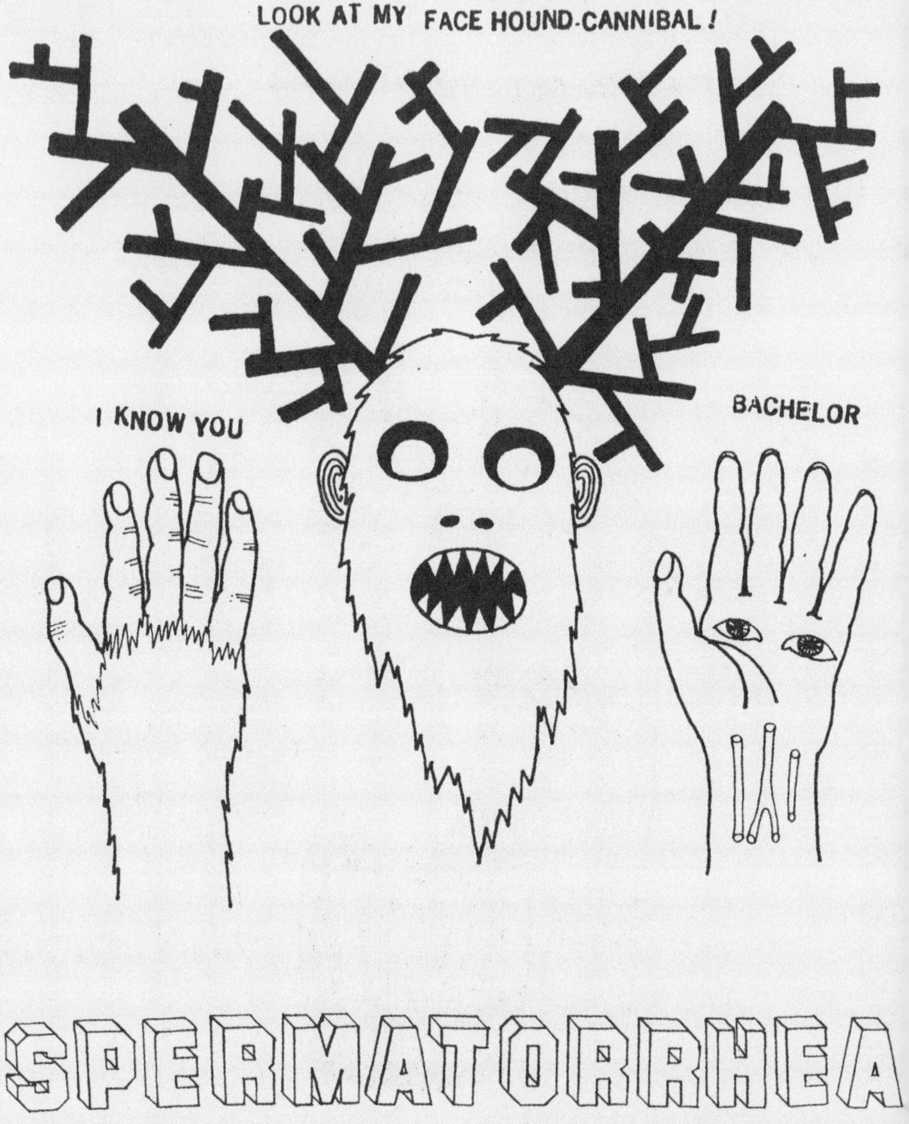
LOOK AT MY FACE HOUND-CANNIBAL!
I KNOW YOU
BACHELOR
SPERMATORRHEA

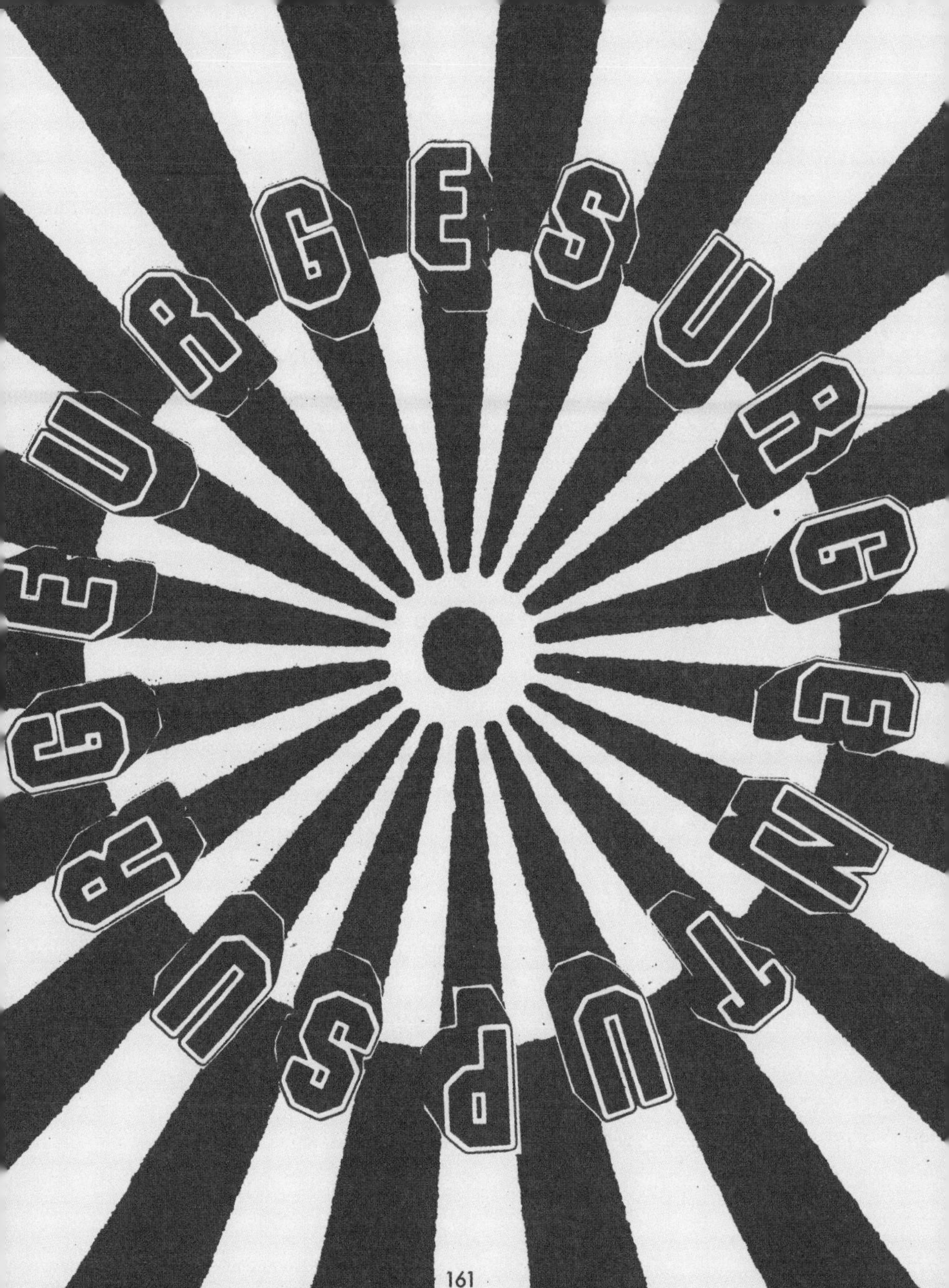
URGESURGENTUPSURGE

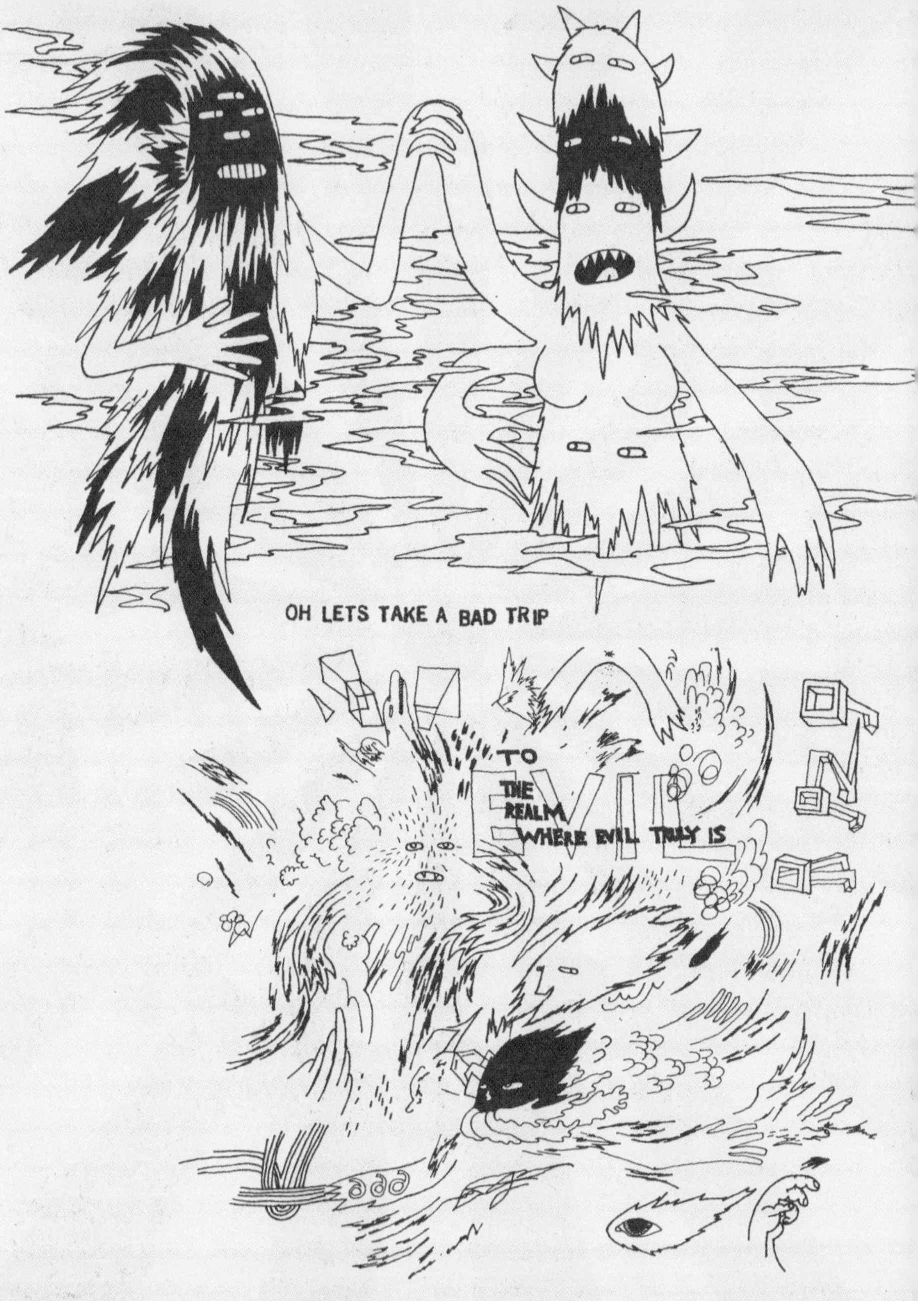
OH LETS TAKE A BAD TRIP
TO
THE
REALM
WHERE EVIL TRULY IS
EVIL

CLOWN-VISION

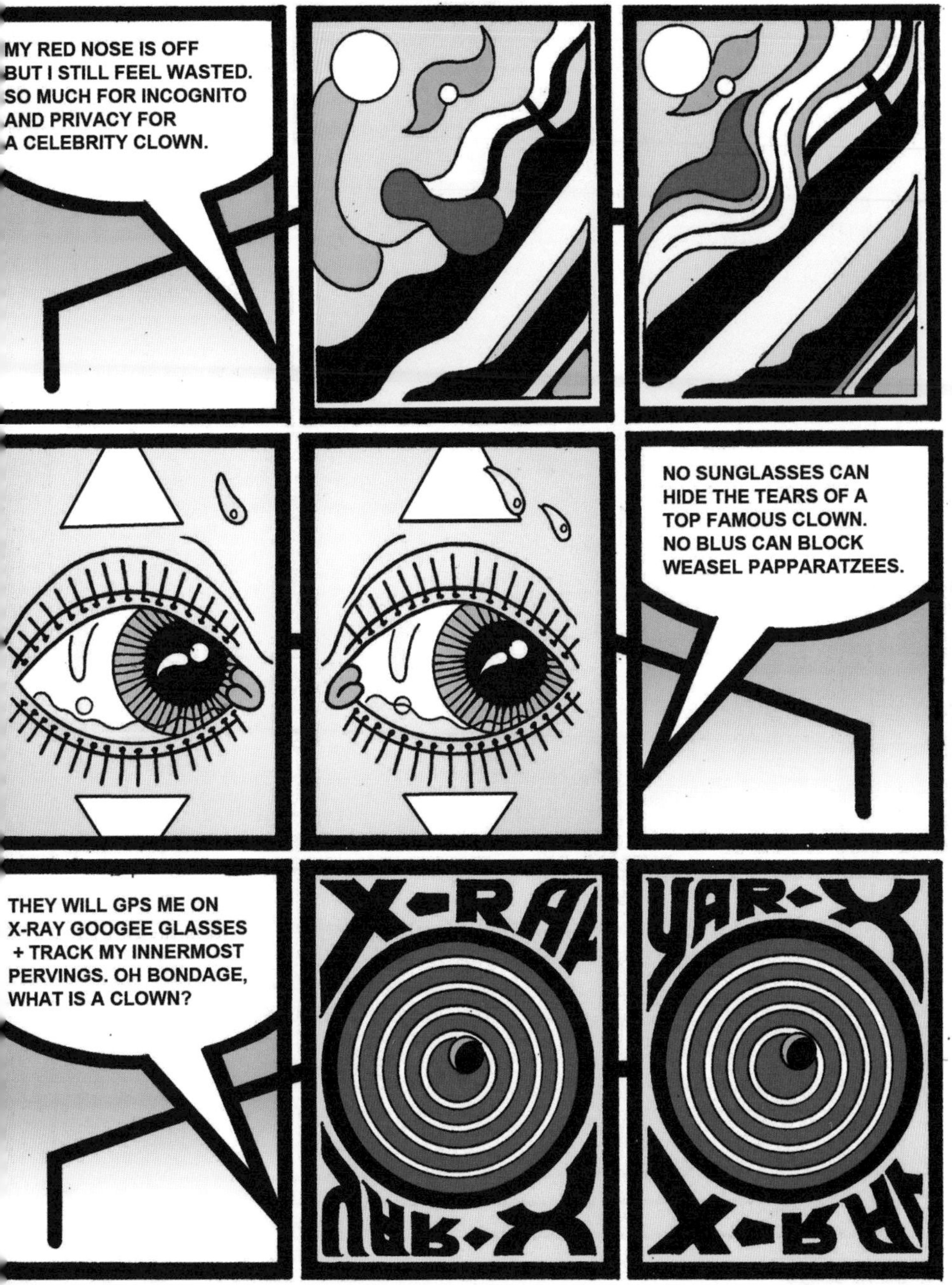
MY RED NOSE IS OFF BUT I STILL FEEL WASTED. SO MUCH FOR INCOGNITO AND PRIVACY FOR A CELEBRITY CLOWN.
NO SUNGLASSES CAN HIDE THE TEARS OF A TOP FAMOUS CLOWN. NO BLUS CAN BLOCK WEASEL PAPPARATZEES.
THEY WILL GPS ME ON X-RAY GOOGEE GLASSES + TRACK MY INNERMOST PERVINGS. OH BONDAGE, WHAT IS A CLOWN?

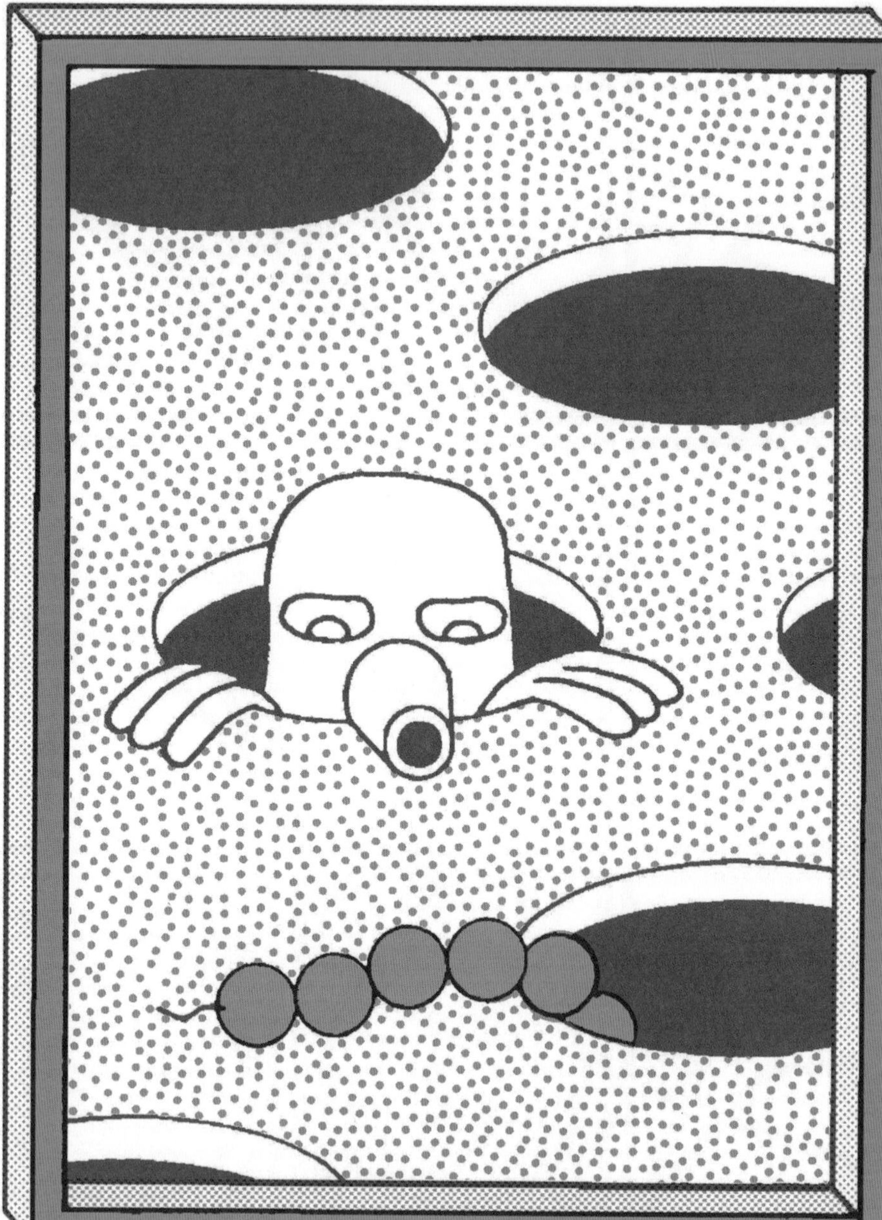

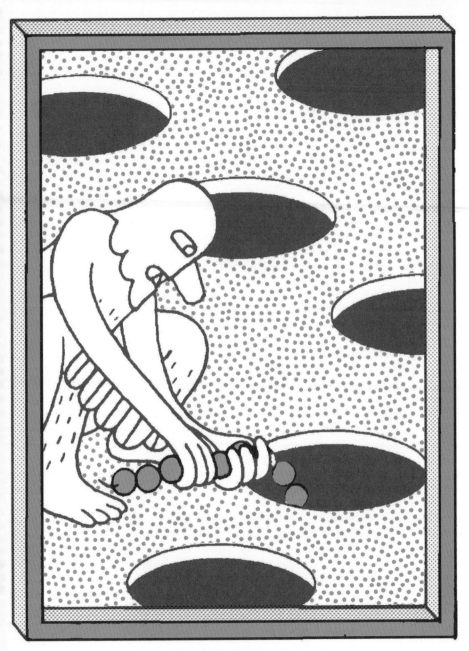

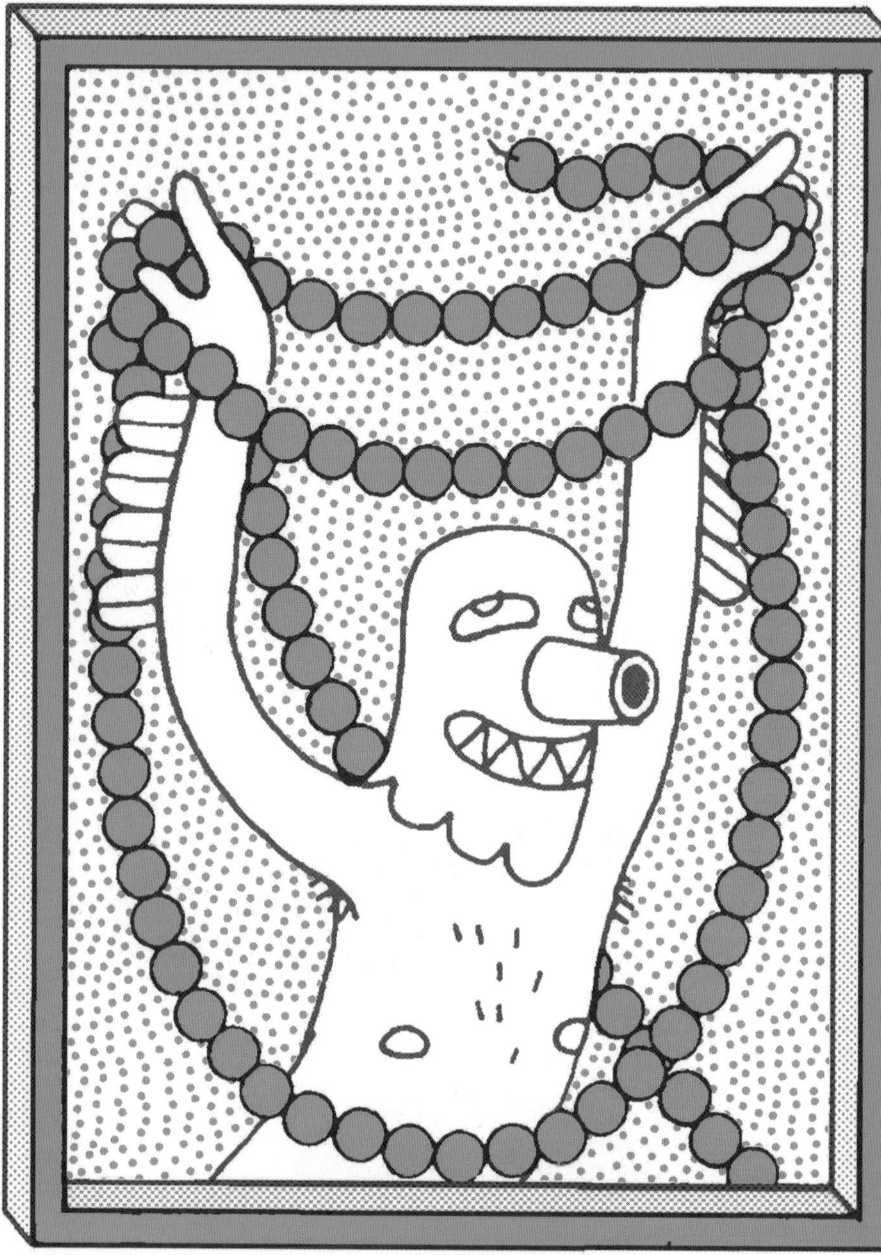

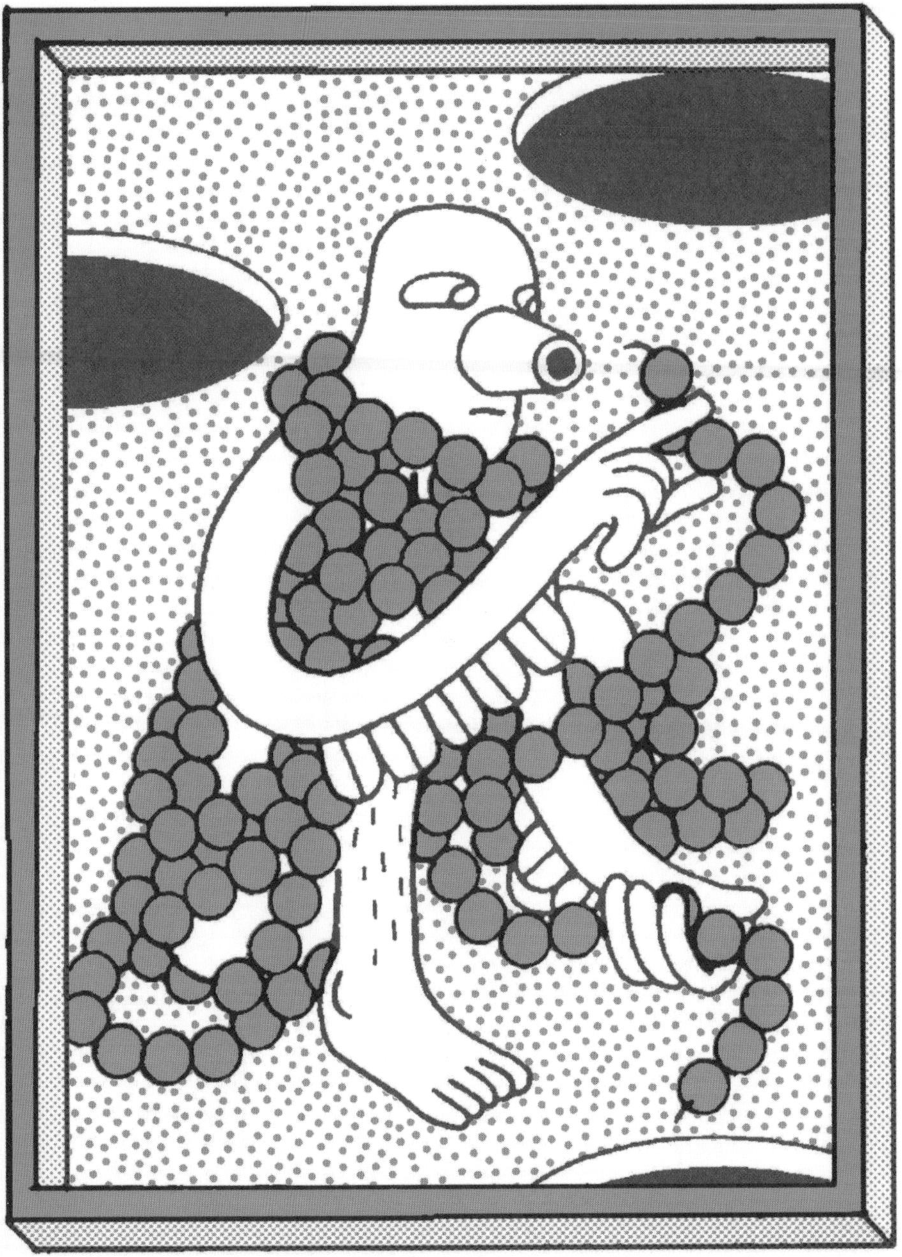

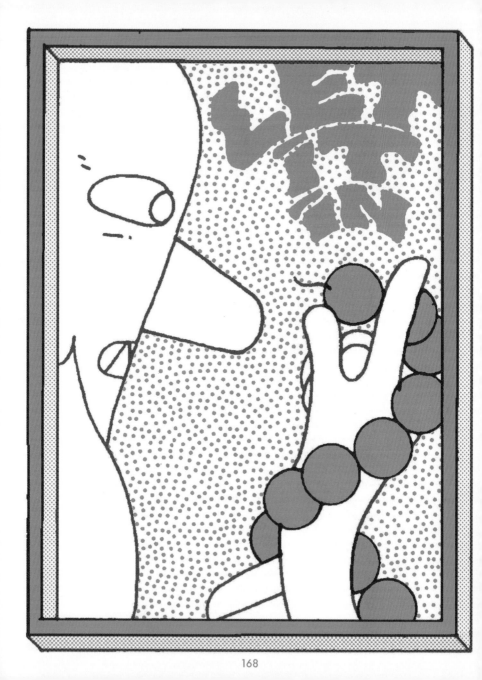

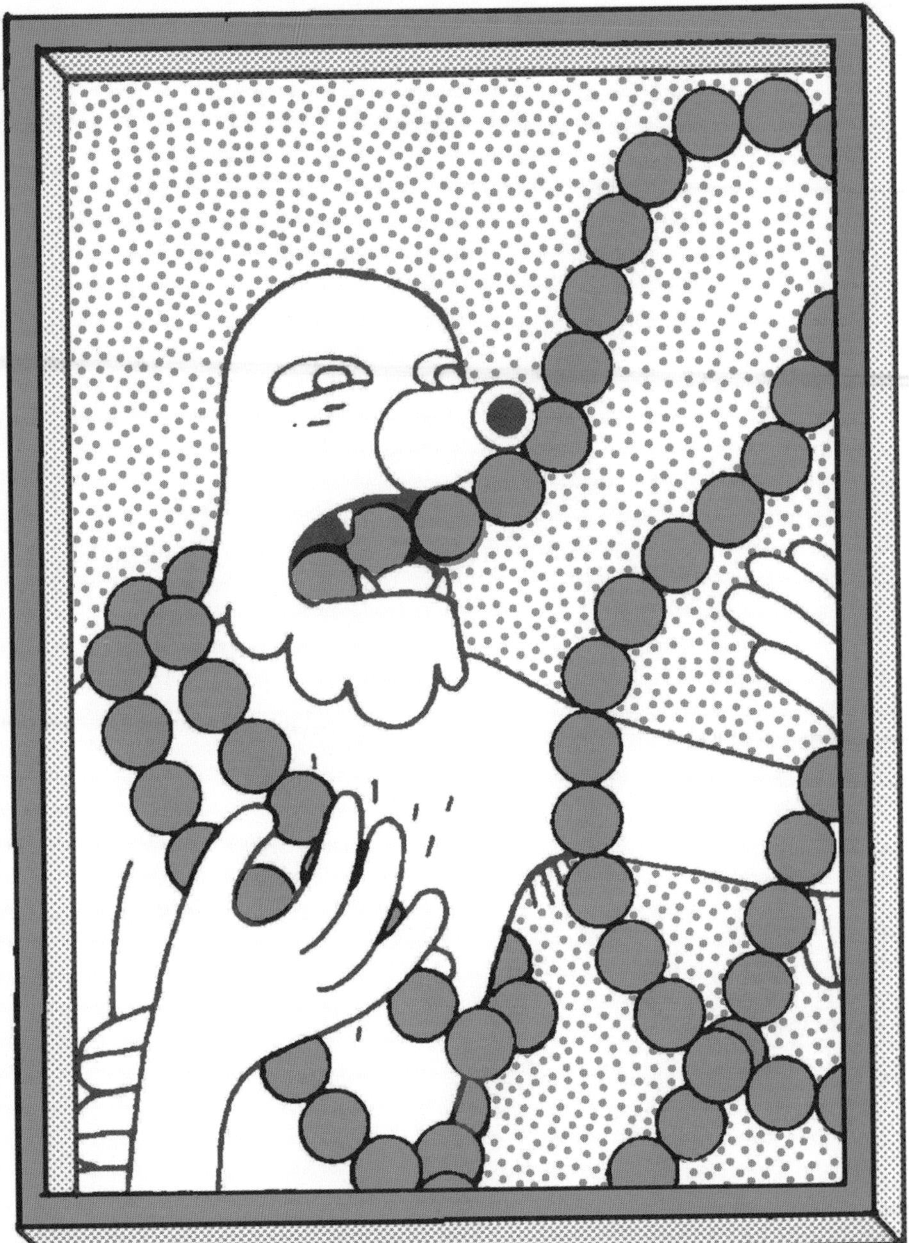

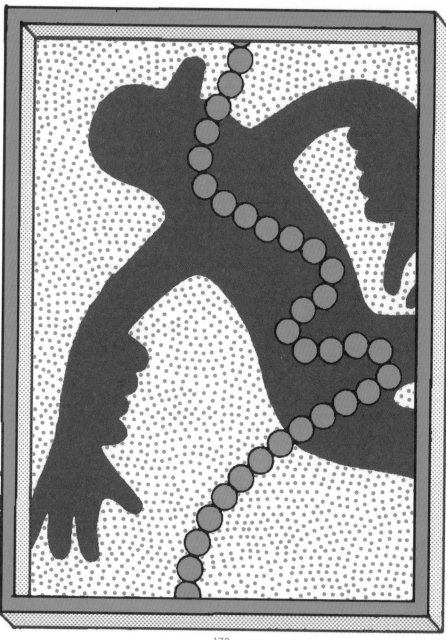

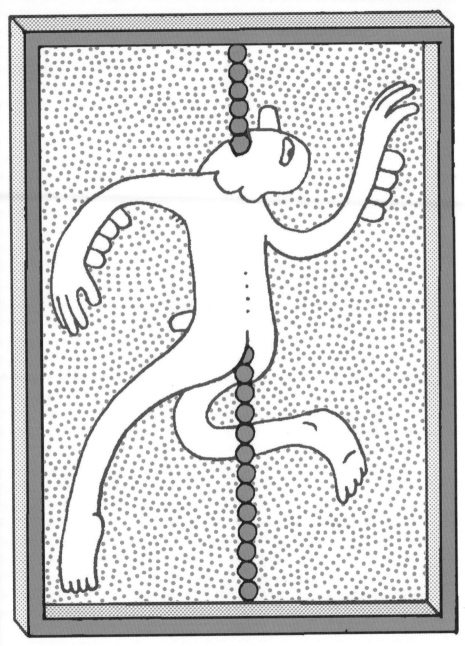

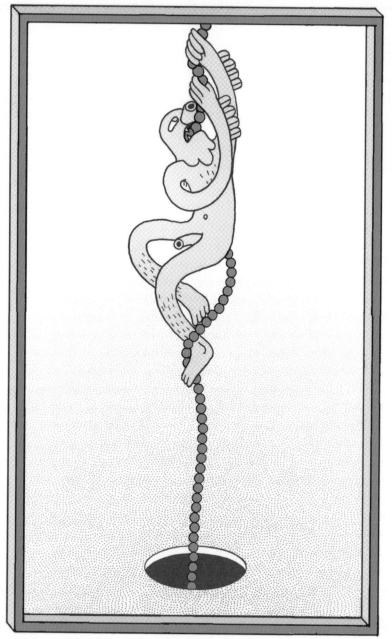

A Very Special Thanks to the friends who encouraged, supported and published these comics:

Caroline Paquita, Max Morris, Midnight Forman, Grace Tran, Joe Tallarico, Marian Runk, Paul Nudd, Ciriza, Annie Murphy, Ruth O-R, Paul Lyons, Ezra Claytan-Daniels, Grant Reynolds, Oscar Arriola, Mona Demone, Conor Stechschulte, Rob Kirby, Jo Dery, Darin Klein, Ed Marszewski, Graham Kolbeins, Simon Bossé, Ryan Sands, Abi Cohen, David Zackin, Lauren Bousfield, Trubble Club, Andy Rench, Neil Brideau, David Cavazos, Barry Matthews, Leon Avelino, and Shannon Michael Cane.

These stories in Little Stranger previously appeared
in the following publications:

Alphabit Snake • Future Tense
Clowns "French Tickler" • CAKE book
The Wine Tree • š! #15
Tête • Têtes De Mickey
Night Taps • Believed Behavior
Clowns "Voyeur" • Lumpen Magazine
Nightcrawlers • Thickness #3
Gobbler • Corpus Corpus #4
Czarnina • Monster 2013
Tight Fit • 4PANEL Project
Farmboy Tales • Sock #2
Creeper • 4PANEL Project
L.A. Silence • Vacuum Horror #1
Sex Club • QU33R
Clowns "Elephant Circus" • Lumpen Magazine
Anal Sex For Perverts • LTTR #4
Coat of Arms • Hot and Cold #1
Hand Full • Gay Genius
Clowns "Camo" • Lumpen Magazine
A Field Guide to Desert Holes • Box of Books #10
Clowns "Clown Vision" • Lumpen Magazine
String of Pearls • Box of Books #9